BOTH ENDS
OF THE AVENUE

BOTH ENDS OF THE AVENUE

The Presidency,
the Executive Branch,
and Congress in the 1980s

edited by Anthony King

American Enterprise Institute
for Public Policy Research
Washington and London

Library of Congress Cataloging in Publication Data
Main entry under title:
Both ends of the avenue.
    (AEI studies ; 361)
    Includes bibliographical references.
    1. Presidents—United States. 2. United States.
Congress. I. King, Anthony Stephen. II. American
Enterprise Institute for Public Policy Research.
III. Series.
JK585.B55 1983   353.03'72   82-20706

ISBN 0–8447–3498–5
ISBN 0–8447–3497–7 (pbk.)

AEI Studies 361

3 5 7 9 10 8 6 4 2

Printed in the United States of America

Contents

Preface

According to the Congressional Research Service—and who should know better?—the distance along Pennsylvania Avenue from the White House to Capitol Hill is approximately a mile and a half. Physically, the distance is not very great; any reasonably fit tourist can walk it in half an hour. But politically, of course, the distance is much greater. The Founding Fathers did not want the relationship between president and Congress to be an easy one, and they succeeded in this as in so much else.

Any time is a good time to explore the presidential–congressional relationship, which is intrinsically fascinating as well as being of crucial importance for the whole American political system; but the early 1980s seem an especially apt time. The presidency is no longer under the clouds of Vietnam and Watergate, but Congress has changed enormously over the past twenty years, not least because of Vietnam and Watergate; and inevitably changes in Congress have produced changes of equal magnitude in that institution's relations with the presidency and the executive branch generally. The dynamics of this new presidential–congressional relationship—or "conversation," as several writers in the following pages term it—is the subject of this book. Each chapter explores a different aspect of the presidential–congressional relationship. The book as a whole seeks to impose coherence on something that is, and was meant to be, incoherent.

Richard Neustadt taught students of American politics a generation ago to think of the presidency and Congress in terms, not of separation of powers but of separated institutions sharing powers. As will emerge, the theme of this book is partly one of sharing but more one of separateness.

Anthony King

Contributors

ERIC L. DAVIS, assistant professor of political science, Middlebury College

HUGH HECLO, professor of government, Harvard University

CHARLES O. JONES, professor of government and senior scholar, White Burkett Miller Center for Public Affairs, University of Virginia

ANTHONY KING, professor of government, University of Sussex, England

MICHAEL J. MALBIN, resident fellow, American Enterprise Institute

NORMAN J. ORNSTEIN, professor of politics, Catholic University of America

NELSON W. POLSBY, professor of political science, University of California, Berkeley

AUSTIN RANNEY, codirector, Political and Social Processes Study Center, American Enterprise Institute

ALLEN SCHICK, professor, school of public affairs, University of Maryland

1

Some Landmarks in Modern Presidential-Congressional Relations

Nelson W. Polsby

In discussions of presidential–congressional relations, two arenas are generally thought to be of primary significance. One arena has to do with the perennial competition between presidents and their staffs, on one hand, and congressmen and congressional staffs, on the other, for the attention and the acquiescence of the rest of the government: the boards, bureaus, commissions, administrations, and agencies of the federal establishment, whether "independent" or formally attached to the executive branch. The other arena is Congress itself, where presidential programs are or are not enacted into law, and where annual decisions must be made about the size and the composition of the federal budget.

This second arena, the congressional, is far more visible than the innards of the executive branch, and so most of the historical experience that is readily available for us to review consists of public reports of congressional–presidential conflict and cooperation on Capitol Hill. The less accessible annals of each and every agency in Washington no doubt record variations—sometimes very great variations—on the themes to be observed in the congressional arena. In any event, in seeking to get our historical bearings on the relations between successive Congresses and presidents in modern times, we turn most readily to those historical moments that mark the emergence of institutional capabilities on one side or the other for doing business in each of these arenas, but with an unavoidable emphasis on Congress. This essay is meant as a sketch for a map of those moments rather than the finished historical atlas the subject deserves—treatment that, at least in part, it is accorded in the rest of this book.

The Establishment of the New Deal Perspective, 1933–1940

The modern era of presidential–congressional relations traditionally opens with the inauguration of Franklin D. Roosevelt in March 1933. In the ensuing three months, the divisiveness and the normal politics of sectional interest that had dominated Congress over the previous period gave way to a depression-induced cooperation between president and Congress that had not been seen for a generation. President Roosevelt proposed various measures, and Congress enacted them very speedily indeed, as the accompanying table from the work of one of the political science profession's foremost Congress-watchers of the time, Pendleton Herring, illustrates.

As Herring says,

> The Chief Executive became the chief law-maker. . . . He displayed remarkable skill in manipulating the attention of Congress and of the public. His messages to Congress were strategically timed and positive and specific in character. Disagreement with his proposals was interpreted by the general public as obstructionism. His swift pace, his boldness in assuming responsibility, and his definite recommendations not only stimulated popular support of his policy, but likewise branded as dissenters and critics congressmen holding to different policies. His radio talks to the nation served the double purpose of reassuring the people and breaking down resistance in Congress. Legislators were made only too well aware of the temper of their constituents.
>
> Congressmen of both parties were willing to follow the President's lead, and he managed his congressional relations with great tact. At the end of the session, he was able to thank both houses for a "spirit of teamwork" between the legislative and executive branches that in most cases "transcended party lines" and made possible "more whole-hearted cooperation" than had been witnessed in "many a long year." Of course the pressure of the emergency and the solid public support behind the President must be understood as modifying normal relations, but even when this is allowed for a full weight of political sagacity remains to account for the satisfactory contacts with Congress. . . .
>
> Measures were put through this Congress with little difficulty that had been turned down repeatedly in previous sessions.[1]

Historian James T. Patterson describes the mood of the time:

> [Roosevelt] did on occasion ask for wide discretionary powers—the economy and banking bills were cases in

2

TABLE 1.1

Progress of Selected New Deal Legislation through Congress, 1933

Number of Bill	Title	Proposed by President	Passed House	Passed Senate	Date Approved	No. of Law or Resolution	Length of General Debate in House
H.R. 1491	Emergency banking relief	Mar. 9	Mar. 9	Mar. 9	Mar. 9	1	40 min.
H.R. 2820	Maintenance of government's credit (economy bill)	Mar. 10	Mar. 11	Mar. 15	Mar. 20	2	2 hr.
H.R. 3341	Permit and tax beer	Mar. 13	Mar. 14	Mar. 16	Mar. 22	3	3 hr.
H.R. 3835	Emergency agricultural relief; farm mortgage; currency issuance and regulation	Mar. 16	Mar. 22	Apr. 28	May 12	10	5½ hr.
S. 598	Unemployment relief (reforestation)	Mar. 21	Mar. 29	Mar. 28	Mar. 31	5	5 hr.
H.R. 4606	Federal emergency relief	Mar. 21	Apr. 21	May 1	May 12	15	2 hr.
H.R. 5980	Supervision of traffic in securities	Mar. 29	May 5	May 8	May 27	22	5 hr.
H.R. 5081	Muscle Shoals and Tennessee Valley Authority	Apr. 10	Apr. 25	May 3	May 18	17	6 hr.
H.R. 5240	Relief of small home owners	Apr. 13	Apr. 28	June 5	June 13	43	1½ hr.
S. 1580	Railroad reorganization and relief	May 4	June 5	May 27	June 16	68	3 hr.
H.R. 5755	Industrial recovery; public construction and taxation	May 17	May 26	June 9	June 16	67	6 hr.

Source: Pendleton Herring, *Presidential Leadership* (New York: Farrar and Rinehart, 1940), p. 44.

point. Congress not only granted such requests but usually did so eagerly. By delegating authority, Congress also delegated responsibility, leaving to executive departments the resolution of troublesome policy matters. Congressional delegation of power was so generous that one veteran newsman sighed, "all my adjectives are exhausted in expressing my admiration, awe, wonder, and terror at the vast grants of power which Roosevelt demands, one after the other, from Congress."

Congressional readiness to surrender cherished prerogatives underscored a significant aspect of the 1933 session: in many areas it was considerably less orthodox than Roosevelt. Far from favoring conservative business interests in the manner of the Congresses of the 1920s, it approved an income-tax amendment requiring incomes to be publicized, and it passed the TVA with remarkable ease. Far from ignoring labor, it enacted the labor provisions of the National Industrial Recovery Act, while the Senate passed the Black thirty-hour-work-week bill in spite of Roosevelt's lack of enthusiasm. And far from wedding itself to orthodox monetary theory, Congress passed the Thomas Amendment, pushing Roosevelt in the direction of devaluation or inflation. Congressmen witnessed the end of the gold standard with scarcely a protest. . . .

Above all, congressmen were eager to spend. Under great pressure from constituents to relieve economic distress, they realized that a simple and tangible solution was to appropriate, appropriate, appropriate, while leaving taxes alone. Budget balancing, an almost sacred conservative panacea, fell by the wayside. The 1933 session, like those throughout the New Deal, was often a more liberal spender than the administration, particularly when strong pressure groups such as farmers or veterans threatened the hapless congressman with electoral extinction. As one contemporary observer commented, Roosevelt's chief difficulties with Congress in 1933 emanated from such pressure groups. The President, he said, could "do little more than keep order in the bread line that reached into the Treasury."[2]

Roosevelt's Hundred Days, so-called, became a benchmark in presidential–congressional relations. This, according to the pro-New Deal consensus that developed among academics and journalistic observers, was how presidential–congressional relations ought to work. This view was not grounded in liberal political preferences alone. It also reflected a taste for the big picture, a preference for assertedly broader, as contrasted with narrower, interests. In addition, it focused upon one leader whose programs and desires could be dramatized and publicized, and gave less emphasis to the unfathomable intricacy of the baroque interiors of the House and Senate. In short, Roosevelt launched American political analysis into a fresh era of what among historians was sometimes called the "presidential synthesis," in which observers tended to see the system from the presidential perspective alone.[3]

Twenty Years of Immobilism, 1940–1960

Roosevelt's unqualified success at being his own prime minister did not last far beyond the hundred days, despite the great Democratic victories in the elections of 1934 and 1936.[4] By 1938, stung in particular by the defeat of his proposal to pack the Supreme Court, Roosevelt undertook to encourage the defeat in primary elections of anti-New Deal Democrats in Congress.[5] The purge was a failure, and the decentralized character of the American party system prevailed. Soon enough, the New Deal went on the shelf as World War II came closer, and for the rest of Roosevelt's life Congress and presidency alike were preoccupied with wartime concerns.

At the time of Harry Truman's succession to the presidency on Roosevelt's death in 1945, the vice-president was still predominantly an official of the legislative branch, as the Constitution, not without ambiguity, provides.[6] Truman's lack of access to Roosevelt, and to the executive branch generally, constituted inadequate preparation for the presidency. We can date the systematic efforts to bring the vice president into a more intimate relationship with the White House to the general feeling that the nation had been ill-served by Truman's isolation.[7] These efforts have failed more often than they have succeeded, the miserable limbos of Richard Nixon (1953–1961), Lyndon Johnson (1961–1963), Hubert Humphrey (1965–1969), Spiro T. Agnew (1969–1973), and Nelson A. Rockefeller (1974–1977) greatly outweighing the more constructive experiences of Alben Barkley (1949–1953) and Walter Mondale (1977–1981).[8]

By World War II, administrative machinery had been put in place that modernized the office of the presidency. A White House office had been created, under the famous battle cry of the Brownlow Commission on Administrative Management, "The president needs help."[9] The expectation had grown up that the president and his program would set the congressional agenda. An executive budget was provided for, and the elite Bureau of the Budget was made a presidential agency.[10]

The precipitous American demobilization after World War II did not extend to the civilian bureaucracies of the Washington community. Ever since the famous Washington wartime housing shortage, Washington has been a boom town.[11] Not all of the growth is attributable to direct employees of the federal government, however. In fact, over the last thirty years the predominant technique by which the federal government has expanded its responsibilities has been to offer grants, subsidies, and contracts to state and local governments, business firms, universities, and other nonprofit entities to perform federally mandated functions of various kinds.[12]

As contemporary times approach, it becomes more difficult to sort out the key events responsible for giving presidential–congressional relations their current shape. Key events in this sense are not necessarily dramatic events, of which there has been an oversupply. Neither the assassination of John Kennedy in 1963 nor the near-impeachment and resignation of Richard Nixon in 1974, surely the two most startling and dramatic events of contemporary American politics, by themselves generated lasting and significant institutional consequences.

More important institutionally were the sorts of relationships that built up over time, the way a muddy river builds its delta. A stalemate existed in presidential–congressional relations within the congressional arena from the late 1930s until the late 1950s. During the later Roosevelt years and all the Truman years, there was no consistent majority available in Congress to sustain the domestic proposals of presidents whose programs were liberal in their ambitions and ready to expand the federal role of ensuring domestic prosperity and a more equal distribution of income, including the expansion of federal responsibility for various sorts of health and welfare benefits. During Dwight Eisenhower's two full terms (1953–1961) the president was not a domestic liberal, and so long as a presidential veto needed a sustaining vote of only one-third plus one in either house of Congress, the overall domestic stalemate dating from before the war could be continued.

The election of 1958 brought the first wave of a series of large postwar Democratic majorities into Congress. One consequence was an increase in demands from the congressional side for the completion of the agenda of the New Deal. The upshot, however, was nothing of the kind; instead the major product of the Eighty-sixth Congress was the Landrum-Griffin bill, greatly disliked by the labor movement.[13] For the first time in this Congress, however, House Democratic liberals organized themselves outside the party structure, which for them had become ideologically too ecumenical.[14]

The Packing of the House Rules Committee

From the 1960s onward the pace of change begins to accelerate, and the twenty years of relative immobilism in presidential–congressional relations is succeeded by twenty years of turbulence. It began with the packing of the House Rules Committee in January 1961. This was an historic event in the institutional history of the House of Representatives, comparable in its impact to the famous revolt against Speaker Joe Cannon in 1909[15] and the day in 1890 when Speaker Thomas B. Reed counted representatives as present although they had refused to answer to their names on a roll call.[16] Like the earlier famous events, it masked substance of enormous importance in a seemingly innocuous procedural matter.[17]

At stake was the fate of the entire program of the incoming Democratic president, John F. Kennedy. For twenty years the House of Representatives had been a graveyard of liberal hopes, because a securely entrenched conservative coalition of Southern Democrats and mainstream Republicans could frequently outmaneuver the majority of the Democrats in Congress even when they could not outvote them. One of the main devices in the House of Representatives for ensuring that proposals the conservative coalition opposed did not pass was simply preventing them from reaching the House floor where a public vote could be taken on them. Even when a congressional committee was dominated by liberal Democrats, as more than one was, conservatives could block committee bills from reaching the floor because of their control of the House Rules Committee, a committee empowered by the rules of the House to screen all bills reported from other committees and to establish orderly procedures for their floor consideration.

Twelve members sat on the committee at the start of Congress in 1960, by tradition the majority party holding a 2-to-1 advantage. So there were four Republicans, all staunch mainstream conservatives, highly responsive to their party leadership. On the Democratic side of the table sat eight members, but only six were loyal to the mainstream Democratic speaker, the venerable Sam Rayburn, who had put them there. The two most senior Democrats—Howard Smith of Virginia and William Colmer of Mississippi—were contemporaries of Rayburn's and were as committed to their brand of Southern conservatism as Rayburn was to the platform of the national Democratic party. This line-up meant that any motion to report to the floor a bill embodying the Kennedy program—or any other progressive measure—could be stopped by a 6-to-6 tie vote in the Rules Committee. Like a highly sophisticated turnpike troll in a children's storybook, old Judge Smith, the committee chairman, could hold up the traffic until his price was met: a program eliminated, a measure watered down, two bills sacrificed in exchange for three bills let through. His craftsmanship in exacting the highest tax the traffic would bear was widely admired by friends and foes alike.

Until 1958, Rayburn's ace in the hole in a Rules Committee battle with Judge Smith was his friendship with the veteran Republican leader, Joe Martin of Massachusetts. In a pinch, Martin could find a Republican vote on the Rules Committee that would relax its death grip on at least some measures where there was bipartisan support. But in the aftermath of their overwhelming defeat of 1958, the Republicans in the House deposed old Joe Martin and replaced him with a self-styled "gut fighter," Charles Halleck of Indiana, with whom there would be no sweetheart deals for Sam Rayburn.

Rayburn lived with the problem during the tag end of the Eisenhower presidency, since an Eisenhower veto could always stop what the Rules Committee let through. But with the advent of a new young president, a Democrat full of partisan vigor and a desire to make a little history, Rayburn had a problem on his hands. Either the House would be the bottleneck that doomed the entire Kennedy program, or something had to be done about the Rules Committee.

What Rayburn did was change the size of the committee, adding two Democrats and a Republican. After a long and subtle series of maneuvers, and with much cooperation from the incoming president, who kept hands off except as directed, Rayburn got the House to vote for the change by a margin of 217 to 212. This meant that when push came to shove the vote in the Rules Committee would be Speaker Rayburn 8 (all of them Democrats) to Chairman Smith 7 (2 Democrats plus 5 Republicans).

Eisenhower had been the first president to maintain within his official entourage a full-time liaison with Congress.[18] Nothing could have been more convincing to the incoming Kennedy administration of the need to continue a White House congressional specialization than their baptism of fire in the fight over the House Rules Committee. And so Lawrence O'Brien's rather vague original assignment to oversee patronage matters in the Kennedy White House rapidly matured into a permanent responsibility for congressional oversight. O'Brien soon had a busy corps of associates, and, as Eric L. Davis shows in chapter 3, the pattern has been maintained—with variations —ever since.

Changes in the Senate

The Senate, meanwhile, had nearly completed its change in the overall scheme of things by the early 1960s. In the post–World War II political climate, where so much responsibility and its attendant publicity had shifted to the federal government, the Senate drifted away from its accustomed role as resting place for grandees from the party machines of the several states. (There had been direct election of senators, after all, rather than selection by state legislatures, for nearly two score years.) Increasingly, the Senate became an arena within which national reputations could be made.[19] In the 1940s and 1950s, Arthur Vandenberg pioneered this new style of senatorial leadership. Vandenberg was a political force in national politics solely by virtue of the impact his senatorial activity was having on national news media, and not, as was the case with his contemporaries, Robert Taft and John Bricker of Ohio, principally because of his access to the political support of party leaders in his home state, or because of the esteem with which he was held by his colleagues in the Senate.[20]

By the 1950s many senators were running hard for president rather than relaxing in the heavy leather chairs that populate the cloakrooms of the Capitol. Backstage heavyweights of the Senate like Richard Russell of Georgia, Bob Kerr of Oklahoma, and Lyndon Johnson of Texas, all were to try their luck in the new arena. Three significant innovations hastened the process of turning the Senate from a remarkably private body into a far more public body.

First was the coming of television, and the wiring up of the entire nation with astonishing speed from 1950 to 1960. Suddenly senators were on the air all the time, giving their imprimatur to the Sunday afternoon discussions of political affairs much favored by stations and networks trying to keep the Federal Communications Commission happy with their public-service programming while they coined fabulous amounts of money from the sale of commercial time. After the astounding success of Estes Kefauver, whose 1951 Senate committee hearings on crime, televised at first only in New York, then more widely, riveted the attention of the entire nation, the ability of television to make stars out of ordinary politicians was lost on nobody. As a result of these hearings, Kefauver, who was rather unpopular in the Senate and was without much wealth, eloquence, or political security in his home state of Tennessee (which in any event was too small to weigh heavily in the electoral college or at a national

9

convention), became a serious contender for the presidential nomination of his party for most of the rest of his life.[21]

The second great innovation came to its most spectacular early fruition in the hands of Hubert Humphrey, senator from Minnesota from 1949 to 1964, vice-president from 1965 to 1969, and again senator from 1971 until his death in 1978. Before Humphrey, many senators maintained solid relationships with national interest groups. But nobody ever matched Humphrey's entrepreneurial flair for conjuring up new and different ways of attracting the attention and stimulating the interest of nationally organized groups in the work of the Senate. By sponsoring flurries of bills and holding hearings on them, Humphrey began to put together a grand coalition of outside clientele groups, not through secret or private alliances, but through the establishment of public commitments. And in turning to Humphrey for leadership, national interest groups in greater profusion than ever learned also to turn to the Senate.[22]

The third innovation was first perfected by the Senate alumnus who in his generation went the farthest the fastest: John F. Kennedy. It was Kennedy who discovered that to become president from the Senate it was sufficient to *be* a senator and not necessary to work at the job. Kennedy, over a protracted period, campaigned for the presidency as a full-time job (as did Kefauver over a shorter span). Far more single-mindedly than any of his contemporary rivals, Kennedy made the Senate a platform from which, rather than an arena within which, he could fulfill his ambitions.[23]

Thus from an encapsulated, somewhat fusty and old-fashioned chamber of dignitaries by 1960 the modern Senate had emerged. Senators hired droves of staff to undertake issue entrepreneurship in their behalf.[24] Great debates were staged and publicized. Policy innovations found champions and a niche in the political system from which to gather the consensus that is the prerequisite of eventual enactment into law.

Kennedy and Johnson: Surge and Decline in Presidential–Congressional Relations

Presidential–congressional relations during the Kennedy presidency were handled gingerly.[25] Lawrence O'Brien learned his job by listening carefully on the Hill and enjoyed an extraordinary measure of confidence both in the White House and in Congress. But despite the great Rules Committee victory, Kennedy feared his margin was too thin in the House to overcome the animosity of conservative committee chairmen. And so he rationed his New Frontier legislation with great—some liberal critics believed with excessive—care. Sam Rayburn's death in the fall of 1961 brought to the speakership John McCormack, head of a rival clan to the Kennedys in the intensely tribal politics of Massachusetts, but a strong, though painfully cautious party loyalist. Over McCormack's objections liberal Democrats began using the party caucus to reshape the pattern of assignments to key legislative committees.[26]

Just at the point when much of this patient gardening could have been expected to begin to bear fruit, John Kennedy was assassinated. His successor, Lyndon Johnson, a devout believer in the efficacy of momentum in legislative affairs, exploited the post-assassination mood and achieved great legislative victories—an unprecedented tax cut, a major civil rights bill.

Johnson was as at home in the congressional arena as any president in American history. In his youth he had been legislative assistant to a congressman from Texas, his home state. Later he was himself a representative, a Roosevelt supporter. Very early in his career in the Senate he became leader of the Democratic majority, and all through the Eisenhower years he applied his monomaniacal energy to the subtleties of arbitrage between a popular, conservative president and a Senate closely divided between Democrats and Republicans, filled to the brim with prima donnas.[27]

Johnson proved equal to the task. He was greatly aided by the fact that he could count on timely assistance from his fellow Texan, Rayburn, who led the House, and matchless favorable publicity from yet another fellow Texan, William S. White, who in those years covered the Senate for the *New York Times*. The Republicans in the Senate, moreover, were for most of the Eisenhower years led by the notably slow-witted and ponderous William Knowland, the perfect foil for Johnson's mercurial talent. Thus by the time he reached the presidency Johnson had already mastered the ins and outs of Congress.

Fate then dealt Johnson an exceedingly strong hand. Barely a year after he succeeded to the presidency and saw the nation through its great, copiously televised trauma, he was faced with the prospect of an election contest against an agreeable Republican senator, Barry Goldwater, then almost universally regarded as an ideological extremist. Indeed, Goldwater cheerfully conceded the point: "Extremism in the defense of liberty is no vice," he intoned in his acceptance speech at the Republican national convention.[28]

No doubt Johnson could have beaten any Republican in 1964, given the skill of his performance in the White House in the wake of his predecessor's shocking and untimely death. But Goldwater's affable maladroitness provoked a landslide of massive proportions against the entire Republican party, visible far down the ballot in electoral results for state assembly seats and local offices. Needless to say, tremendous Democratic majorities rode into Congress, and Johnson was ready for them.

What followed was the historic Eighty-ninth Congress, in which the unfinished agenda of the New Deal was more than completed. As the authoritative *Congressional Quarterly Almanac* said,

> . . . the first session of the 89th, starting early and working late, . . . passed more major legislation than most Congresses pass in two sessions. The scope of the legislation was even more impressive than the number of major new laws. Measures which, taken alone, would have crowned the achievements of any Congress, were enacted in a seemingly endless stream.
>
> In the course of the year, Congress approved major programs which had long been on the agenda of the Democratic party; in the case of medical care for the aged under Social Security, for as long as 20 years. Other long-standing objectives were met by enactment of aid to primary and secondary schools, college scholarships and immigration reform.
>
> The pace of the session was so breathless as to cause a major revision of the image, widely prevalent in preceding years, of Congress as structurally incapable of swift decision, prone to frustrate demands for progress. The change was due to three primary factors not always present in past years: The decisive Democratic majorities elected in 1964, the personal leadership of President Johnson, and the shaping of legislation to obtain maximum political support in Congress. On a number of occasions (most notably in connection with the Elementary-Secondary Education Act) the word was passed to approve the bill and worry about perfecting details later.[29]

Within four years of Johnson's landslide he had worn out his welcome. The Vietnam War, a responsibility he had inherited from Kennedy but which he greatly and, to a certain extent, underhandedly escalated, caused enormous dissension within the Democratic party and in the country at large. Notably influential among the opponents of the war by 1966 was the Senate Foreign Relations Committee, under the leadership of J. William Fulbright of Arkansas.[30] Bitterness over the war spread like blight in Washington and elsewhere. It erupted at the 1968 Democratic national convention in Chicago where Mayor Richard Daley's police, provoked by "obscene epithets . . . rocks, sticks, bathroom tiles and even human feces . . . [and] by widely published threats of attempts to disrupt both the city and the Convention," indulged in a week-long rampage aptly described as a "police riot."[31]

One immediate consequence of the greatly disproportionate disarray of the Democratic party was the election of a Republican, Richard Nixon, to the presidency.

Presidential–Congressional Tensions Further Institutionalized

Democrats, however, still controlled Congress and, in Mr. Nixon's view, the bureaucracies of the federal government as well. Greatly politicizing and rebaptizing the Bureau of the Budget as the Office of Management and Budget, the Nixon administration undertook to limit the functions and the effectiveness of the vast new programs in the federal agencies that had sprung to life under the massive expansion of the Johnson years.[32] On Capitol Hill, Democrats grew suspicious of Nixon's good faith in routine dealings, and began to expand their staffs.[33] The idea was to be able to evaluate, not merely to receive, information from the executive branch. The legislative branch embarked on a seemingly endless program of building and real estate acquisition to house thousands of new workers.

Reforms of their nomination process institutionalized the Democratic party's disarray of 1968, and the party was unable to mount an effective electoral challenge to President Nixon in 1972.[34] Instead Nixon won a great personal victory over Senator George McGovern even while the Democrats once again carried Congress.

Two years later, Nixon resigned in disgrace barely in advance of certain impeachment and conviction of high crimes and misdemeanors. Nixon was merely the second high official of his administration to resign: he was preceded by his vice-president, Spiro T. Agnew, who pleaded *nolo contendere* to formal charges of having received payoffs from contractors in his home state of Maryland while serving as vice-president.[35]

A curious interlude that followed the Agnew resignation tells much about the underlying stability of the American political order. Under the provisions of the recently enacted Twenty-fifth Amendment, a vacancy in the vice-presidency was to be filled by presidential appointment, subject to confirmation by vote of both House and Senate. Mr. Nixon was by then in extremely bad odor in Congress, and impeachment was already in the air. There was a strong presumption that his choice of a vice-president would be far from trivial. It was known that his first preference was John Connally, lately the Democratic governor of Texas, more recently a convert to the

Republican party. The word was passed that Connally might well fail to receive confirmation, and so Nixon turned to the House Republican minority leader, Gerald Ford, who was easily confirmed.[36]

At no time, evidently, did the Democratic majority in both houses demand that Nixon select a Democrat. While the Connally trial balloon suggests that the confirmation process was no perfunctory matter, the Ford nomination shows that the president's congressional opposition operated within self-imposed but strict norms of self-restraint. This was all the more remarkable in that they did so in dealing with a president who strove to compete with the worst behavior of all his predecessors simultaneously in his disregard for tacit limitations upon presidential aggrandizement.[37]

In spite of the fact that the impeachment process had lain unused for a century in its application to the president, it was by no means a constitutionally novel procedure. At each step in the unfolding of the process, Congress was able to find ample guidance. It is, as it was intended to be, a political process, conducted by politically accountable officials in a judicial manner. Nixon's abrupt resignation, and his acceptance of a blanket pardon from his successor a month later, concealed only from his most obdurate political partisans the plain truth that his guilt on at least three counts of high crimes and misdemeanors had been established to the satisfaction of virtually all those who had any access to the facts at all.

The first article of impeachment accused Nixon of numerous acts "in a course of conduct or plan designed to delay, impede and obstruct the investigation" of the break-in of the Watergate offices of the Democratic National Committee, "to cover up, conceal and protect those responsible; and to conceal the existence and scope of other unlawful covert activities." The second article charged that Nixon "repeatedly engaged in conduct violating the constitutional rights of citizens, impairing the due and proper administration of justice and the conduct of lawful inquiries"—including misuse of the Federal Bureau of Investigation, the Central Intelligence Agency, and the Internal Revenue Service. The third article charged him with obstructing the impeachment investigation of the House Judiciary Committee itself by "willfully disobeying" subpoenas requiring him to produce material in his possession believed necessary for their inquiry.

Rejected articles of impeachment accused President Nixon of unjustly enriching himself by tax evasion, of unlawfully spending federal money on private property belonging to him, and of unlawfully concealing from Congress bombing operations in Cambodia.[38]

In the two years and four months Gerald Ford served as president, he cast a great many vetoes—on a month-by-month basis, more vetoes than any but four of his predecessors.[39] Congress swarmed with Democrats after the 1974 elections: up from 243 to 289 in the House, from 58 to 62 in the Senate. The House Democratic caucus, burning brightly with post-Watergate indignation, overturned the seniority of three committee chairmen and sliced into the formal powers of the rest.[10] A new congressional budgetary process was begun, in which House and Senate budget committees were established along with an independent congressional agency, the Congressional Budget Office (CBO), staffed by professional budget analysts.[41] In very short order much of official Washington as well as Congress came to rely on the work of the staffs of these committees and the CBO in a field where once the Bureau of the Budget had held exclusive sway.

The election of 1976 returned a Democrat to the White House along with large Democratic majorities to House and Senate. Yet relations between Congress and the president deteriorated. President Jimmy Carter so cherished his status as an outsider to the Washington political scene that he never made friends on Capitol Hill.[42] Only in the last months of his presidency, when the exigencies of a reelection campaign loomed, did he take seriously the need to pay close attention to the grand coalition of Democrats that had elected him and each of his Democratic predecessors since Franklin Roosevelt. An engineer by training, Carter worked hard and successfully to master the essentials—as well as many of the inessentials—of the programs he advocated, but, in the rueful words of a frustrated congressional ally, he never acted as though the politics of being president was a branch of human relations.

> The President sent a flotilla of major proposals to the Congress in the first eighteen months of his administration—cuts in water projects, social security finance, a comprehensive energy program, a tax rebate scheme, hospital cost containment legislation, comprehensive tax reform, welfare reform. Many of these proposals went to the tax-writing committees of the Congress: Senate Finance and House Ways and Means. And because the President had overloaded the Congress and those committees with reforms that would not command ready assent, because he was not able to marshal the administration's resources and develop political support for all the major battles that were required, and because many of his top political lieutenants were untutored

15

in the ways of the Congress (and at the outset didn't seem to care), most of these proposals were either sunk or badly damaged. President Carter's reputation as less than skillful in dealing the affairs and with the Congress was thus firmly established.[43]

Carter sponsored a major reorganization of the civil service, which in short order helped to stimulate a significant and unintended flight of senior civil servants into retirement.[44] He embarked upon such administrative gimmicks as "zero-based" budgeting, a demand that each part and program of the executive branch be justified annually as though it were a new proposal, but which quickly became in the description of a polite observer a "new way to do incremental budgeting."[45] He ignored advice from all sides on how to organize his legislative liaison, insisting that if Congress failed to see the merits of his prepackaged posposals he would reach over their heads to the people as he had done with the legislature when he was briefly governor of Georgia.[46] Perhaps the best emblem of his relationship with his own party in Congress came on election day 1980 when it became apparent early on that he would be defeated for reelection. Before the polls closed throughout the West, President Carter conceded publicly to his opponent, despite the pleas of his supporters and staff that an early concession would lower turnout and hurt Democratic candidates further down on the ticket. It seemed to observers that he was placing a cosmetic need of his own, to appear to be a gracious loser, ahead of the survival needs of congressional colleagues.[47] For an explanation of the great difficulties between Carter and Congress in the preceding four years, it was understandable that an analyst would look no farther.

Yet it was true, as Carter apologists claimed, that Congress had become an awesomely complex place, and coordination difficult. Sunshine laws and regulations had vastly increased the number of recorded votes.[48] This demanded more grandstanding by members. Legislation was more often written on the floor than negotiated out in committee, where an ethic of give and take could prevail and a coordinated legislative strategy could be agreed upon.[49] The capacity of committees to inspire the loyalty of members declined, as did the atmosphere of comity and trust between committees. It was a rare subcommittee chairman who, in the manner of the powerful committee chairman of a few years before, could protect his subcommittee's legislation on the floor from the intrusion of every element in the entire House. And the Speaker, despite significantly enhanced powers, could only deliver the goods as long as the White House was willing to cooperate with him. So in the end, the dismal relations between Congress and president during the Carter years boiled down to President Carter's reluctance to adopt the members of his own party in Congress as full partners in the development of legislative alternatives and in the assignment of priorities to them.

President Reagan and Congress: A New Era?

President Ronald Reagan's decisive victory over Jimmy Carter in the 1980 election presaged a remarkable new beginning in presidential–congressional relations. Several elements contributed to this renewal.

First, the election results were unexpectedly lopsided. Although two weeks before the election the polls were uncertain about the outcome, Reagan won 489 out of 538 electoral votes. Moreover, the Republicans won the Senate, their first majority in either house of Congress in twenty-six years. Commentators—and especially Reagan supporters among them—were strongly disposed to read these results as an unequivocal mandate, if not, indeed, the first wave of a conservative groundswell that would change American politics for a generation.

Careful analysis could not sustain the more extravagant of these claims, but the political climate in Washington does not always respond to careful analysis. Reagan, almost as much of an outsider to the nation's capital as his predecessor, took pains initially to court rather than to ignore Congress. He installed a professional legislative team in the White House and gave them his confidence. And he sharpened his legislative priorities down to a very fine point. These were, at first, all budgetary.

He appointed an able and phenomenally energetic young congressman as his director of the Office of Management and Budget and gave him free and immediate rein to cut federal spending. At the same time, the new administration was slow in making appointments to the top of the agencies and departments that were going to be cut the hardest. So in effect there were few inconvenient voices in the new administration disturbing plans for budgetary cutbacks with unwelcome substantive defenses. That sort of defense would have to be made, if it was to be made at all, in Congress, as the appropriations subcommittees each took up their part of the whole budgetary package.

It was the special innovation of the Reagan administration that a way was found to short-circuit the congressional process as well. The device was "reconciliation," a procedure in which the Congress votes an overall appropriations ceiling and then orders its committees to shape specific programs to accommodate to the total. In the Senate, newly controlled by Republicans, it was a foregone conclusion that a vote would be taken, and won, to reconcile federal spending to the Reagan ceilings earlier in the budget cycle than was originally provided. The great procedural victory on the same issue came in the House, where the Republican–conservative Democratic coalition reemerged in full vigor after some years of hibernation.[50]

Some Lessons from the Historical Record

There are at least a few lessons hidden, and perhaps not so hidden, in the recent history of presidential–congressional relations. One is that electoral results are constantly reshaping the terrain over which presidential–congressional relations are battled out. To come to fruition, presidential initiatives demand tractable congressional coalitions. These coalitions are formed out of the raw materials supplied by voters in the several states and in the 435 congressional districts. It is voters who decide how many Democrats and how many Republicans sit in Congress. And it is voters who decide from what party the president shall be chosen.

In the half-century surveyed in this essay, Democrats held the presidency for thirty-two years and Republicans eighteen. For a good part of the time, however, Democratic programs were stalled and frustrated because congressional sentiment was more evenly divided, regardless of the party labels of incumbents.

So a second lesson is that electoral results must be turned by acts of institutional leadership into legislative coalitions, a set of transactions separate and apart from the voting that puts presidents and members of Congress in office. In general, two great coalitions have dominated congressional business.[51] One consisted mostly of Democrats variously divided into genera and species: liberal Democrats, mainstream Democrats, urban Democrats, Northern Democrats, Western Democrats, and more than a handful of Southern liberal Democrats. These, plus a few maverick progressive, silk-stocking, or suburban Republicans, make up the more liberal coalition. The "conservative coalition" has generally consisted of almost all the Republicans plus conservative Democrats, mostly Southern (recently called "boll weevils"), with a few Westerners.[52] Most commentators on presidential–congressional relations over the last fifty years have spent a lot of time and energy with sharp pencils, calculating the ways in which ebbs and flows in the electoral results have added to and subtracted from these coalitions.

These sorts of calculations led to propositions of the following kind:

1. Over a twenty-year period there has been a significant shift among the congressional delegations of the South from Democratic to Republican. In 1960 there were 107 congressional seats in the thirteen states of the old Confederacy. Seven of those seats were held by Republicans. After the 1980 election, 39 Republican House members came from the 108 seats allocated to the South.

2. This does not mean, however, that Southern conservatism has become more influential in Congress. On the whole, Southern Republicans filtered into open seats instead of knocking off incumbents, and these seats had predominantly been held by conservative Democrats.[53] There has always been a modest number of mainstream or liberal Democrats from the South, from rural areas where the New Deal brought electricity and farm price supports, for example, or from big cities like Houston or New Orleans, with large working-class and black populations, or from areas, like Miami or San Antonio, heavily populated by Spanish-Americans. In 1960 twenty-five Southerners voted with the rest of the Democratic party on House roll calls more than twice as often as they voted against; that number was still twenty-five in 1981, which means that the net gain of Southern Republicans in Congress has *all* been at the expense of conservative Southern Democrats.[54]

3. Consequently, for those significant decisions taken in the House Democratic caucus, as in the 1970s many were, the voice of conservative southerners was greatly diminished. This helps to explain how, in the late 1960s and 1970s the caucus became an instrument of the Democratic party's mainstream.

Behind micropolitical movements of this kind we can see lurking larger forces such as were once identified by E. E. Schattschneider as "the nationalization of American politics," the reduction in the distinctiveness of regional political trends, owing in part to migration, in part to the advance of technological innovations like air conditioning and television.[55] Almost certainly the influence of television has been very great in accelerating the tendency for political information and political sentiment in the United States to be uniform across the country.

Over the fifty-year span, both the Congress and the president have grown greatly in their institutional size and capabilities. At the beginning of the era, the executive office was a few clerks and assistants, and Congress made do with comparably small professional staffs. Now both institutions are burgeoning establishments, capable of waging titanic battles employing bales of memoranda, sophisticated word-processors, and all the other weaponry of modern bureaucratic warfare. On the whole, other democratic governments do not equip themselves in this way, but none is anywhere near as large as the U.S. government, none employs a fully worked out separation of powers, and all devolve far greater responsibility upon career civil servants.[56]

In the longer view, perhaps the most interesting development of the fifty-year period is the emergence of a presidential branch of government separate and apart from the executive branch. It is the presidential branch that sits *across* the table from the executive branch at budgetary hearings, and that imperfectly attempts to coordinate both the executive and legislative branches in its own behalf. Against this development—this growing estrangement if not outright hostility of the presidential branch—the executive branch has been helpless, and that is the root cause of the decline in the caliber of the career bureaucracies, which is only beginning to become visible to thoughtful students of public administration.[57] The legislative branch, on the other hand, has taken measures to protect its territory by greatly expanding its staff capacity. The U.S. Congress remains a uniquely capable and independent legislature even in the face of the enormous development of the presidency in modern times.

Notes

1. The foregoing quotations are from Pendleton Herring, "First Session of the Seventy-Third Congress, March 9, 1933 to June 16, 1933," *American Political Science Review*, vol. 28 (February 1934), pp. 65, 67, and 75. See also his description of congressional handling of the banking crisis, ibid., pp. 70ff., and, in general, Herring, *Presidential Leadership* (New York: Farrar and Rinehart, 1940), and Herring's periodic reviews of congressional activity for the *American Political Science Review:* "1st Session of the 72nd Congress," vol. 26 (October 1932), pp. 846-74; "2nd Session of the 72nd Congress," vol. 27 (June 1933), pp. 404-22; "1st Session of the 73rd Congress," vol. 28 (February 1934), pp. 65-83; "2nd Session of the 73rd Congress," vol. 28 (October 1934), pp. 852-66; and "1st Session of the 74th Congress," vol. 29 (December 1935), pp. 985-1005.

2. James T. Patterson, *Congressional Conservatism and the New Deal* (Lexington: University of Kentucky Press, 1967), pp. 4-5. See also, William E. Leuchtenburg, *Franklin D. Roosevelt and the New Deal* (New York: Harper & Row, 1963), pp. 41-62.

3. I am using this term in a sense slightly different from the usage of its coiner, Thomas C. Cochran, who in "The 'Presidential Synthesis' in American History," *American Historical Review*, vol. 53 (July 1948), pp. 748-59, argued for a greater infusion of social science theory and methods into historical inquiry and for an understanding of the lives of ordinary people in the past and not just political elites.

See also Martin Shapiro's discussion of what he calls the "New Deal myth" about the Supreme Court. "The Supreme Court from Warren to Burger" in Anthony King, ed., *The New American Political System* (Washington, D.C.: American Enterprise Institute, 1978), especially pp. 188ff.

4. See Patterson, *Congressional Conservatism.*

5. See Jasper B. Shannon, "Presidential Politics in the South: 1938," *Journal of Politics,* vol. 1, nos. 2 and 3 (May and August 1939), pp. 146-70, 278-300.

6. The relevant provisions of the Constitution on the vice-presidency are art. I, sect. 3, para. 4: "The Vice President of the United States shall be President of the Senate, but shall have no vote, unless they be equally divided."; art. II, sect. 1, para. 5: "In case of the removal of the President from office, or of his death, resignation, or inability to discharge the powers and duties of the said office, the same shall devolve on the Vice President, and the Congress may by law provide for the case of removal, death, resignation or inability, both of the President and Vice President, declaring what officer shall then act as President, and such officer shall act accordingly, until the disability be removed, or a President shall be elected." (This clause has been modified by the Twentieth and Twenty-fifth Amendments.)

7. In "Truman's Global Leadership," *Current History,* vol. 39 (October 1960), p. 226, Louis W. Koenig says:

> Roosevelt was not in Washington a month altogether during the 82 days that Truman was vice-president. The Roosevelt papers disclose that the two met by appointment only twice. Truman himself estimates that he saw Roosevelt only eight times the year before his death, and these meetings contributed little to Truman's preparation for the Presidency.

8. Gerald Ford was vice-president from December 6, 1973, to August 9, 1974, the first person to be appointed and confirmed by Congress under the provisions of the Twenty-fifth Amendment (paragraph 1: "In the case of the removal of the President from office or of his death or resignation, the Vice President shall become President.") He succeeded to the presidency so rapidly he scarcely had time to find out what the vice presidency was all about.

9. President's Commission on Administrative Management, *Administrative Management in the Government of the United States* (Washington, D.C., January 1937), p. 5.

10. See Richard Neustadt, "Presidency and Legislation: The Growth of Central Clearance," *American Political Science Review,* vol. 48 (September 1954), pp. 641-71; and Neustadt, "Presidency and Legislation: Planning the President's Program," *American Political Science Review,* vol. 49 (December 1955), pp. 980-1021.

11. See Nelson W. Polsby, "The Washington Community, 1960–1980," in Thomas E. Mann and Norman J. Ornstein, eds., *The New Congress* (Washington, D.C.: American Enterprise Institute, 1981), pp. 7-31, for a general overview.

12. See Frederick C. Mosher, *The GAO* (Boulder, Colo.: Westview

Press, 1979), pp. 310-14; W. Brooke Graves, *American Intergovernmental Relations* (New York: Charles Scribner's Sons, 1964), pp. 540-73.

13. See Alan K. McAdams, *Power and Politics in Labor Legislation* (New York: Columbia University Press, 1964)

14. See Kenneth Kofmehl, "Institutionalization of a Voting Bloc," *Western Political Quarterly*, vol. 17 (June 1964), pp. 256-72; Mark F. Ferber, "The Formation of the Democratic Study Group," in Nelson W. Polsby, ed., *Congressional Behavior* (New York: Random House, 1971), pp. 249-69.

15. On the revolt against Cannon, see Blair Bolles, *Tyrant from Illinois: Uncle Joe Cannon's Experiment with Personal Power* (New York: Norton, 1951); Charles O. Jones, "Joseph G. Cannon and Howard W. Smith: An Essay on the Limits of Leadership in the House of Representatives," *Journal of Politics*, vol. 30 (August 1968), pp. 617-46.

16. On Reed's counting of the House, see Samuel W. McCall, *The Life of Thomas Brackett Reed* (Boston: Houghton Mifflin Co., 1914), pp. 162-72.

17. For good overviews see H. Douglas Price, "Race, Religion, and the Rules Committee," in A. Westin, ed., *The Uses of Power* (New York: Harcourt Brace & World, 1962), pp. 1-71; Neil MacNeil, *Forge of Democracy* (New York: McKay, 1963), pp. 39-60.

18. See John Hart, "Staffing the Presidency: Kennedy and the Office of Congressional Relations," *Presidential Studies Quarterly*, vol. 3, no. 1 (Winter 1983).

19. See Nelson W. Polsby, "Goodby to the Inner Club," *Washington Monthly*, vol. 1 (August 1969), pp. 30-34. Good pictures of the Senate "before" are given in Allen Drury, *A Senate Journal, 1943-1945* (New York: McGraw-Hill, 1963); and William S. White, *Citadel* (New York: Harper & Row, 1956). A summary of the Senate "after" is Michael Foley, *The New Senate: The Senate Liberals and Institutional Change, 1959-1972* (New Haven: Yale University Press, 1980).

20. Secretary of State Dean Acheson had a great hand in promoting Vandenberg's position. See Dean Acheson, *Sketches From Life of Men I Have Known* (New York: Harper & Row, 1961), pp. 123-46; and Acheson, *Present at the Creation* (New York: Norton, 1969); also, James T. Patterson, *Mr. Republican: A Biography of Robert A. Taft* (Boston: Houghton Mifflin, 1972).

21. Joseph B. Gorman, *Kefauver: A Political Biography* (New York: Oxford University Press, 1971).

22. See Hubert H. Humphrey, *Education of a Public Man: My Life & Politics* (Garden City, N.Y.: Doubleday, 1976).

23. On Kennedy in the Senate see Herbert S. Parmet, *Jack: The Struggles of John F. Kennedy* (New York: Dial, 1980); Theodore H. White, *The Making of the President 1960* (New York: Atheneum, 1961); Theodore C. Sorensen, *Kennedy* (New York: Harper & Row, 1965), pp. 43-70.

24. See Michael J. Malbin, *Unelected Representatives: A New Role for Congressional Staffs* (New York: Basic Books, 1980).

25. See Lawrence O'Brien, *No Final Victories* (Garden City, N.Y.:

Doubleday, 1974), pp. 104-36. On Kennedy and Congress in general see Randall B. Ripley, *Kennedy and Congress* (Morristown, N.J.: General Learning Press, 1972).

26. See Richard W. Bolling, *Defeating the Leadership's Nominee in the House Democratic Caucus,* Inter-University Case Program No. 91 (Indianapolis: Bobbs-Merrill, 1965).

27. On Johnson as majority leader, see Rowland Evans and Robert Novak, *Lyndon B. Johnson: The Exercise of Power* (New York: New American Library, 1966), pp. 88-224; Nelson W. Polsby, *Congress and the Presidency* (Englewood Cliffs, N.J.: Prentice-Hall, 1976), pp. 95-102.

28. On the effects of the 1964 election on the Republican party see Robert Novak, *The Agony of the GOP 1964* (New York: Macmillan, 1965); Robert J. Donovan, *The Future of the Republican Party* (New York: New American Library, 1964). On Goldwater as a candidate, see Richard H. Rovere, *The Goldwater Caper* (New York: Harcourt Brace and World, 1965).

29. "Congress 1965—The Year in Review," *Congressional Quarterly Almanac,* vol. 21 (Washington, D.C.: Congressional Quarterly Press, 1965), p. 65.

30. See Haynes Johnson and Bernard M. Gwertzman, *Fulbright: The Dissenter* (Garden City, N.Y.: Doubleday, 1968), pp. 193-224.

31. Daniel Walker, *Rights in Conflict* (New York: Grosset & Dunlap, 1968), pp. vii, ix.

32. See Richard Nathan, *The Plot That Failed: Nixon and the Administrative Presidency* (New York: Wiley, 1975); Polsby, *Congress and the Presidency,* pp. 48-61.

33. See Charles O. Jones, "Congress and the Presidency," in Mann and Ornstein, eds., *The New Congress,* pp. 223-49 (especially pp. 229-37); also James L. Sundquist, "Congress and the President: Enemies or Partners?" in Lawrence C. Dodd and Bruce I. Oppenheimer, eds., *Congress Reconsidered* (New York: Praeger, 1977), pp. 222-43.

34. The literature on this subject is massive. For varied views, see William J. Crotty, *Decision for the Democrats: Reforming the Party Structure* (Baltimore, Md.: Johns Hopkins University Press, 1978); Austin Ranney, *Curing the Mischiefs of Faction: Party Reform in America* (Berkeley: University of California Press, 1975); Theodore H. White, *The Making of the President 1972* (New York: Atheneum Publishers, 1973), pp. 25ff.

35. See Richard M. Cohen and Jules Witcover, *A Heartbeat Away: The Investigation and Resignation of Vice President Spiro T. Agnew* (New York: Viking Press, 1974).

36. On the Ford nomination see Jerald F. terHorst, *Gerald Ford and the Future of the Presidency* (New York: Okpaku Publishing Co., 1974), pp. 139-69; John Osborne, *The Fifth Year of the Nixon Watch* (New York: Liveright, 1974), pp. 167-72; Robert T. Hartmann, *Palace Politics: An Inside Account of the Ford Years* (New York: McGraw-Hill, 1980), pp. 14-28.

37. The literature on the Nixon impeachment episode is very large. See Sam J. Ervin, Jr., *The Whole Truth: The Watergate Conspiracy* (New York: Random House, 1981); Leon Jaworski, *The Right and the Power: The Prosecution of Watergate* (Houston: Gulf Publishing Co., 1976); Philip Kurland, *Watergate and the Constitution* (Chicago: University of Chicago Press, 1978).

38. See Report of the Committee on the Judiciary, House of Representatives, *Impeachment of Richard M. Nixon*, August 20, 1974.

39. Grover Cleveland was the all-time champion caster of presidential vetoes (8.6 per month in his first term, 3.54 per month in his second) followed by Franklin Roosevelt (4.41 vetoes per month), Harry Truman (2.60), and Dwight Eisenhower (1.89). Ford, who like the others served with a Congress controlled by the opposing party, comes in at 1.83 vetoes a month. Next is Ulysses S. Grant with 0.97. See Louis Fisher, *The Politics of Shared Power* (Washington, D.C.: Congressional Quarterly Press, 1981), p. 26.

40. See Norman J. Ornstein and David W. Rohde, "Shifting Forces, Changing Rules, and Political Outcomes: The Impact of Congressional Change on Four House Committees," in Robert L. Peabody and Nelson W. Polsby, eds., *New Perspectives on the House of Representatives* (Chicago: Rand McNally, 1977), pp. 186-269.

41. See Allen Schick, *Congress and Money: Budgeting, Spending, and Taxing* (Washington, D.C.: Urban Institute, 1980).

42. See Haynes Johnson, *In the Absence of Power: Governing America* (New York: Viking Press, 1980); Betty Glad, *Jimmy Carter: In Search of the Great White House* (New York: Norton, 1980).

43. Ben W. Heineman, Jr., and Curtis A. Hessler, *Memorandum for the President* (New York: Random House, 1981), p. xix.

44. "About 95 percent of top bureaucrats reaching retirement age—those between 55 and 59 with 30 years of federal experience—are deciding to leave, compared with about 18 percent in 1978, the General Accounting Office (GAO) reports" (p. 1296). William J. Lanouette, "SES: From Civil Service Showpiece to Incipient Failure in Two Years," *National Journal* (July 18, 1981), pp. 1296-99.

45. See Thomas H. Hammond and Jack H. Knott, eds., *A Zero-Based Look at Zero-Based Budgeting* (New Brunswick, N.J.: Transaction Books, 1980), pp. 98-102. "ZBB has so metamorphosed into incremental budgeting that the only thing left is its smile floating in the air" (p. 102).

46. See Eric L. Davis, "Legislative Liaison in the Carter Administration," *Political Science Quarterly*, vol. 94 (Summer 1979), pp. 287-301.

47. This among other things led to complaints about the effects of election day information on turnout. See Raymond Wolfinger and Peter Linquiti, "Tuning In and Turning Out," *Public Opinion*, vol. 4 (February/March 1981), pp. 56-60. On Carter's role, see John Fogarty, "Carter Saw No Harm in Conceding Early," *San Francisco Chronicle*, November 7, 1980; John Balzar, "Demos Hurt by Early TV Vote Report," ibid., March 11, 1981; Kenneth Reich, "State Democrats Bitter on Carter's Early Conces-

sion," *Los Angeles Times*, November 5, 1980; William Endicott, "Anti-Carter Vote Seen in State Races," ibid., November 6, 1980; and Roger Smith, "Early Concession Costly: State Party Leaders Sure Carter 'Paralyzed' Effort," ibid., November 7, 1980.

48. "As characterized by one member, the House has become a 'fast breeder reactor' for amendments. Between 1963 and 1970 the total number of appropriations amendments, for example, was 441 but within the 1971-77 period, the number increased to 715." Joseph Cooper and Melissa P. Coolie, "Structural Adaptation in the House: Multiple Reference and Interunit Committees in Organizational Perspective," a paper delivered at the 1981 annual meeting of the American Political Science Association, September 3-6, 1981, p. 34. See also, Barbara Sinclair, "The Speaker's Task Force in the Post-Reform House of Representatives," *American Political Science Review*, vol. 75 (June 1981), pp. 397-410 (especially p. 399).

49. See Norman J. Ornstein, Robert L. Peabody, and David W. Rohde, "The Contemporary Senate: Into the 1980s," in Lawrence C. Dodd and Bruce I. Oppenheimer, eds., *Congress Reconsidered* (Washington, D.C.: Congressional Quarterly Press, 1981), pp. 13-30.

50. On President Reagan and Congress, see Dick Kirschten, "The Pennsylvania Ave. Connection—Making Peace on Capitol Hill," *National Journal*, vol. 13 (March 7, 1981), pp. 384-87; Richard E. Cohen, "The 'Revolution' on Capitol Hill: Is It Just a Temporary Coup?" ibid., vol. 13 (August 19, 1981), pp. 1537-41.

51. See Nelson W. Polsby, "Coalition and Faction in American Politics: An Institutional View," in S. M. Lipset, ed., *Party Coalitions in the 1980's* (San Francisco: Institute for Contemporary Studies, 1981), pp. 153-78.

52. See John F. Manley, "The Conservative Coalition in Congress," *American Behavioral Scientist*, vol. 17 (November-December 1973), pp. 223-47.

53. See Raymond Wolfinger and Robert B. Arsenau, "Partisan Change in the South, 1952-1976," in Louis Maisel and Joseph Cooper, eds., Sage *Electoral Studies Yearbook*, vol. 4: *Political Parties: Development and Decay* (Beverly Hills, Calif.: Sage Publications, 1978), pp. 179-210.

54. Calculations based on *Congressional Quarterly* statistics.

55. E. E. Schattschneider, "United States: The Functional Approach to Party Government," in Sigmund Neumann, ed., *Modern Political Parties* (Chicago: University of Chicago Press, 1956), pp. 194-215 (especially pp. 210ff.); and E. E. Schattschneider, *The Semisovereign People* (New York: Holt, 1960), pp. 78-96.

56. For comparative perspective, see Nelson W. Polsby, "Legislatures," in Fred I. Greenstein and Nelson W. Polsby, eds., *Handbook of Political Science*, vol. 5 (Reading, Mass.: Addison-Wesley Publishing Co., Inc., 1975), pp. 257-319; and Kenneth Bradshaw and David Pring, *Parliament and Congress* (Austin: University of Texas Press, 1972).

57. For glimmerings of this see Hugh Heclo, *A Government of Strangers: Executive Politics in Washington* (Washington, D.C.: Brookings Institution, 1977).

2
One Executive Branch or Many?

Hugh Heclo

Recent presidents have felt a need to avow a commitment to governing through their cabinet officers, President-elect Carter no less than President-elect Nixon. President-elect Reagan predicted that his agency heads would function as a team of emissaries to the departments rather than as departmental advocates to the White House. "I am more confident than ever," he said, "that Cabinet Government can and will work."[1]

Such statements seem to arise out of a president's natural desire to reassure an apprehensive public rather than out of well-worked-out plans for his administration. They are meant to show that the new man is a leader but not power-hungry, presidential but not imperial.

If cabinet government is weakly defined to mean improved two-way communications between the White House and the departments, or if it means restraining White House staff from taking over the statutory duties of cabinet officers, then no one can object. But if cabinet government is defined in the strong sense—as the president governing only indirectly through the way his department and agency heads decide to act as a group—then the proposition is dangerously unrealistic. It is significant that no president has ever left office extolling the virtues of cabinet government.

Beyond Cabinet Government

Beyond the talk of cabinet government lies the reality of the president's managerial task in the executive branch. Through his initial personnel appointments and periodic expressions of general aims, a president gives structure to his administration. But no administrative structure goes into motion without continual presidential involvement. The fundamental reason for this fact lies beyond any questions of

I wish to thank the National Academy of Public Administration for its support during the early stages of preparing this paper.

personality, competing ambitions, or policy disagreements. It is instead embedded in a political constitution that does two things. First, the Constitution binds executive bureaucracies to a powerful legislature independent of the president. And, second, our constitutional system vests executive branch leadership in a president and department heads whose personal and political fates are not closely tied together.

The effect of these arrangements is that no public official short of the president has a vested interest in coordinating political management in the executive branch as a whole. But by the same token no president has more than a tenuous capacity himself to perform such a coordinating role. *If* Congress were to hold executive departments and bureaus accountable only through the president, his hand as executive coordinator would be in little doubt. *If* presidents and department heads were elected and dismissed as a team, their interests would tend to converge. Neither condition has ever existed or is likely to exist in the near future. A true cabinet (or collegial) government neither has existed nor will exist in the United States.

The president's role as executive branch manager is therefore inherently necessary and inherently ambiguous under our system of government. For the president, there can be no answer to the conundrum, One executive branch or many? Should a president readily defer to departmental and congressional opinion, his administration will soon lack all coherence. Should the president, however, seek thoroughgoing conformity with his views within the executive branch, he will soon run afoul of Congress's and courts' administrative power and will also lose valuable diversity of advice. Twentieth-century American presidents have typically engaged in a constant struggle to find a middle ground between a "oneness" they cannot achieve and a "manyness" they cannot accept, between directionlessness and groupthink within their executive families.

To cope with this tenuous relation to the rest of the executive branch, presidents and their advisers have used a variety of mechanisms. The 1921 law giving the president power to prepare a coordinated budget of the executive branch for submission to Congress was one landmark. So too was the gradual evolution—still under way—of the president's budget agency (the Bureau of the Budget, renamed in 1970 the Office of Management and Budget) into something like a general management agency after 1939. President Eisenhower's staff secretariat for cabinet deliberations was an interesting experiment that did not survive. There has been greater staying power in individual staffs responsible for helping the president to develop and coordinate policies in particular functional areas. The

Council of Economic Advisers for economic management, the National Security Council staff for Defense/State Department affairs, and the domestic policy staff for social programs are the central examples.

The story of these institutional developments has been told many times.[2] But perhaps because they are so pervasive, the underlying forces shaping presidential management and institutions have aroused less attention. It has been over twenty-five years since the appearance of Richard Neustadt's classic articles concerning presidential programming and legislative coordination within the executive branch. Since that time, major changes in the political environment for executive branch management have occurred. This essay examines that changed environment and goes on to argue that presidential strategies required to cope with the changes are serving to undercut the institutional capabilities of government. In this respect, the successful managerial strategy of the Reagan administration has simply given stronger impetus to a trend that has been under way for a generation. A good way to appreciate what has happened is to start where Richard Neustadt did, with the beginnings of the Eisenhower presidency, and to contrast that situation with the launching of the Reagan presidency. A few brief glimpses will do.

Then and Now. President-elect Eisenhower entered office committed to cutting taxes and spending, balancing the budget, and reducing government interventions in the economy. During the transition period after the November 1952 election, he received several reports from private consultants that identified basic organizational means for putting his administration in place—perhaps a thousand pages of paper in all. At a series of private meetings at New York's Hotel Commodore, General Eisenhower discussed with his designated cabinet secretaries some of the general aims and methods he wished to adopt. These meetings resulted in no significant leaks of the transition reports.[3]

The new president's budget cuts were worked out gradually through established bureaucratic routines within the executive branch. During Eisenhower's first six months in office, some reductions were proposed in the outgoing Truman administration's budget for fiscal 1954 (running from July 1953 through June 1954), but the president's main budget-making activities during 1953 were devoted to cutting projected spending in the fiscal 1955 budget. By and large, the budget cutbacks were negotiated within the confines of the executive branch. Proposals from the career staff of the president's Budget Bureau were argued back and forth with the spending agencies, under general presidential guidelines calling for a 10 percent to 15 percent reduction in total spending so as to move toward a balanced budget. On a few particularly sensitive matters, such as Eisenhower's insistence on defense cuts, discreet consultations were held with selected congressional leaders.

President Eisenhower's first major legislative program was unveiled one year after he took office. The program presented in early 1954 was developed mainly from agency proposals that worked their way upward toward the president through well-established bureaucratic channels. The bulk of the day-to-day work involved in screening these proposals for the president fell to a handful of White House aides (six to ten) working in intimate consultation with a senior career bureaucrat and his staff in the Bureau of the Budget; most of these civil servants had been in government since the 1930s. As a general rule, this legislative programming, like the new administration's budget-cutting exercise, was a process confined to a fairly small circle of people who could best be described as political generalists—Republican party moderates, bureaucratic insiders, and key congressional leaders. The electoral pendulum had clearly swung in 1952, but in doing so the political process had produced a government that could best be described as vaguely conservative and comfortable with (if not always wholly trusting of) holdover bureaucrats from the executive establishment. It was a vagueness and comfortableness that infuriated more hardline conservatives such as Robert Taft.

President-elect Reagan entered office espousing many of the same themes of reducing spending, taxation, and government intervention. But unlike Eisenhower, Reagan moved toward office with a transition staff of roughly 300 persons supported by a $2 million tax-paid budget. Transition staff work concentrated not so much on administrative procedures as on complex policy issues and priority actions, so that the new administration could begin changing the course of policy within the first 100 days. The transition reports filled several file cabinets. Designated cabinet members, subordinate appointees, and many conservative policy analysts with little involvement in the Republican party were deeply involved in this transition process well before the president-elect had met with his cabinet secretaries as a group. Various transition reports were leaked, generally with the aim of building pressure for particular presidential policy choices.[4]

Weeks before Reagan took the oath of office, various groups were far along in preparing highly detailed lists of deep cuts in the outgoing Carter administration's budget. Transition staff worked on the budget mainly from a list of item-by-item cuts prepared by the

Republican staff of the Senate Budget Committee, but other lists were pushed by other congressional staff arms, conservative think tanks, and political action groups. The net result was a series of White House budget proposals that reflected not merely a means for staying within general presidential guidelines for budget stringency and balance, but a more or less comprehensive attack on the structure of existing domestic policy.

At the same time the new president achieved a very fast start on major policy commitments—a green light for massive defense spending, a new supply-side approach to tax cutting, a more belligerent, anti-Communist foreign and human rights policy, and so on. These initiatives were not undertaken as part of a comprehensive legislative program laid before Congress, but were worked out largely in advance of the administration's assuming office and were refined in a complex system of White House and cabinet councils. It is fair to say that no senior career official of the executive branch was centrally involved in any of these developments. Within six months of taking office, the new president was heavily committed to a multiyear program of domestic spending cutbacks, defense increases, and tax reductions.

Compared with the vagueness of an earlier period, the Reagan group was clear and specific (if not always consistent) on the meaning of its conservative orientation for detailed government programs and policy choices. It seemed to distrust not only individual bureaucrats held over from the previous Democratic administration but also the very idea of a Washington executive establishment. If many of Eisenhower's budgetary and legislative proposals grew out of work in the bureaucracy, the Reagan officials' fast start seemed to reflect little thinking from inside government—and proud they were of that fact.

Of course personalities, philosophies, and public demands change over time. The year 1980 was not 1952, and Ronald Reagan was not Dwight Eisenhower. It would be foolish to think that one set of factors can explain all of the differences in the ways in which the two presidents settled into office. But it would be no less shortsighted to think that our governing system is simply a compound of a particular presidential personality, political philosophy, and election. In fact the 1980 election results were much less decisive than Eisenhower's 1952 mandate and seemed, in and of themselves, to dictate nothing like a major policy realignment.[5] The point is that the years since 1952 have produced important changes in the deeper background factors affecting presidential management in the executive branch. Taken together these factors have made it more difficult for any president to find and hold onto a working middle ground between oneness and manyness in the executive branch. And that in turn is likely to upset many of the conventional ideas old-time Washingtonians cherish about the working relations between the president and the Congress. If Jimmy Carter or Gerald Ford often symbolized the directionless end of the range, Richard Nixon and Ronald Reagan and his team seemed intent on epitomizing the unidirectional, groupthink end of it. But before risking any prognosis for the 1980s, we should look more deeply into the changed, post-Eisenhower setting for presidential management.

The Environment for Political Management

A full comparison of the Eisenhower and Reagan transitions would indicate that important aspects of the president's position in the executive branch and his relations with Congress have not changed greatly during the past thirty years. The president is still expected to present Congress with an inventory of legislative proposals reflecting the coordinated views of his administration. His initiatives play the key role in setting the agenda for Congress and often define the terms of debate. The main, enduring source of staff manpower at the center of the executive branch remains the budget agency in the Executive Office of the President. And today, as in all earlier times, major portions of activities in the executive branch continue to be outside the president's direct control, a function of the powers of administrative supervision exercised by Congress and the courts. In other words, basic contours on the landscape of presidential management remain familiar.

But these easily recognizable features are no longer the full picture, if they ever were. Today's president also faces a more fluid, complex managerial situation, open to more outside forces and contingencies and therefore less predictable. His operating environment is less like the fixed geographic contours of a topographical map and more like the shifting atmospheric contours of a weather map. It would be convenient if we could describe what had happened as simply an increase or a decline in presidential power. But the changes are more subtle than that. Some developments work in the president's favor, helping him navigate through crosscurrents and even to chart the course for others. Offsetting tendencies help to push him aside and scatter his administration to the winds. A system that many observers see as breaking down in the Carter years seems a breeze to manage (at least at the outset) in the Reagan presidency. If the much-discussed volatility of the electorate has increased in recent years, the volatility and uncertainty of our governing system seem to have increased even more. Before deciding what they add up to, let us consider three developments in the setting for presidential management: policy congestion, political mobilization, and institutional estrangement.

The Effects of Policy Congestion. Traditionally, presidents have been thought to be in the key position to help set the national policy agenda. Indeed, it has been this need for a working agenda that has generally led congressmen, bureaucrats, and others to support various presidential mechanisms for coordination of the executive branch.[6] Presidents are in their turn, however, greatly affected by the changing agenda of government activities and particularly in recent years by the crowding of that agenda. The point is not simply that the federal government is doing more things, but that it is doing more things that affect one another. A general awareness has grown that one issue impinges on another, one government activity on another.

In domestic programs, the expansion and interaction of government activities have become pervasive. For example, federal assistance to local governments, individuals, and profit and nonprofit organizations has grown rapidly in the past twenty years and now accounts for over half of federal spending. In 1980 there were over 1,100 such assistance programs. Their number, however, is less important than their layering and overlap. Overlap results because any given recipient typically acquires federal assistance from more than one program administered by more than one agency, but no one is responsible for supervising the cumulative impact of each agency's requirements for its program. Layering results because, in trying to bring at least some coordinated thrust to these programs, so-called crosscutting requirements are laid down to apply to programs in more than one agency (for example, prohibiting racial, sexual, or age discrimination, safeguarding the environment, or providing for the handicapped). At last count there were fifty-nine such cross-agency requirements, half of which were promulgated just within the last nine years. Yet each of these coordinating requirements is itself run by an individual department or agency with no one responsible for supervising the cumulative impact of these crosscutting requirements.[7] Hence complexity builds on complexity, circles within circles.

Federal assistance programs are but a miniature reflection of the larger interactions created by a congested policy agenda. Newspaper stories typically refer to an "explosion" of government spending and regulation, but the more salient public-management problem is a growing "implosion" of government activities—an inward bursting of pressures across traditional policy and organizational boundaries.

In 1954 President Eisenhower could propose a new interstate highway program that was just that: a plan for building roads. The issue was initiated, debated, and executed with minimal attention to nonhighway considerations. Today we would expect, almost without thinking about it, that consideration of such an issue should include the implications for private-car versus mass-public transportation, energy conservation, environmental impacts, effects on urban development and neighborhoods, regional economic development programs, minority hiring by road-construction contractors, and on and on. We may disagree about how trade-offs among these various concerns should be struck, but few would deny the legitimacy of their presence in any agenda of highway building.

The situation becomes even more complex if we expand the terms of reference beyond purely domestic affairs to international affairs. During the past thirty years, America's ability to dominate any single nation or grouping of nations has diminished. At the same time, we have grown to need other nations more and so find our domestic interests enmeshed in their decisions.[8] This further congests the policy agenda with what in former times could be more easily dismissed as extraneous considerations. Today, our relations with foreign ministries interact with agricultural policies in ways that affect farmers at home as much as consumers abroad. What we can or cannot persuade other governments to do has a direct impact on our industrial policies, which put Americans into or out of jobs. A young couple's ability to buy a house depends not only on their own savings or on decisions made in Washington but more and more on reactions by foreigners to our economic performance. No single set of priorities or neat regrouping of organizational units can conceivably encompass the relevant interactions among policy issues Thus in 1977 President Carter proposed a new Energy Department "to bring immediate order" to the conduct of national energy policy. One and a half years after the creation of this department, it was necessary to assemble a group representing no fewer than twenty-two other federal departments and agencies "to provide for the coordination of Federal energy policies."[9]

It seems that during the 1960s sensitivity to the interrelatedness of issues began to increase—poverty problems and economic management; civil rights and the workings of labor markets and educational bureaucracies; housing and transportation programs, financial markets, and urban decay. Crowding onto the public agenda during the 1970s were issues—energy, inflation, economic revitalization—with even more intense crosscutting qualities. Seen from the president's desk, all of this has produced a dual complexity. There are more issues to be coordinated affecting any given agency, and there are more agencies in need of coordination for any given issue.

As a practical matter, these tendencies mean that the president, rather than simply deciding on a government agenda, is increasingly involved in sorting out relationships among agendas—for economic management, international affairs, social policy, intergovernmental relations, and so on. The resulting product of this synthesizing process inevitably appears diffuse and unfocused. Consider, for example, the "thrusts" of such programs as a presidential perspective might imply:

- anti-inflation policies retaining a commitment to full employment
- an energy program that combines incentives for increased conservation and greater production
- a national trade policy that protects domestic interests and promotes international cooperation
- a taxing and spending package that both benefits the disadvantaged and enhances the wealth-generating capacities of the advantaged
- a national security stance that counters Soviet expansionism and reduces the risks of war

Of course it is easy to dismiss such stands as political hypocrisy that allows the president to duck hard choices. Yet in a deeper sense modern presidents are driven to these positions because they manage in a policy environment in which there are no acceptable final choices on such matters. Presidents have found it increasingly difficult to make the executive branch speak with one voice because we as a nation have become increasingly aware that one unrelinquishable value interferes with another and that no final choice can be made between the environment and profitability, between social compassion and economic competition, or between the risks of peace and those of war. A president who tries to meet the injunction to represent all of the people in his leadership of the executive branch tends, therefore, to become a study in ambiguity.

The New Political Mobilization. The president's task of synthesizing a meta-agenda does not link the office to any coherent, preexisting constituency. Indeed the fact that there is such an office charged with applying an overarching national perspective serves as a ready-made excuse for every other political actor to leave that coordinating task to the president. That much is scarcely novel. It has always proved difficult to argue the general against the particular, the common interests against particular interests.

What policy congestion adds to this picture is a higher level of ambiguity in presidential leadership at a greater distance from any concrete constituency. It does so because the president must try to represent and execute our own unreconciled policy preferences. There is a way out, however. The antidote to ambiguity is simplification. If the president can impose one or another grand simplification upon the system—the aim of a balanced budget, some foreign threat, or the like—then complex policy agendas lose their power to diffuse the president's program and confuse his bases of support. The president's task of coordinating the executive branch then adds to rather than detracts from his comprehensibility as a leader (so long as most of those who matter believe in the simplification in question).[10]

Here a second major development intervenes. Even if presidents are inclined to adopt simplistic formulas and to deny the ambiguity of reconciling differing policy agendas, major portions of the U.S. political system are now mobilized to frustrate any drive for simplification. This mobilization includes but also goes beyond the "single-issue" groups President Carter warned against in his farewell address to the nation.

Political mobilization is a process by which otherwise passive individuals and groups are brought to a point of actively impinging upon the work of government. Clearly, many forces must combine to generate such a process. What distinguishes the most recent period seems, however, to have little to do with the moving power of political parties, personalities, or grand ideological theories. It is government programs and policy issues that have mobilized more and more political activists in the American political system during the past two decades.

The federal government has itself encouraged much of this development, sometimes intentionally, often accidentally. In the more deliberate category, for example, fall numerous efforts in the 1960s to reach out beyond traditional power centers for the development of federal social programs. The Kennedy administration and, on a much more massive scale, the Johnson administration deliberately broke with the tradition of relying on agency proposals in the development of the president's domestic program. Instead, task forces were created with a heavy contingent of outsiders to generate innovative policy ideas and break the grip of established bureaucracies and interest groups.[11] Many of the programs they proposed and Congress enacted similarly sought to reach out beyond established interests to activate the disadvantaged, bypass routine administrative channels, and break the crust of old-fashioned political and bureaucratic structures. Anti-poverty programs, civil rights laws, urban development and housing programs, education, environmental and employment initiatives, and new judicial enforcement mechanisms—all helped to shape a new group politics as much as they were shaped by it.

The federal government also encouraged a new political mobilization around programs and policy issues in a less deliberate way. Rather than being directly administered from Washington, the expanding activities of the national government during the past several decades have been delivered largely through intermediary groups: state and local governments, professional associations, profit and nonprofit organizations.[12] This fact goes far to explain why, despite higher federal spending and mounting regulatory activity, the federal work force has expanded very little in this generation. Of all federal spending, only 15 percent to 20 percent is directed to activities that the federal government itself performs. Thus in 1978 for every employee working within the Department of Health, Education, and Welfare, there were approximately seven workers outside the department with salaries being paid indirectly by that department.

Not surprisingly, this indirect, de facto federal work force has developed a vested interest in particular programs and policy issues. But the political mobilization created by government activity goes beyond that. Washington has learned that it can pursue many of its purposes without actually administering, directly or indirectly, a spending program. A spreading web of positive and negative inducements has been used to make businesses, communities, and other groups the executors of federal purposes. Negative inducements have grown primarily in the form of government regulations regarding such matters as the environment, consumer protection, occupational safety, and antidiscrimination requirements. In 1976, for example, eighty-three federal agencies were engaged in regulating some aspect of private activity, thirty-four of these agencies having been created since 1960. Positive inducements have increasingly taken shape through federal loans, loan guarantees, and special tax provisions. Thus outstanding direct and guaranteed loans by the federal government (for everything from housing to college education) totaled $405 billion in 1979, most of the growth occurring in the past ten years. Special tax provisions to encourage certain types of activities resulted in $150 billion in forgone federal revenues in 1979, up from only $40 billion a decade earlier.

The important point for present purposes is that all of these federal activities, whatever their policy impacts, have had the political effect of activating more people with a conscious, specialized stake in Washington. The residue left by Johnson's Great Society, Nixon's

New Federalism, and the sheer momentum of government inventiveness is a jumble of policy activists. They range in style and substance from lawyers engaged in the hushed maneuverings of new Washington law firms to members of grass-roots neighborhood groups raucously voicing their demands.

Political mobilization has not, as some observers argued in the 1970s, been a phenomenon confined to a new political class of highly educated, pro-ecology, antibusiness activists. The election of 1980 made clear that there has been at least as much mobilization occurring on the right as on the left end of the policy spectrum. Any current survey could identify dozens of conservative organizations engaged in the kind of loosely structured, day-to-day trench warfare that goes with policy activism—program analysis, fund raising, public relations, publication, selective mailings, conferencing, lecturing, and all the rest. The conservative Heritage Foundation in Washington, for example, has established a so-called resource bank of 450 research groups and 1,100 public policy experts who can serve at short notice to testify before Congress and administrative hearings, to engage in panel discussions and press interviews, to produce publications, and to take part in that most vital of Washington activities, the working luncheon.[13] To think that political mobilization has embraced only the new right of 1980 or the new left of the 1960s is to trivialize what has been a societal phenomenon of the past generation.

Presidents have, of course, always had to contend with interest groups in American politics. But the proliferation of groups, their professionalization, their expanding financial and voting power in politics, and their in-depth concentration on particular programs and policy issues have added up to a significantly different environment for presidential management in the executive branch. Large umbrella organizations that a president might deal with on a number of cross-cutting issues have yielded ground increasingly to more specialized groupings focused on a narrow range of policy concerns. Hence, the 1978 congressional debate on natural-gas pricing involved no fewer than 117 lobby organizations. Included were representatives not only from the vested industrial interests but also from many of the eighty or so public-interest groups, most of which have appeared within the past ten years. A 1979 directory of Washington representatives lists what must be a conservative estimate of 5,000 individuals and 500 law and public relations firms providing direct representation in the city. Political parties, the largest umbrella organizations with which presidents once bargained, have now been largely eclipsed by the financial, analytic, and organizing power of newly mobilized groups.

These developments are important because they can easily close the president's escape route from policy congestion. Quite apart from their election activities, political parties have traditionally served as grand simplifiers. People mobilized through the new group politics, in contrast, serve as grand complicators. By organizing political activity around a few themes or even just a general mood, the political party helps to make the president's leadership comprehensible both at the lowest level of clubhouse politics and at the most intricate management structures atop the executive branch. But the newer environment of policy activists scattered throughout various issue networks makes it highly unlikely that any president can sustain such a position. Any simple faiths the president might espouse will eventually become ensnared in a web of counterarguments, many of which are comprehensible only to the specially initiated. Premises are disputed. Data are inadequate. Projections are wrong. The inevitable contradictions with other items on the crowded policy agenda are trumpeted. Each policy specialist has a vested interest in complicating the president's sketch of a grand design. Each group is, of course, promoting its own brand of simplification, but the cumulative effect of each group's doing so is to deny the president *his* chance at simplifying the inevitable ambiguities of modern public policy.

An Institutional Estrangement. There never was a golden age when presidents worked harmoniously with Congress, the bureaucracy, or the courts. The word "estrangement" is used here to indicate, not a breakdown of once harmonious relations, but a diminishing sense of mutual needs between the presidency and these other major political institutions.

In any survey of the history of presidential management of the executive branch, one proposition seems unexceptionable. Presidential capacities to coordinate the executive branch have been created and countenanced because they meet the needs of institutions other than the presidential office. Any managerial device that fails to meet this test, however much desired by the president, is doomed to extinction. Thus the presidency acquired powers for enforcing a comprehensive executive branch budget not simply because presidents demanded such powers, but because an alliance could be formed with Congress's appropriation committees, which were newly empowered by the executive budget process.[14] Central presidential clearance of agency views on proposed or pending legislation was initiated and developed at the request of Congress as an aid to its own committees' work. Likewise, it is now commonly forgotten that as the president's Bureau of the Budget grew in prominence during the

1930s and 1940s, senior careerists in that organization devoted considerable effort to serving the needs of Congress, usually through informal consultations and occasionally even through temporary assignments to congressional committees. It is revealing, too, that the exception to this tradition, the bureau's division of administrative management, which developed its reorganization plans and strategies in complete isolation from Congress, suffered a continuing decline in influence as soon as the war emergency was over in 1945. Major advances in planning the president's legislative program in the late 1940s and early 1950s were improvised, at least in part, as a means of meeting congressional needs for information and of helping Congress to organize its work. The list could be extended for many pages, but the implications would be the same. The client for strengthening presidential management in the executive branch has not been and probably cannot be simply the president, his staff, or his view of the public good.

The changes in Congress discussed elsewhere in this volume add up to a significant reduction in the extent to which Congress needs the president. Major staff increases have given Congress the capacity to draw up its own detailed proposals for complex legislation, frame its own alternatives, and often outanalyze the president's own staffs of experts. The president's budget, once the only game in town for taking a comprehensive look at the fiscal situation of the nation, is now only one of several points of departure for a reformed congressional budget process that is able to form its own independent view of the budgetary and fiscal situation as a whole. Congressional delegations of authority to executive bureaucracies, which might once have carried a vague expectation that the president would oversee the operations, have increasingly been tied to provisions for detailed congressional review and oversight of operations.

One should not push this argument too far. Clearly Congress still finds it useful for the president to help organize its debate by bringing forward his own legislative packages for tax reform, spending cuts, energy production, and so on. But while the president may be useful, he seems less essential to congressional deliberations. His capacities for coordinating the rest of the executive branch seem more detached and less tied in any organic way to what major parts of Congress need in order to do their work.

The courts and the executive bureaucracies, as well as Congress, seem to need the president less. Resort to litigation to achieve public policy goals has increased greatly in the last several decades, and the courts have obliged by applying their own administrative remedies and program directives. Public pressures that might once have served to strengthen the president's hand in managing the executive branch have flowed instead into the various tributaries of judicial activism. The resulting administrative standards and policy guidelines may or may not themselves be coordinated, but they certainly bear no conscious relation to the role of the president in managing the executive branch. To go back to an earlier example, the overlapping and layered jumble of federal assistance programs has not produced any significant groundswell of support for more rational presidential oversight of the system.[15] What it has produced in the past twenty years is a whole new body of "assistance law" pressed by recipients against federal agencies and developed by the courts without any reference to the Executive Office of the President.

And what of the bureaucracy? Like all the other participants, officialdom supports presidential leadership in the executive branch when there is some net advantage to itself in doing so. If a presidential presence can be calculated to help agencies get what they want or at least avoid trouble that they do not want, especially in Congress, support for central coordination grows. Otherwise there are opportunities aplenty for the bureaucracy to go its own way. Experience with the string of presidents since the end of the 1960s has not helped much in that regard. There is no need here to rehearse the batterings to presidential prestige that grew out of Vietnam, Watergate, problems of the economy, energy, and presidents' own mismanagement of their jobs. Each new arrival in the White House has raised and disappointed bureaucratic hopes. No one can say for sure, but it is a good bet that during many of the sixteen years since 1966 it has hurt more than helped for agencies to be known as pressing cases with a White House imprimatur.

Compared with the ups and downs of recent presidents, the lines of force created by the new political mobilization and by a Congress flush with staffs and subcommittees are reassuringly stable for the bureaucracy. That is not to say that all the groups, analysts, staffers, and policy kibitzers are necessarily cooperative. But, with time to learn, one can find ways of operating through this thicket. That is true particularly because the increasingly fragmented Congress and the mobilized networks of policy activists have an inherent stake in concentrating on the narrowest, least presidential policy choices: specific project budgets, particular regulations, personnel assignments, and so on. Time to learn is one thing that bureaucrats have. Concentration on discrete programs and activities is one thing that comes naturally to them. And a good measure of stability is one thing they yearn for in their work plans. Contrast all this with what presidents have to offer—impatience, a commitment to pulling things together, and fits of unpredictable influence—and the question seems to answer itself. What does a modern president have to offer that meets the bureaucracy's long-term needs?

When Congress, courts, and bureaucracies need presidents less, presidents find it more difficult to create a presumption for coordinating operations in the executive branch. If we add to this the legislative and judicial strictures put on presidents in response to executive misdeeds of recent decades (as described in chapter 6), we find ample reason for institutional estrangement. But in the background there has also been something more subtle at work than the presence of a War Powers Act or an Executive Impoundment Act on the books. It amounts to a kind of governmental sociology problem.

When people do not know and trust one another, they are apt to put things in writing. People in governmental institutions are no different. Washington in the last thirty years or so has ceased to be a place where people know and trust one another (trust not in the Boy Scout sense but in the sense of understanding both one another and the rules of mutual restraint). With trust, much of the inevitable friction between government organizations can be worked out or contained informally by those with the discretion and the skill to work at points where institutions grate on one another. That is no longer the case in Washington. Increasingly, political institutions rub up against one another formally through set procedures that must be followed, reports that must be made, data that must be supplied, consultations that must occur, and on and on. Formalization is the symptom of estrangement.

Of course none of this can be proved. At most there are impressions and hints. One hint is simply the number of bodies involved. During the period in which the classic central management functions for budgeting, legislative clearance, and programming were developed in the presidency (1921–1950), counterpart staffs were largely underdeveloped in the departments and agencies. Since then staffs and specialized units within the executive branch have proliferated beyond anyone's plans, in part because the president's Bureau of the Budget devoted considerable effort to building up such departmental units. The large numbers of executive staff and their rapid turnover do not constitute an environment in which personal knowledge and informal understandings can be readily established or sustained. As President Reagan took office, a directory of federal executives identified more than 12,000 senior positions, of which 30 percent were in line to change during the first three months and the rest during the next nine months of the president's first year.[16] There were, for example, 200 health offices, 190 environmental offices, and 145 energy offices in the executive branch.

The exact numbers are not as important as what they imply: a more impersonal atmosphere, more points for possible misunderstanding and friction in relations among government institutions. They add up to a fragmentation of an already disjointed governing community in Washington. Estrangement seems to have been facilitated by a generational shift in the way top people in government look at their work. This impression is difficult to describe, much less to prove. One way, probably simplistic, of labeling the development is to say that congressmen, executive managers, and their staffs have come to take a greater interest in policy than in institutions. To control the substantive choices about what government does has seemed more interesting, important, and "savvy" than low-key work to facilitate the operation and meshing of organizations. And deeper than this, no doubt, lie forces more appropriately left to the social psychologist. The chore of institutional nurturing requires a kind of self-subordination that seems out of favor. Whatever abstract need one institution may have for another, it is people who establish and sustain linkages, people such as higher bureaucrats, congressional staffers, and White House aides. For them to play a facilitating role and avoid unnecessary estrangements in government requires an unfashionable set of attitudes: a desire to spread rather than take credit; a passion for anonymity rather than for celebrity; a concern for the propriety of how things get done no less than a preference for what things get done. It is this kind of staff work that seems to have been in short supply in recent years.

The Triumph of Reagan Management

The executive end of the avenue operates in a more complex and fluid managerial environment. It may seem that the three changes I have sketched present only disadvantages for any president interested in bringing coherent leadership to the executive branch. Certainly that would have seemed a plausible conclusion at the end of the Carter administration. Experiences in the first two years of the Reagan presidency show, however, that, at least in the short term, there are considerable advantages for presidents and their staffs to exploit. As policy agendas collide, as new groups mobilize, and as government institutions drift apart, there are opportunities to find new ways of pulling things together within the executive branch. More than any other modern president, Ronald Reagan succeeded in creating a more or less unified and coherent system of political administration during his first two years in office.[17] How did he do it? At least four factors can be identified.

In the first place, the new president and his immediate staff were willing to limit drastically the number of presidential priorities. There was of course the familiar need to deal with crises, usually in foreign affairs (for example, Libya, El Salvador, the PLO in Beirut, the AWACS sale). But in terms of commitment of presidential time and effort, these were sporadic and ad hoc affairs. Likewise defense issues, once given the go-ahead for more spending, seemed to exhibit little presidential involvement, certainly nothing like the Eisenhower presence in the Pentagon's business. The economy was the president's first, second, and third priority; it was here that Ronald Reagan engaged in sustained struggles with Congress, launched his major public appeals, and staked his reputation. And it is important to add that the president's commitment was not to all areas of economic policy. The narrow compass of presidential priorities included little about industrial policies for particular sectors, regional development, industrial relations and wage bargaining (apart from air traffic controllers), or international economic relations. The presidential priority in economic affairs was to reduce the role of government—its taxes, spending, and regulations—and stand aside for an economic revival in the private sector.

The simple message contained in this presidential agenda was that a vast amount of government activity was of no interest to the president, except as it might be cut back. Departmental bureaucracies found it hard if not impossible to gain White House attention for their roles and missions. To put it into the language we have used earlier, by drastically narrowing his priorities to a few economic road signs, the president appeared to rise above the prevailing policy congestion. In place of ambiguity and trade-offs appeared simplicity and decision.

The second feature of the Reagan management system might at first sight seem to contradict the first, but in fact complemented it. Below the level of the president's own absolute priority were a host of concrete, actionable objectives to be carried out by the new administration. In general these were consistent with the president's theme of cutting back in domestic affairs, and their presence helped ensure that the theme would be a guide to action rather than a melody that was forgotten in the day-to-day conduct of departmental business. More than in any earlier administration, the Republicans entered office with a program. It was not so much a party program as a product evolved within the conservative networks of policy intellectuals and activists. The most formal expression of this program occurred in the Heritage Foundation's 1980 electoral publication *Mandate for Leadership,* a 1,080-page compilation of 1,270 recommendations for action in the new administration; a year later the same foundation identified 61 percent of these actions as having been taken.[18] It would be a mistake, however, to overstate the formal nature of the new Republican agenda. More important than any published document was agreement among like-minded people as they looked at particular areas of government, whether this was an assessment of Soviet military intentions or of food stamps.

Defined in this way, the program of the Reagan administration possessed several substantial advantages for creating unified political management. Much of it was budget oriented, thereby tying programmatic actions to the one powerful, action-forcing process that exists on a government-wide basis. Moreover, an agenda of budget reduction made far fewer demands on the knowledge of government leadership than did government activism. To be sure, considerable knowledge was still required, and the new budget director, David Stockman, acquired a deserved reputation for brilliance. But it was a brilliance that could be confined to knowing a great deal about budget numbers and their politics. Advocates of government activism in earlier administrations needed to know how to use government to solve problems, a very complicated matter indeed. Adherents of the Reagan program saw themselves as solving problems to the extent that they knew how to impose cuts in government. It seems fair to say that no one could have known enough to run the Great Society program as a whole, but it was quite possible to know enough to run the Reagan program; if the former was driven to the expedient of throwing money at problems, the latter began with a clear idea of how to throw government cutbacks at problems.

Narrowly defined presidential priorities and a subpresidential program capable of concrete, fairly simple action provided two elements of a successful management strategy. The third was finding the body of like-minded people to help do the job. From the beginning, the Reagan administration procedures for political appointments made it clear that loyalty and compatibility with the Reagan philosophy were the sine qua non for White House endorsement. Despite some early objections from the conservative right that non-Reaganites were being appointed, it now seems clear that the White House personnel office pursued a fairly consistent policy of scrutinizing and clearing candidates on the basis of their sympathy with previously established Reagan positions on the issues. This applied not only to major presidential appointments but also to lower-level positions filled by department heads. The clarity and simplicity of the administration's program facilitated this personnel process. Both President Nixon and President Carter were said to have regretted the free hand given their department heads in filling lower-level positions, and political scientists have waxed eloquent in urging stricter White House scrutiny of personnel choices. But it has been largely useless advice, for only with the Reagan administration has there been a more or less coherent philosophy and program against which job applicants' loyalty could be checked. And by the same token, the conservative networks of policy activists that helped generate the administration's program also provided a manpower pool for filling political executive positions. Thus the new political mobilization provided a resource here, too, that could be exploited in executive branch management.

The final element of a successful management strategy lay in the continuing attempt to reinforce central rather than departmental loyalties among executive branch managers. This became clear during the transition process. Transition teams named on November 12, 1980, were required to submit their first reports on departmental activities to the president's staff by November 24 (with the draft of the final report due the second week of December). This tight scheduling was an excellent device to reaffirm preconceptions rather than to learn very much about departmental work and advice, and few transition teams seemed inclined in any event to consult closely with predecessors. Likewise the administration got off to a very fast start in framing its new budget and legislative economic package by maintaining arm's length relations with the permanent government. With little chance to consult with lower-level departmental officials, new cabinet secretaries were called in individually to negotiate their budgets with a team of OMB and White House officials who had already largely agreed on the cuts that were to be made. As the administration progressed, all important issues requiring bargaining with Congress tended to be managed through a permanent working group of eight to ten senior White House officials (with isolated instances of cabinet member attendance) that came to be known as the legislative strategy group. The group marshaled the president's resources for legislative bargaining, meshing strategy with day-to-day tactics for when and how to push the legislature and—equally important—when not to push and let the White House fade into the background. An important byproduct was the effect of the group in disciplining others in the executive branch. The work of the legislative strategy group, and the president's support of it, left departmental officials with little real power to negotiate with Congress on their own. Any "deals" they might strike would probably be disavowed by the White House, and the leverage they could supply in guiding White House strategy decisions was uncertain at best. Hence departmental executives tended to be rendered impotent before Congress except as they fit in with the White House designs.

In a curious way the widely publicized cabinet councils—the symbols of commitment to cabinet government in the Reagan administration—complemented the centralization of strategy and tactics in the White House. These six councils were chaired by a cabinet secretary in their working sessions and administratively coordinated by White House aides. By mid-1982 the informal as well as the pro forma functions of these councils had become clearer than they were in the first heady days of pronouncements on cabinet government (when the president and his counsellor Ed Meese considered housing cabinet secretaries in an office building adjacent to the White House). In general the councils massaged issues in the early stages of coming to a White House decision: facts were presented, differing viewpoints registered, and areas of agreement and disagreement outlined among the departments and agencies. All of this was strictly preparatory to the major decisions on policy management that occurred in the White House: analysis of the place of issues in administration strategy; decisions on what to back, what to oppose, and what to let departments take the heat on; decisions on what packages of positions to put together and how to sell them to Congress and the public; and so on. For most of these major decisions cabinet members were brought in only individually, not as a group, and only on a need-to-know basis. For example, as befitted the president's own priorities, the cabinet council on economic affairs was by far the most active, meeting more than ninety times in the first fifteen months of the administration. But the guiding decisions on the Reagan economic program were not taken in this group setting. They were taken in a much less formal, nonroutinized way by the president-in-council—a continuing swirl of discussions involving the Treasury secretary, the OMB director, and a handful of senior White House aides. As a result of this process, a mid-1982 economic assessment for the nation was not agreed to by the man who was formally the chief adviser to the president on economics, the chairman of the Council of Economic Advisers.

Thus the cabinet council system has reenforced central White House policy management. It has done so in the past, by forcing departmental policy development into a system of strategic decision making closely held in the White House. That tendency was strengthened in 1982 when the president's office of policy development in the

46

Domestic Council was given responsibility, not only for coordinating cabinet councils and interdepartmental issues, but for scrutinizing policies developed solely within the confines of single departments and for tying its work to the analysis of the White House public opinion pollsters. In part, too, the cabinet council system has helped insulate political executives from the permanent departmental bureaucracies and from the congressional committees by continually convening the executives in meetings under White House auspices. The hoped-for sociological effect of the busy round of council meetings, usually held within the White House, was to add a presidential presence to the lives of cabinet secretaries, lives that normally are preoccupied with congressional hearings and departmental briefings. As Ed Meese, the man who devised the cabinet council system, put it, "The difference in this presidency is that Reagan has used his system so that the Cabinet members all feel closer to him than they do to their departments. And he gives them a lot of opportunity to remember that."[19] Some of these opportunities occur in the never-ending round of council meetings; others occur after the meetings in the rejection observed being meted out to those the White House regards as poor "team players."

Thinking Institutionally

Taken together, the four elements of Reagan management have, so far at least, constituted a powerful system for bringing coherence and centralized loyalties to executive branch leadership. It is a system that is fully consistent with the advice political scientists have offered to presidents in recent years, although anyone would be naive to think that it is the result of practical politicians consciously deciding to follow such academic advice. On the contrary. Reagan management has evolved, I would argue, as shrewd political managers have tried to cope with today's troublesome setting for presidential leadership. The four strategic features we have identified are ways of exploiting the larger changes in political environment that have been occurring since the Eisenhower presidency.

By drastically limiting White House priorities, the president seems to rise above the confusion and squabbling of a congested policy environment. By adopting a fairly ideological approach to government programming and political appointments, the administration makes use of the interests and personnel generated by the new political mobilization. And by trying to insulate political executives from the traditions of the permanent government in Washington (which includes bureaucracies, interest groups, and congressional committees), the Reagan administration builds on the institutional estrangement that was already under way.

A good case can be made that the Reagan administration had no choice except to strive for central strategic direction if it wished to launch its intended massive changes in the role of the federal government. And yet neither should one minimize the drawbacks of what has happened, drawbacks that relate not to one's particular policy preferences but to the institutional capabilities of government. The problem is—and it arises whatever party wins the White House—that strategies required to cope with the changed political environment have as their byproduct a tendency to further deinstitutionalize the machinery of government. Consider again each of the factors we have discussed. Severely limiting presidential priorities may help keep the president out of trouble in a complex policy system, but it also sends out signals throughout the administrative structure that the bulk of government work is of little interest to central policy makers. It has always been difficult in American government to sustain any presidential interest in the unglamorous tasks of administrative management—that is to say, overseeing improvements in the way government carries out its work. Under current conditions that sort of presidential attention to "good government" issues is even more problematic. Institutional staff in the presidency who are concerned with government-wide managerial capabilities find their functions downgraded and their work taken less seriously in the bureaucracy. Longer-term perspectives, which is to say a concern for issues beyond the life of one administration, are likely to give way to a succession of faddish and well-publicized management improvement campaigns. In this situation the "government can't work" attitude may well become a self-fulfilling prophecy.

Other elements of the Reagan strategy point in much the same direction. The stress on ideological consistency in government programming and personnel appointments does much to bring managerial unity to an administration, but it also defines managerial success exclusively in terms of making particular policy preferences prevail in the decision-making process. Longer-term considerations of maintaining government machinery in good working order tend to be discounted as naive and old fashioned. If the "bottom line" in government management is only about policy choices, institutional considerations can be shunted aside; to the true ideologue there is no next time when the machinery must be intact to change policy directions or recalculate policy preferences. Discontinuity and the atrophy of routine governmental processes become positive virtues. Likewise, estrangement of the new leadership from established institutions becomes an asset to be exploited, not a weakness in government.

To value discontinuity, to discount the long term, to elevate specific policy preferences over the maintenance of enduring relationships, to prize content over process—these are the obverse of what might be called institutional thinking. To think institutionally is to be sensitive to the idea that there is an organizational life and value that is larger than the preferences of any individual or policies of the passing moment. Of course an excess of institutional sensitivity can lead to mindless routine and stagnation. But that is hardly the direction the forces of our political environment are now pushing. These forces point toward deinstitutional thinking and politics, and it is difficult to foresee anything that might counteract that tendency.

To be fair one should add that the forces at work run deeper than the strategies of the Reagan administration's managers or even the political environment lying behind these strategies. When financial experts complain about a "go-go" entrepreneurial spirit in financial institutions that is displacing traditions of fiduciary soundness; when business school professors trace economic problems to short-term profit orientations taught in business schools at the expense of longer-term values and organizational operations; when legal scholars criticize the tendency for Supreme Court decisions to express the individual views of justices with diminished regard to the opinion of the Court's majority or the development of a coherent body of law [20]—these can be taken as indicators of a society-wide phenomenon that endorses short-term personal calculations at the expense of institutional values. And so too it becomes rational at the highest levels of political management to measure success by short-term policy decisions and allow the institutional capacities of government to go to seed.

What then is the prognosis for presidential leadership in the executive branch? Uncertain, of course, but it seems reasonable to begin with three premises. First, there will be no change in our basic political constitution. As we approach the bicentennial of our federal Constitution later in this decade, there will undoubtedly be much talk, but probably little action, about reformulating the 200-year-old institutional design. In particular, cabinet government will remain a dead letter, and the presidency will remain as the only office constitutionally established to bring a government-wide perspective to bear on problems facing the nation as a whole. Individual presidents may fail in that task. Changes in the managerial environment such as we have discussed earlier may conspire to frustrate them, as indeed occurred with President Carter. But this integrating task must be the inherent duty of the presidential office if the office is to have any functional meaning.

Second, there will be no political demobilization. Political apathy in the general public may increase or decrease in the years ahead. But it seems highly unlikely that, once having realized their stake in government policy issues, the activists concerned with the environment, government deregulation, civil rights, nuclear threats, and so on are going to disappear or be rendered impotent. Thus during its first two years, the Reagan administration did manage to achieve remarkable coherence throughout the top levels of the executive branch and to score major legislative victories. But rather than quitting the field, the policy interests that were defeated (environmentalists and consumer advocates, equal rights groups and social policy activists, détentists in foreign policy, and so on) brought renewed pressures in other arenas such as the courts, congressional subcommittees, state and local governments, and electoral organization. If anything, the successful mobilization of the right around the Reagan candidacy is likely to provoke greater efforts at countermobilization elsewhere along the political spectrum in the years ahead.

Finally, there will be no decongestion of the policy agenda. This is, of course, implied by the premise of a continuation of the new group politics. And yet even without organized or semiorganized groups, we are not likely to go back to the days when highway programs could be left to the road builders, economic policy to the economists, or civil rights, welfare, and environmental concerns solely to the variable outcome of state and local politics. Once having been raised, our national consciousness of competing policy objectives and national responsibilities is unlikely to be suppressed. Calls for decentralization under some version of new federalism will probably not change that basic fact.

In other words, at least two of the three developments sketched earlier seem likely to continue. These two carry both advantages and disadvantages for a president. A congested policy environment may render his synthesizing efforts ambiguous and detached from any active constituency. But such an environment also generates a sense of stalemate and demands that someone rise above the melee and take an overview of our national problems. That we instinctively look to the president to perform this task is his advantage and his burden.

Likewise, the continued mobilization of policy activists inevitably frustrates presidential attempts to impose some grand simplification on the system. But the activities of these groups also tend to be incomprehensible and suspect to ordinary citizens who do not spend a great deal of their time watching public affairs. Often they do not understand what the president is doing either, but at least he, of all the participants, is able to command the attention of these non-active citizens. If he can manage to mesh his persona with their concerns, the "special interests" may become a foil as well as a frustration. President Carter tried this and failed. Other presidents may do better; if not, it will not be for want of a hearing before the general public.

The one remaining development of recent decades contains, in the long run, unalloyed disadvantages for presidential management in the executive branch. Institutional estrangement means that the president's coordination efforts lack the broad base of support that they need. Presidential management must continue to wither unless it has roots extending to other political institutions, especially Congress. Their needs nourish his performance.

Hence, major developments in the years to come seem likely to occur in this area: a search for nontraditional management devices drawing political institutions somewhat closer together. The evidence of political fragmentation is easily observable. What we often fail to see are the subtle ways by which public officials begin to try to work around the difficulties. In time their efforts at coping may evolve into new government processes. For now, there are only omens. Three in particular are worth attention for what they may portend.

1. More precooking. In the current unpredictable environment for management, presidential initiatives have become risky. To allay the dangers, presidents and their staffs are likely to become involved in earlier and more regular consultations with those who are essential to the success of the president's plans; indeed, future presidents may find it prudent to have very few specific plans until extensive collaboration has occurred.

The process by which President Carter produced his second, emergency budget in 1980 may prove to be a significant example. On that occasion, as never before in recent history, the president's budget proposal was worked out in intimate discussion with leaders of the congressional budget process. When the emergency budget reached the Hill, there were important people there with a stake in its adoption, and individual spending plans from various committees were forcefully "reconciled" to meet the terms of the first budget resolution. Likewise, the administration's welfare reform was worked out in extensive discussions with the affected interests. Its initial energy program was not. Both initiatives eventually failed to prevail in Congress, but in the former case many groups carried the blame. In the latter case, the president alone took it on the chin.

There are strong incentives for presidents and other political leaders who feel they are being pulled apart by the new group politics to develop new processes for collaboration. Whether they will respond to these incentives remains to be seen, and in this regard the Reagan administration provides an interesting test case. Far from precooking policies with other leaders, the new Republican administration arrived in Washington carrying its own distinctive approaches to spending cuts, tax reduction, and economic management. Some compromises naturally had to be made along the way, but in general the new administration sought, with considerable success, to impose its policy approach on Congress and on business and labor leaders in the private sector. If the initial economic package of the Reagan administration had produced all the results it promised, the president's hand would have been immensely strengthened. As it turned out, high deficits forced the administration in 1982 to consider new ways of increasing government revenues, and collaboration became more necessary than ever to pick up the pieces of its economic program. The outcome of this collaboration came with the tax bill of 1982, a bill whose genesis lay with discreet consultations among OMB, Senate, and House leaders in economic policy operating as an informal group that became known as the Gang of 17. This leadership crystallized around the work of the chairman of the Senate Finance Committee, Robert Dole, and the president only belatedly signed on to push for final enactment of this major shift in economic policy.

Handled carelessly and in a shortsighted way, White House efforts at precooking policies with the affected groups will draw a president into problems and premature commitments. Handled well, it will reduce the riskiness of his managerial environment. In the final analysis, only the president can determine which it will be. To be president in fact as well as in name, he himself must hold the line between the collaboration he needs and the collegiality that would make him a figurehead.

2. *New processes for allocating scarcities.* Each of the traditional devices for presidential management has been effective only so long as it was perceived as distributing something in short supply. For the budget process, both the assumption of continuing economic growth to produce more tax revenues and the Keynesian breaking of a preoccupation with the linkage between revenues and spending served to undercut this perception of scarcity. The legislative clearance process likewise remained powerful so long as it monopolized

most of another scarce resource: decisions about what was or was not "in accord with the president's program." The more that proposals outside this process could win presidential support, the more that financial decisions were tolerated outside the admittedly narrow confines of budgeting, the less these mechanisms could serve as a framework for coordination.

Certainly there has been no lack of a sense of growing scarcity in the last several administrations—in the economy, in energy supplies, in clean air and water, in living space, and more; there has also been a growing scarcity of public patience with excuses as to why government is not working as well as it should. The problem is that little of this raw emotional force seems to be connected in any reliable way with the ongoing momentum of government.

The search has already started for new mechanisms to make some of these necessary connections. Groundwork has been prepared for some kind of comprehensive regulatory review, that is, for a mechanism to assess individual regulations in light of the cumulative impact of government regulatory activity. A beginning has been made in construction of a federal "paperwork budget" aimed at giving the president's budget agency a means of creating and administering (it is hoped) a new scarcity: the number of "burden hours" on the public that federal bureaucracies can impose through requests for written information. Along the same lines are recent efforts to centralize review of overlapping standards in federal assistance programs.

No one should want to make too much of these particular straws in the wind. What they have in common is a greater reliance on central management of government processes through the presidency. What they seem to lack is a close relation to the work of Congress affecting the same issues. If either collaboration or new presidential allocational mechanisms are to work, each has to reinforce the other. Collaboration without enduring procedural mechanisms will remain erratic and opportunistic. Presidential management processes that do not help Congress organize its own work are easily overwhelmed.

Consider an extreme case of allocational innovation. Suppose that the president let it be known that he would veto any legislation not previously cleared through his (let us call it) policy coordination staff; that if his veto were overridden he would impound funds for such legislation; that if his impoundments were overturned by congressional review, he would delay the mandated spending, or withhold administrative support, or impose similar sanctions. The president would surely have a coordinated device for allocating a scarce resource, namely his acquiescence in legislation. Such a device would also coalesce all the disparate forces of Congress and the bureaucracy

53

against the president, a situation not too distant from what had happened to the Nixon administration well before Watergate revelations.

Consider now the consequences if the president gave the same warnings, but laid down the requirement that it was, say, a leadership caucus of each house of Congress whose clearance he required before signing legislation. Suppose too that that leadership caucus, to protect itself from the unrestrained demands of each outside group and subcommittee of Congress, let it be known that their clearance was contingent on a White House report as to the consistency of proposed legislation with the president's program. And suppose even further that presidential staff were willing to take the blame for not reporting on proposals that the congressional leadership informally indicated it preferred not to deal with (excepting, of course, issues on which the president had a strong preference). There indeed would be an organic linkage between the forces of coherence in the executive and legislative branches. It is also a somewhat exaggerated description of what commonly occurred during the days when legislative clearance was in its prime during the late 1940s.

It is at least conceivable that some similar process, with a broader mandate to take account of the interaction among policies, might be discovered or some such existing process strengthened. The budget is the most obvious example. During its first year in office, the Reagan administration did much to strengthen the centralizing power within Congress of House and Senate budget committees at the expense of the many other spending committees and subcommittees. But important as this development was, it may also be a dead end. Heavy-handed use of the budget reconciliation process to meet presidential priorities left many congressmen of both parties hostile to a repeat performance. Moreover, a preoccupation with budget numbers and total spending ceilings often increases discipline at the expense of understanding. Budget ceilings are typically arbitrary and, as events after the summer of 1981 showed, easily outdated by changing circumstances in the economy and spending programs. Getting the budget numbers "right" can readily displace a broader analysis of true costs and public objectives to be served. Thus narrowly conceived budget making is an excellent means to suppress innovative policy making, of either a liberal or a conservative nature.

3. *Presidential party building.* The president remains at a disadvantage so long as there is no reliable link between his own actions in Washington and organized political resources at the grass-roots level. The perception of this disadvantage seems bound to increase in the White House for several reasons.

Efforts to precook the president's program constantly run into the difficulty that there are few reliable bargaining partners. National representatives of mobilized groups typically have only the most tenuous control over their memberships. Congressmen know that their political survival is a function, in most times and under most circumstances, of how closely they cultivate their local districts. It is that tending of home fences, rather than collaboration with the president, that protects the congressman against the pressures of mobilized groups cutting across districts.

The president can, of course, fall back upon his general prestige with the public and his ability to command attention. But the media are blunt instruments for dealing with the specific issues around which groups are mobilized. Any allocative mechanisms he might use to coordinate the executive branch—budgets, clearances, regulatory reviews, or others—require clear, sustained political backing if they are not to become unglued under the disintegrating power of groups, congressional subcommittees, and bureaus. Against the president's attempts to allocate scarcities there are hundreds of forms of self-defense, all drawing their nourishment from grass roots activity: write-in campaigns, lawsuits, state referendums and initiatives, news exposés, and so on.

Facing these pressures, the White House will be under a growing temptation to find ways of generating organized presidential support at precisely the same grass-roots level. President Carter tried, unsuccessfully, with town meetings, intimate sessions with local editors and publishers, a presidential office for intergovernmental relations, and other devices. A new president may try the novel idea of using his political party for similar purposes. Or the old idea of political field offices for the president may be revived. Whether any of this could actually succeed for the president is another question. The track record is not promising.

More precooking of policies, the search for devices for allocating scarcities, and efforts at presidential party building will all fit poorly with the traditional methods by which presidents and Congresses do business with each other. Precooking means that congressmen will be under more pressure to commit themselves early and not simply to respond to executive proposals, that they will have to do more sharing than claiming of credit. Above all, to be seriously engaged in the early stages of policy development with the president and executive officials will mean exhibiting some loyalty to a constituency of collaborators as well as to the traditional home constituency. And that is a tall order.

Any presidential attempt to allocate scarcities will make little sense unless it is fitted into congressional procedures, but Congress always finds it difficult to use procedures that distribute costs (and easy to use those that distribute benefits only). It is for this reason that the current experiment in reconciling spending committees' decisions with budget committees' firm ceilings is so important. And yet, as noted above, a disciplined budget process may be only a small—and by itself distorting—part of a more rational policy-making system.

Efforts at presidential party building will be the most explosive development of all for Congress. Grass-roots politics is the vital subsoil of congressional politics, and for the White House to mix in this area is dangerous and unpredictable. Some of these dangers have already begun appearing among congressmen themselves, as some single-issue groups (such as the pro-life groups) mobilizing the grass roots have asked their congressional backers to join in efforts at defeating fellow congressmen who are not "right" on the issue. White House functionaries, particularly the large numbers who are now more experienced and interested in policy issues than in party politics, may feel less restraint about pressuring congressmen where they live, namely locally. Eyebrows were raised in 1981 when White House officials used lists of conservative campaign contributors to Democratic congressmen to push the president's budget cuts in the House of Representatives. The years ahead may well see much more of the same.

Whether or not these particular elements of a prognosis are correct, presidential relations in the executive branch seem destined for some unsteady times. Under our political constitution, this relationship is necessarily a marriage of inconvenience, and in recent years a more complex family situation (more issues to fight about, more in-laws and onlookers, more formalized exchanges, fewer accepted routines in the household) has only added to the natural suspicions.

The problem is not, fundamentally, the absence of a sufficiently tough budget process or other coordinating mechanism inside the executive branch. What is missing from the relationship between president and bureaucracy is an overarching political process within which particular management strategies can work. Political parties no longer seem to help very much in that regard. Neither do presidential appeals to the people at large. A particular foreign crisis may be exploited as a substitute for a political process, but any resulting consensus seems to be increasingly short-lived.

The presidency will be a threat to institutional capabilities in government so long as efforts by presidents at coordination within the executive branch are not linked to a larger set of understandings with leaders in other political institutions. Policy, we know, is not something that gets made in an organization or on a chart. It is a conversation that occurs among people in various organizations. In the past it has been possible to hold that conversation, to build those political understandings across institutions, in fairly quiet tones among presidents, congressional leaders, top bureaucrats, and others. Today, in a more open, mobilized period, that no longer seems possible. New political traditions will have to be invented to carry on the essential conversation.

Notes

1. Quoted in the *National Journal*, December 20, 1980, p. 2174.
2. A listing of the major studies can be found in Richard M. Pious, *The American Presidency* (New York: Basic Books, 1979), pp. 440-42.
3. The general, public transition is described in Laurin Henry, *Presidential Transitions* (Washington, D.C.: Public Affairs Press, 1960). For details of Eisenhower's budget process as well as copies of the studies by private consultants, see Eisenhower Presidential Library, *Papers of Joseph M. Dodge*, Box 6, "Budget Reviews," and Boxes 10 and 11, "Management Handbook for the Next President" and "Reorganization."
4. *National Journal*, December 20, 1980, pp. 2152-57.
5. Everett C. Ladd, "The Brittle Mandate," *Political Science Quarterly*, vol. 96 (Spring 1981), pp. 1-25; Gerald M. Pomper et al., *The Election of 1980* (Chatham, N.J.: Chatham House, 1981). For counterevidence, see Adam Clymer and Kathleen Francis, "The Realities of Realignment," *Public Opinion*, vol. 3, no. 4 (June/July 1981), pp. 42-47.
6. See, for example, Richard E. Neustadt, "Presidency and Legislation: The Growth of Central Clearance," *American Political Science Review*, vol. 48 (September 1954), pp. 644, 660-62, and Richard E. Neustadt, "Presidency and Legislation: Planning the President's Program," *American Political Science Review*, vol. 49 (December 1955), pp. 980-1021.
7. Office of Management and Budget, *Managing Federal Assistance in the 1980s* (Washington, D.C., March 1980), pp. 18-20.
8. During the past twenty years, the U.S. share of world steel production has fallen by approximately one-third, the U.S. share of total military spending by almost two-fifths, and the U.S. share of world oil production by three-fifths. In each case, America has been unable to maintain its share of such instruments of power not because the nation is doing less, but because other countries have been doing so much more. During the years that U.S. dominance has receded, U.S. dependence on the rest of the world has increased. The share of the U.S. national product that is exported doubled between 1965 and 1980, and the share of national product imported doubled in half that time. The return on activities abroad makes up one-third of all corporate profits in America. The nation is dependent on foreigners for more than half of its needs in nine of its thirteen key industrial raw materials.

9. Executive Order 12083, September 27, 1978.

10. It now seems clear, for example, that Eisenhower's use of the budget as a coordinating device was vastly simplified by a widespread conviction that budget numbers should add up to a given total related to tax revenues without a sideways glance at conditions in the economy, much less at the social distribution of what later became known as "tax expenditures." See David C. Mowrey et al., "Presidential Management of Budgetary and Fiscal Policymaking," *Political Science Quarterly*, vol. 95, no. 3 (Fall 1980), pp. 395-425.

11. See Norman C. Thomas and Harold L. Wolman, "Policy Formulation in the Institutionalized Presidency: The Johnson Task Forces," in Thomas E. Cronin and Sanford D. Greenberg, eds., *The Presidential Advisory System* (New York: Harper and Row, 1969), pp. 124-43.

12. Samuel H. Beer, "The Modernization of American Federalism," *Publius*, vol. 3 (Fall 1973), pp. 49-95; and Frederick C. Mosher, "The Changing Responsibilities and Tactics of the Federal Government," *Public Administration Review*, vol. 40 (November/December 1980), pp. 541-48.

13. *National Journal*, March 20, 1982, p. 505. See also Hugh Heclo, "Issue Networks and the Executive Establishment," in Anthony King, ed., *The New American Political System* (Washington, D.C.: American Enterprise Institute, 1978), pp. 87-124.

14. Ladd, "Brittle Mandate," pp. 1-25; and Clymer and Francis, "Realities of Realignment," pp. 42-47.

15. In 1978 Congress did pass the Federal Grant and Cooperative Agreement Act (Public Law 95-224), but its main reference to the presidency was a provision that the Office of Management and Budget should study and report on the problem of coordinating grant requirements.

16. *Federal Executive Directory* (Washington, D.C.: Carroll Publishing Co., 1980).

17. For reports on White House management during the early stages of the Reagan administration, see articles in the *National Journal*, November 15, 1980, pp. 1924-26; November 29, 1980, pp. 2028-30; January 17, 1981, pp. 88-92; February 21, 1981, pp. 300-307; April 4, 1981, pp. 564-67; April 25, 1981, pp. 675-77; August 1, 1981, p. 1387; January 23, 1982, pp. 140-44; and April 3, 1982, pp. 584-89. A midterm assessment of cabinet government in the Reagan administration is contained in a three-part series in the *Washington Post*, July 18-20, 1982.

18. Heritage Foundation, *Mandate for Leadership: Policy Management in a Conservative Administration* (Washington, D.C.: Heritage Foundation, 1980); and Richard N. Holwill, ed., *The First Year* (Washington, D.C.: Heritage Foundation, 1982).

19. *National Journal*, April 3, 1982, p. 588.

20. Henry Kaufman, quoted in the *Washington Post*, August 22, 1982; Robert Hayes and William Abernathy, "Managing Our Way to Economic Decline," *Harvard Business Review* (Summer 1980); Archibald Cox, *Freedom of Expression* (Cambridge, Mass.: Harvard University Press, 1981), pp. 88-89.

3

Congressional Liaison: The People and the Institutions

ERIC L. DAVIS

Congress is often responsible for determining whether a president will be able to accomplish his policy goals. For this reason Congress is important for the president, and he must pay a good deal of attention to legislative developments. There are, however, many other concerns impinging on his time—international relations, the economy, and coordination of the administrative and regulatory apparatus of government, among others—so the president cannot handle the task of congressional relations entirely by himself. Over the past thirty years, the institution of the legislative liaison staff has developed to provide the president with the assistance he needs in the area of congressional relations.

This legislative liaison staff is the focus of this chapter. I will discuss the historical development of the legislative liaison function, the career patterns of liaison staffers, the different ways in which legislative liaison staffs have been organized, some of the ways in which liaison staffers attempt to accomplish their goals, and the sorts of relationships one finds between liaison staff and staff responsible for the formulation of new policy proposals. I will conclude with some reflections on the state of legislative liaison at the beginning of the 1980s. Most of my analysis will concentrate on legislative liaison at the White House, not on department and agency liaison activities.

Historical Development of Legislative Liaison Staffs

Although Franklin D. Roosevelt is widely regarded as the first modern president, the legislative liaison staff did not become an integral part of the White House until nearly two decades after the New Deal. The New Deal proposals were presented to Congress on an ad hoc basis. If Roosevelt felt that one of his programs was encountering difficulties on Capitol Hill, he would assign an assistant or two the short-term task of selling the program and getting the congressional roadblocks removed. However, FDR never established a staff within the White House that would have as its sole responsibility liaison with Congress.[1]

Roosevelt's catch-as-catch-can approach to congressional relations was, for the most part, successful during the first six years of his presidency, from 1933 to 1938. It was quite compatible with his generally unstructured approach to administration. In a situation of grave economic emergency, Congress was not inclined to question the president's proposals for recovery. The overwhelming Democratic majorities in the first three Roosevelt Congresses meant that those few members who did want to oppose the president on a regular basis could find few allies in either the House or the Senate.

After the 1938 congressional elections, however, Roosevelt's record on Capitol Hill was more mixed. The Republicans made substantial gains in the elections, and the GOP members joined with their Southern Democratic colleagues, many of whom had become disaffected from the New Deal once the economic recovery was under way, to form the congressional "conservative coalition." This coalition would be the bane of Democratic presidents on Capitol Hill for the next thirty years. Even when faced with this new legislative obstacle, Roosevelt, his attention increasingly focused on the rise of dictators abroad, did not establish a permanent congressional liaison staff.[2]

Following Harry Truman's election in 1948, he assigned two relatively junior White House aides to the task of legislative liaison. One was responsible for the Senate, the other for the House. These agents were not seen on Capitol Hill as being able to speak for the president, nor did they influence legislative strategy or tactics. They were primarily messengers, responsible for servicing requests for presidential favors coming from the Hill. When it came to matters of substance involving liaison with Congress on important pieces of legislation, Truman operated in much the same way as had his predecessor, relying, on an ad hos basis, on assistants like Charles Murphy and Clark Clifford.[3]

Dwight D. Eisenhower was the first president to establish an Office of Congressional Relations (OCR) as a formal organization within the White House. For the first time, members of the White House staff had liaison between the president and Congress as their sole responsibility.

Eisenhower had a number of reasons for wanting to have a legislative liaison group. First, his White House was characterized by hierarchical and specialized patterns of organization. Eisenhower preferred a strict division of labor among his advisers. Specific individuals were assigned specific functions. He was uncomfortable with the more free-wheeling styles of administration practiced in the Roosevelt and Truman White Houses.

Eisenhower also wanted the liaison staff to be a buffer between himself and what he feared would be hordes of importuning members of Congress. Since the Republicans, in the 1952 elections, regained control of both Congress and the presidency for the first time in more than twenty years, Eisenhower expected the White House to be deluged with requests for patronage and other favors. He was not comfortable with this style of politics, nor did he consider it an appropriate area for presidential involvement. The Congressional Relations Office, made up of individuals with extensive political and congressional staff experience, would, it was hoped, be well equipped to insulate Eisenhower from demands for political rewards.[4]

The Eisenhower liaison staff was not very active, compared with its successors, in attempting to obtain the passage of the president's program on Capitol Hill. In large part, this was because the Eisenhower administration did not submit an extensive legislative program to Congress. The Eisenhower staff did spend considerable time trying to prevent Congress from passing legislation considered undesirable by the White House. In this task, liaison personnel worked closely with the Republican congressional leadership.

Eisenhower had complete confidence in those who headed the legislative liaison effort, first General Wilton Persons, then Bryce Harlow. Members of Congress soon came to see that a commitment on the part of either of these men was the equivalent of a commitment from the president himself. By establishing a formal, professional, and politically experienced congressional relations staff, which was able to speak for the president and which worked closely with the legislative leadership of the president's party, Eisenhower set in motion the process that led to further development of the liaison effort under his successors.

After some initial hesitation, President Kennedy decided to retain the Office of Congressional Relations as part of the White House staff structure. He did not particularly care for the formal staff system of the Eisenhower years, but he wanted to propose a wide-ranging legislative program. The composition of Congress in 1961, with the Southern Democratic–Republican conservative coalition having a potential majority in both houses and controlling most of the important committees, did not seem particularly auspicious to a president who wanted to move the country in a liberal direction

61

on issues such as health care, civil rights, education, and economic development. Kennedy concluded that maintaining a formal organization within the White House to coordinate the liaison process was necessary if he were to make any headway in Congress.

Kennedy selected Lawrence O'Brien, his chief political aide in the 1960 campaign, to direct the office. O'Brien was one of the most skilled political operatives in the Democratic party. He had been associated with Kennedy since 1952 and had had much experience in the thickets of Massachusetts Democratic politics. O'Brien's long-time personal relationship with Kennedy was an asset in his work. When he and his staff went up to Capitol Hill, it was clear to members of Congress that they were acting not only on their own authority, but on the president's as well.[5]

In many ways, Lawrence O'Brien can be considered the father of modern legislative liaison. The decisions O'Brien made regarding the organization and functioning of the White House Congressional Relations Office established the framework within which the liaison effort was conducted not only in the Kennedy White House, but also under Presidents Johnson, Nixon, and Ford. Indeed, the continuity in the organization and functioning of the liaison staffs across the transition from a Democratic to a Republican administration in 1969 is noteworthy. Major changes in the Office of Congressional Relations were, however, introduced at the beginning of the Carter presidency in 1977.

What were the decisions O'Brien made on taking up his position in 1961 that established continuity in legislative liaison for the next sixteen years? Unlike the Eisenhower staff, the Kennedy people were presenting an activist legislative program of their own to Congress, not just responding to items on the congressional agenda. O'Brien considered it important that White House liaison officers should not spend all of their time on Capitol Hill only asking for support for the president's programs. It was equally important for them to create a general climate of favor and receptivity toward the president and the administration among members of Congress, and to use these positive perceptions as a resource when attempting to obtain support for particular pieces of legislation.

O'Brien also considered it important that the White House liaison effort be organized along lines paralleling the organization of Congress itself, with specialists for each of the blocs and factions that come together to form majority coalitions in the House and Senate. The individuals O'Brien selected for his staff were, in almost all cases, chosen for their political, not their substantive, backgrounds. O'Brien deliberately decided not to organize his congressional relations office along issue lines. (This decision will be discussed at greater length in a later section of the chapter.)

Finally, O'Brien recognized that the White House liaison staff was not an organization with sufficient resources of its own to meet the goal of building majorities in Congress behind the president's programs. Cooperative efforts with other participants in the legislative process—department and agency legislative staffs, the Democratic congressional leadership, and interest groups supportive of the president—were essential. (This topic will be discussed more extensively later.)

Considering all of these decisions, one would think that the professional and politically sophisticated liaison effort in the Kennedy White House would have helped the president set an extensive record of legislative accomplishment. Such was not the case, however. In part, Kennedy himself was hesitant to take the initiative on legislation likely to arouse intense controversy. The president, for example, had to be pushed by his congressional supporters to introduce a more far-reaching civil rights package in 1963 than he originally intended. Additionally, though, the Kennedy liaison office was constrained by the congressional arithmetic. With more than 250 Republicans and Southern Democrats in the House throughout his presidency, and with the Northern Democrats invariably in a minority in the Senate, there were simply not very many members inclined to look with favor on the administration, regardless of the efforts of the liaison team.

The legislative logjam built up from 1961 to 1963 was not broken until after the 1964 election. This was probably less a consequence of the activities of the Johnson White House than of Barry Goldwater's presidential candidacy. By taking thirty-eight Republican House members down to defeat with him, Goldwater ensured that the Northern Democrats would be close enough to a majority in the House that Lyndon Johnson would be able to achieve passage of much of the Great Society program.

The congressional liaison staff operated in much the same way in the Johnson White House as it had during the Kennedy years. There was a rather high degree of continuity in liaison personnel between the two administrations. O'Brien continued to head the liaison effort during much of the Johnson period. Johnson himself was a much more active partner of the staff than Kennedy had been, a development by no means unexpected, considering Johnson's extensive prior legislative experience, much of it in positions of party leadership.[6]

Personnel in the liaison office changed completely during the transition from Johnson to Richard Nixon in 1969. The basic structure of the office, though, as well as the orientation of most of its members, remained the same. Individuals continued to be selected because of their political, not their substantive, skills; the organization of the liaison office continued to parallel the organization of Congress; and the office continued to look to the congressional leadership and to interest groups for coalition-building assistance.

The Congressional Relations Office was much further removed from the process of policy making in the Nixon White House than it had been during the Johnson years; for example, staffers were rarely consulted before proposals were sent to Capitol Hill. In part, this was due to the more formal channels of communication that characterized the Nixon White House. In addition, however, it reflected Richard Nixon's general attitude toward Congress and the legislative process. Nixon was uncomfortable with the give-and-take of congressional politics. He was quite unwilling to bargain with members of Congress or to seek compromises on policy problems through the building of coalitions. When Congress would not accept his ideas, Nixon resorted to extra-constitutional devices such as large-scale impoundment of funds and extensive use of executive privilege to get his way. The liaison staff, experts in the arts of persuasion, were thus a rather peripheral part of the Nixon operation.

The Congressional Relations Office was one of the few components of the Nixon White House that never became entangled in the net of Watergate. Nixon's director of congressional relations, William Timmons, continues to be a highly respected and sought-after figure in Washington politics. Such cannot be said about many of Nixon's other senior aides.

Legislative liaison in Gerald Ford's White House was in many ways similar to liaison in the White House of Lyndon Johnson. Working under the close supervision of a politically skilled and legislatively experienced president, the liaison staff was an important part of the policy-making process. The strategic environment facing the Ford team, however, was quite different from that in which the Johnson staff worked. Rather than attempting to build majority coalitions behind presidential programs, as did Johnson's aides, the Ford staff was often seeking to assemble the blocking coalition of one-third needed to uphold presidential vetoes. Even though the Democrats held a more than two-to-one edge in House seats during most of Ford's term, only twelve of his sixty-six vetoes were overridden, a record for which the Congressional Relations Office was in large part responsible.

Jimmy Carter, after his election, was advised by former White House aides of both parties such as Democrat Henry Hall Wilson and

Republican Bryce Harlow to keep in operation the forms of liaison that had been relatively successful for previous presidents. Perhaps because this advice represented the conventional wisdom of the Washington community as well, Carter and his senior advisers considered it suspect. Upon taking office, Carter decided not to continue the styles of legislative liaison that had become standard over the previous sixteen years.

Carter did not consider it necessary to keep in operation a legislative liaison system that emphasized cultivating members of Congress on a personal basis and establishing cooperative lobbying relationships with a wide range of participants in the legislative process. Legislative liaison was for Carter simply a matter of convincing members of Congress of the correctness of his positions on the issues. If the rightness of his cause could not be demonstrated on Capitol Hill, Carter proposed to use the media to go over the heads of Congress to appeal to the public for support, as in his frequent attacks on Congress for not passing his energy programs in the form submitted.

The Carter liaison office was organized along issue lines, not along lines paralleling the organization of Congress. Some of those selected for liaison positions at the outset of the Carter administration lacked the political skills necessary to be successful in their jobs. Frank Moore, for example, who was appointed by Carter to head the Office of Congressional Relations, had the advantage of being Carter's own man; he was perceived on Capitol Hill as someone close to the president. But he had no previous Washington experience. He had been Carter's director of legislative relations when Carter was governor of Georgia, but to many in Washington he seemed unwilling to learn the folkways of Congress, unable to recognize that the Georgia Legislature and the U.S. Congress were not quite the same thing.[7]

Carter did achieve some legislative successes during his presidency: the ratification of the Panama Canal treaties, the "windfall" profits tax on oil companies, the deregulation of natural gas prices, and the deregulation of a number of transportation industries. It often seemed, however, as if these successes were attained in spite of the work of the legislative liaison staff, not because of it. More importantly, Carter suffered a number of major defeats on Capitol Hill. The House, for example, defeated the conference report on the Energy Mobilization Board by a nearly two-to-one margin, and in both 1978 and 1980 the Democratic majority in Congress took the initiative on tax policy completely away from the administration and, in the first of those years, passed a tax bill containing many provisions that the president had opposed. A more politically skilled liaison office might have been able to prevent these defeats, by keeping Democratic members of Congress in line behind the president's programs and picking up Republican support for those programs where possible. After all, there were almost as many Democrats in the Congress during the Carter years as there had been during the Johnson period, yet Carter and his congressional relations staff did not seem able to capitalize on this resource.

Other chapters in this volume discuss the changes in the organization of Congress and the party system that became manifest during the 1970s. The implications of these changes make Congress less permeable to the exercise of presidential influence, even if the same party is in power at both ends of Pennsylvania Avenue, and more generally reduce the importance of party ties as a link between Congress and the presidency. For these reasons, it would seem incumbent upon presidents in the 1980s to have a politically skilled legislative liaison staff to tie together two institutions that are increasingly drifting apart.

Career Patterns of Legislative Liaison Staffs

What kinds of work have legislative liaison staffers done before joining the White House staff? Where do presidents and their advisers look when hiring liaison personnel? What happens to the staff after they leave office? Do they continue to work on legislation-related matters? Tables 3–1 and 3–2 attempt to provide the answers to these questions.

One would think that most individuals working at the White House on congressional relations would have had previous political experience at the national level. Table 3–1 shows that this is indeed the case: sixty-one of the sixty-five persons who have worked on liaison staffs since 1961 have had experience on Capitol Hill, as congressional staff members, as private or public lobbyists, as officials of the national party organizations, or in some combination of these. Approximately two-thirds of the White House liaison personnel (forty-five out of sixty-five) have worked in Congress at some point in their careers prior to joining the White House. For all presidents since Kennedy, previous congressional experience seems to have been the major criterion in hiring liaison staffers. Some lobbying experience appears to have been a desired qualification as well; twenty-seven out of the sixty-five White House staffers had worked as legislative representatives for private or public interest groups or for government agencies. Party and elective experience

TABLE 3–1

EXPERIENCE OF CONGRESSIONAL LIAISON STAFF BEFORE COMING TO THE
WHITE HOUSE, 1960–1981

Experience	Kennedy Admin.	Johnson Admin.	Nixon Admin.	Ford Admin.	Carter Admin.	Reagan Admin.	Total
Congress	3	0	9	3	5	4	24
Lobbying	0	1	2	0	2	2	7
Party	2	1	2	0	1	0	6
Congress and lobbying	0	0	4	5	2	4	15
Congress and party	1	0	2	0	0	1	4
Lobbying and party	0	3	0	0	0	0	3
Congress, lobbying, and party	0	1	1	0	0	0	2
None	0	0	0	0	2	2	4
Total	6	6	20	8	12	13	65

SOURCES: For Kennedy through Ford: Joseph A. Pika, "White House Boundary Roles: Linking Advisory Systems and Presidential Publics," paper presented at 1979 annual meeting of American Political Science Association, p. 39; for Carter: Congressional Quarterly, Inc., *The Washington Lobby*, 3d ed. (Washington, D.C., 1979), p. 29; for Reagan: *Congressional Quarterly Weekly Report*, January 24, 1981, p. 174.

were never as important as the other criteria (only fifteen out of sixty-five lobbyists had such backgrounds) and appear to have become less so in recent years. Of the fifteen individuals with party or elective backgrounds, thirteen worked for Presidents Kennedy, Johnson, or Nixon. This appears to be yet another example of the decline in importance of the political parties at the presidential level.

Only four of the sixty-five liaison aides had had no national political experience before joining the White House staff. It should be noted that one of these was Frank Moore. Moore's lack of Washington experience placed him in a definite minority among his liaison colleagues, not only from other administrations, but within his own.

As can be seen from table 3–2, the principal occupation to which liaison staffers moved after they left office was lobbying. More than half (twenty-two out of forty) of the ex-liaison staffers became lobbyists of one sort or another; only eight out of the forty became congressional staffers. After their White House service, the

TABLE 3–2

EXPERIENCE OF CONGRESSIONAL LIAISON STAFF AFTER LEAVING THE
WHITE HOUSE, 1960–1981

Experience	Kennedy Admin.	Johnson Admin.	Nixon Admin.	Ford Admin.	Total
Lobbying	4	2	13	3	22
Congress	0	2	3	3	8
Other[a]	2	2	3	2	9
Unknown	0	0	1	0	1
Total	6	6	20	8	40

a. Included in this category are lawyers and political consultants who may have done lobbying on occasion.
SOURCE: Pika, "White House Boundary Roles," p. 41.

liaison staffers, with their wide range of contacts in both the legislative and the executive branches of government, became attractive personnel to a wide range of organizations seeking to influence the legislative process.

These generalizations about career patterns can be illustrated through the presentation of "professional biographies" of a number of liaison staffers in recent administrations, both Republican and Democratic:

Mike Manatos was the chief Senate lobbyist during the Kennedy and Johnson administrations. From 1937 through 1961, he worked as a staffer for four different senators from Wyoming, his home state. After leaving the White House in 1969, he worked as director for national government relations for the Procter & Gamble Company in Washington, D.C., where he was an associate of Bryce Harlow, who had been Eisenhower's director of congressional relations and who served at times as an aide to President Nixon.

James R. Jones was a legislative aide to President Johnson from 1965 to 1969. Prior to joining the Johnson staff, Jones was an assistant to Congressman Ed Edmondson (Democrat, Oklahoma). In 1972, Jones was elected to the House in his own right. He now serves as chairman of the House Budget Committee.

William Timmons was a senior member of the Office of Congressional Relations during the Nixon and part of the Ford administrations. He first came to Washington in 1955 and spent the next fourteen years working as an assistant to Senator Ernest Wiley and Congressman William Brock, both of Tennessee. After leaving the

Ford White House, Timmons set up his own lobbying firm, Timmons & Co., in Washington. He worked on the Reagan campaign in 1980 and was an adviser on legislative liaison to President-elect Reagan during the 1980–1981 transition.

Tom C. Korologos was another member of the Nixon-Ford OCR. Originally a journalist, he came to Washington in 1962 as press secretary to Senator Wallace Bennett (Republican, Utah). After working for Bennett for eight years, he joined the White House legislative liaison staff. He left the Ford White House shortly after Timmons and joined his former colleague on the staff of Timmons & Co. Like Timmons, Korologos was a consultant on congressional relations to the Reagan transition team.

Harold Barefoot Sanders was Lyndon Johnson's director of congressional relations from 1967 through 1969, after O'Brien left the White House to become postmaster general. Sanders had had a long career in Texas politics, having been a member of the Texas House of Representatives from 1952 through 1958 and an unsuccessful candidate for the U.S. House in 1958. President Kennedy appointed Sanders a U.S. attorney in Texas, and President Johnson brought him to Washington, first as an assistant deputy attorney general, then as an assistant attorney general (where he had responsibility for the Justice Department's legislative program), and finally as his chief White House lobbyist. Unlike many of his colleagues, Sanders did not stay in Washington after his service on the legislative liaison staff. He returned to Texas and his law practice. He was an unsuccessful candidate for the U.S. Senate in 1972. In 1979, President Carter appointed him to the federal bench in Dallas.

Organization of Legislative Liaison Staffs

To understand the reasons presidents have adopted particular schemes for organizing their legislative liaison staffs, it is necessary to be aware of the organization of Congress, the institution that is the focus of the liaison staffs' attempts at influence. The U.S. Congress is a highly differentiated institution in which patterns of power differ considerably from one decision-making site to another. Furthermore, although Congress is formally organized around two competing political parties, the important cleavages on many issues are not those between the two parties, but those between coalitions drawing their members from both parties.

The differentiated and fragmented nature of the congressional power structure has implications for the White House liaison office, as well as for any other set of individuals seeking to influence Congress. In particular, the majority-building tactics used by the

White House must vary depending on which voting unit is the object of influence at any particular time.

How have recent presidents organized their liaison staffs so that they might succeed on Capitol Hill? As I have already noted, Presidents Kennedy, Johnson, Nixon, and Ford structured their congressional relations offices along lines paralleling the organization of the Congress itself. The liaison staff during these four administrations typically had from six to ten members at any one time.

The director was responsible for coordinating the entire operation and for meeting regularly with the president. Kennedy, Johnson, and Ford selected for this position individuals who not only had some exposure to national politics but who were also personal associates. Before coming to the White House, Kennedy's choice, Lawrence O'Brien, had been a presidential campaign executive; Johnson's choice, Barefoot Sanders, had been a departmental executive; and Ford's choice, Max Friedersdorf, had been a congressional staffer. Perhaps more importantly, each one of the three had had a political relationship with the president (O'Brien more so than the others) before being asked to head the OCR.

President Nixon, in contrast, selected as his directors of congressional liaison first Bryce Harlow (a corporate lobbyist in Washington and Eisenhower's OCR director) and then William Timmons (a congressional staffer). While these men were experienced on the national political scene, they were not particularly close to the president prior to their appointment to OCR.

Typically, one or two members of the staff worked with the director of liaison inside the White House. These aides normally had two principal responsibilities. The first was to coordinate the activities of the departmental and agency liaison officers. This was often a monumental task, far too much for just one or two people. Although the president is head of the executive branch in name, he often encounters substantial difficulties in getting the departments and agencies to carry out his agenda rather than their own. The area of legislative liaison is no exception. White House liaison staff frequently complained that department liaison personnel did not spend sufficient time working on the president's program—that they concentrated their efforts on what the White House perceived to be rather unimportant departmental bills that were bound to pass in any case. Furthermore, department liaison staffs were at times accused of making end runs around the Office of Management and Budget, trying to get congressional budget writers to restore appropriations that had been cut out in the Executive Office. One liaison aide expressed this sentiment rather well:

You might want to look at how administration positions get changed during the liaison effort. Say a department or an agency is in a fight with OMB as a new policy is being put together, and the department or agency loses. But the agency is then responsible for most of the liaison work on the Hill. Whose position do the agency liaison people present to the Congress, their own or the administration's? Or say someone introduces an amendment to the Transportation Appropriations Bill to add a billion for something or other. The Transportation liaison man is asked what the administration's position is. He says, "OMB is against it." He doesn't answer the question directly, but the message gets out that the department was for it, but lost to OMB. So, since most of the liaison work is done by the departments, administration positions may get changed during the liaison process.[8]

There were a number of approaches that the White House liaison staff could try to bring more unity to the administration's legislative liaison activities. Most presidents scheduled regular weekly meetings of all of the departmental and agency lobbyists, which they themselves would periodically attend. The purpose of these meetings was to develop a sense of teamwork and camaraderie among the various liaison agents and, on occasion, to seek the help of one department in another department's liaison efforts. During the Kennedy-Johnson administrations, for example, Agriculture Department lobbyists were often asked to contact rural members of Congress on a whole range of programs. As a White House lobbyist described this departmental effort, "The Agriculture people were a great asset to the White House, first because they were knowledgeable and hard-working, and secondly because they would work bills outside their own department's issues."

Additionally, Presidents Johnson and Nixon attempted to gain greater White House control over the liaison process by parachuting their own appointees into departmental liaison positions. Assistant secretaries for legislation (the usual title for departmental liaison officers) were selected not by the departmental secretaries but by the White House. Ralph Huitt, for example, a political scientist who had once worked for Lyndon Johnson in the Senate, was selected by the president to be chief of legislation for the Department of Health, Education, and Welfare in 1965. Johnson would rarely appoint anyone to such a position without first clearing the nominee with O'Brien and Joseph Califano, his chief domestic policy aide in the White House. Similarly, when the Nixon administration was being shaken up following the president's 1972 reelection, H. R. Haldeman and John

71

Ehrlichman, Nixon's two principal aides, made most of the decisions regarding staffing of departmental liaison offices. One Carter White House aide regretted that his administration did not follow such a centralized personnel selection process. Referring to department lobbyists, he noted that:

> We should have filled those jobs with Jimmy Carter people, but we didn't. The president believes very strongly in cabinet government. But a result of that is that you have in the departments not Jimmy Carter people, but Joe Califano people, or Brock Adams people, or Bob Bergland people.

In addition to coordinating departmental liaison efforts, the second task of the White House lobbyists who spent their time at 1600 Pennsylvania Avenue was to be responsible for serving as a central clearing house of legislative intelligence. First, they tried to keep track of the exchanges of favors between the White House and Capitol Hill. Who owed what to whom at any given moment? How could pens from bill signing ceremonies, tickets to the president's box at the Kennedy Center, rides on Air Force One, and invitations to state dinners be used to cultivate favorable opinions of the White House on the part of members of Congress? Perhaps more important, these White House aides also assembled the head-count information collected by the liaison aides who worked the Hill. This information was presented to the president on a regular basis, sometimes accompanied by a recommendation that he place a call to a particular member of the House or the Senate in an attempt to pick up a vote. Furthermore, as we will see shortly, this information was often shared with the congressional leadership of the president's party and with interest groups seeking the same legislative goals as the president.

Most members of the White House liaison staff, though, spent most of their time not in the White House but on Capitol Hill, regularly talking to members of Congress and their staffs.[9] The liaison agents who "worked the Hill"—numbering from four to seven in most administrations—would typically assemble at the White House for a morning meeting and then spend the rest of the day in the House and Senate office buildings. Unlike some of the executive agencies (particularly the military departments and the Veterans Administration), the White House did not have office space assigned to it on Capitol Hill, so the White House liaison officers spent most of their time working out of the rooms of the leadership of the president's party. During the Kennedy-Johnson period, for example, the House lobbyists worked out of the offices of Speaker John McCormack (Democrat, Massachusetts) and Majority Leader Carl Albert (Democrat, Oklahoma). The effort to break the Southern filibuster on what became the Civil Rights Act of 1964 was coordinated by the White House from the office of Senate Majority Whip Hubert H. Humphrey (Democrat, Minnesota). Similarly, the liaison staffers of Presidents Nixon and Ford worked out of the offices of the House and Senate minority leaders. The vice-president is provided with a suite of rooms on the Senate side of the Capitol Building; these quarters have also proved useful to White House lobbyists responsible for the Senate.

Most of the liaison staff's communications with members of Congress took place in the members' offices or in committee rooms. Only rarely did White House liaison staffers use social functions as opportunities for lobbying on behalf of the White House. Many White House lobbyists did not wait to be called by members in order to visit them. Henry Hall Wilson, a Kennedy-Johnson lobbyist, tried to visit each Southern Democrat (the members for whom he was chiefly responsible) at least once a week, and President Ford's lobbyists tried to see the ranking Republican member of each House and Senate committee on a weekly basis as well.

With the White House lobbyists spread out all over Capitol Hill, some communications system was needed to enable them to keep in touch with their headquarters at the White House. Since the mid-1960s, all White House lobbyists working on Capitol Hill have been given paging devices, which enable them to contact each other and which enable the director of OCR or someone else back in the White House to get in touch with his forces on Capitol Hill. Members of the House and Senate who wanted to get in touch with the White House lobbyists would usually leave a message for them at the White House or, if the matter was urgent, would reach them through the party leaders' offices.

When organizing his liaison office at the beginning of his administration, any president has two options. First, he can organize his legislative staff in terms of *issues*, with staffers (probably substantive specialists) assigned particular policy areas and talking about those issues with the members who are influential in those fields. Or, the president can organize the liaison staff in terms of *people*, with staffers (probably not substantive specialists) assigned to talk about all issues, and other matters as well, to groups of members—the same groups of members whatever the issues involved.

If the president chooses to organize his staff in terms of people, he then has all sorts of ways in which he could, in principle, define the groups that staffers are to deal with. Members of the House and Senate could be divided up according to geography (North, South, "Sunbelt," "Snowbelt"); ideology (liberals, moderates, conservatives);

location in the Senate and House office buildings (one staffer per building); previous acquaintance with the staffers on the Hill; alphabetical order; or even at random.

Presidents Kennedy, Johnson, Nixon, and Ford all chose the people-centered approach for the organization of their liaison staffs. All four valued this approach because it enabled the White House to keep in regular touch with a large number of members of Congress. The presidents did not want to be in a situation where the only time their staffs would contact members was when those members' votes were needed. This mode of organization enabled the liaison staffs to spend their time trying to find out what was on members' minds, occasionally providing them with benefits under the control of the White House, and hoping that the climate of favor and receptivity thus created would lead to votes in support of the president. These presidents did recognize that this form of organization meant that the liaison staff could not be counted on for detailed negotiations with members of Congress on the substance of legislation, particularly during the policy formulation process. However, the White House domestic policy staff (most of whose members were substantive specialists) was available to be used in such negotiations.

From 1961 through 1976 all the administrations also chose similar strategies for dividing up members of Congress for purposes of the people-centered approach. First, there were separate lobbying staffs for the Senate and the House, with, as would be expected, a considerably larger staff for the larger chamber. Then, within each chamber, members were assigned to lobbyists on the basis of a combination of geographical, ideological, and partisan considerations. The approach of the Kennedy-Johnson liaison team to the House was typical. Three White House lobbyists were assigned to the House, each with responsibility for keeping in touch with a different group of House Democrats. One was responsible only for the Southern Democrats, a key group because their voting behavior determined whether the conservative coalition would form and be successful. The Northern Democrats were divided up among two members of the staff. One dealt with the big-city Democrats, often elected with the support of a party organization, while the other was responsible for the more issue-oriented liberals who formed the backbone of the Democratic Study Group. This last staffer was also responsible for liaison with moderate Republicans who might support the administration's programs. In the Ford White House, while there were separate lobbyists for the House and the Senate, there was not the attention to finer subdivisions of members that characterized the Kennedy-Johnson years. Perhaps this was because the congressional Republicans, the prime target of the Ford team's efforts, were a more homogeneous party than the congressional Democrats.

Structuring the liaison staff in terms of particular blocs or factions within Congress was of considerable assistance to presidents in their majority-building tasks on Capitol Hill. This form of organization was quite compatible with the building of majority coalitions by means of assembling groups of members. Rather than dealing with members on a one-on-one basis, the White House could concentrate its efforts on groups of like-minded members. Such an approach, by preventing needless waste of White House liaison resources, was likely to lead to more presidential legislative successes.

Jimmy Carter began his presidency by organizing his liaison office along lines quite different from those of his predecessors. Carter adopted the other organizational option mentioned earlier, that of structuring the office along issue lines. In the Carter White House, instead of having specialists for the various blocs of members in the Senate and the House, there were specialists in energy, foreign policy, health, environmental issues, and so on.

One of the reasons for Carter's choosing this form of organization had to do with his attitude toward the Washington community. The president and his closest advisers thought of the established Washington community in some senses as the enemy. They had been elected, they believed, by having run against Washington. They would not govern according to the accepted norms of Washington. As I noted earlier, the fact that previous presidents had all organized their liaison offices in the same way was reason enough for Carter to call this form of organization into question.

Carter was elected in 1976 thinking he did not "owe" any other political organization or politician anything. He had not had to build a coalition of party leaders, interest groups, and other elected officials in order to attain the presidency. Rather, in large part because of the changes introduced into the presidential selection process in 1972 and 1976, Carter had been elected through a process of "retail" politics, interacting with individual citizens through the media, instead of through a process of "wholesale" politics, in which he would have had to interact with political brokers and elites on a face-to-face basis.[10]

If Carter felt that he did not owe anything to other elements of the Washington community, he certainly believed that he did not owe anything to the U. S. Congress. The president's feeling that he owed nothing to the Congress was one reason he believed it unnecessary to establish a liaison staff structured around people. Since the politics of bargaining and coalition building was unfamiliar to Carter, he did not recognize the importance of personal relationships as a means of facilitating the bargaining process, nor did he see the need to be aware of the various groupings on Capitol Hill that might be brought together to form a majority.

Since politics for Carter was to be a process of solving policy problems by discovering the best technical solutions to them, what was more logical than to organize the legislative liaison staff along issue lines? The matter of preparing Congress to look favorably on presidential initiatives without regard to specific issues was apparently not even considered as Carter and his associates went about organizing their liaison effort. Senator Hubert Humphrey gave his opinion of this strategy in an interview with Haynes Johnson of the *Washington Post*:

> You see, part of Carter's problem is that he really doesn't know the little characteristics of our colleagues up here. You've got to know what makes 'em tick, you've got to know their wives, you've got to know their families, you've got to know their backgrounds. You know, I used to say Johnson was a personal FBI. The son of a gun was incredible, but so was Kennedy, and so in a sense was Ford. All of the last four Presidents were creatures of Congress. Kennedy, Johnson, Nixon, Ford—when they went to the White House, they had connections up here, buddy-buddy connections.
>
> There is a fellowship in the Congress which is unique. It's different and better than anything that you ever have in a lodge or even a church. Now that changes when you go down to the White House; even as Vice-President, I experienced it. But still, you've got the connections and you still know a lot about the members.
>
> But here comes Carter, and he's a new boy in town. Institutionally, Congress hasn't sized him up yet. And he still doesn't know all the players here—their idiosyncracies, their characteristics. He gets the stereotypes: he knows that Humphrey is garrulous, for example, or that Russell Long can be a good storyteller, and so on. But he doesn't know all the little things that make 'em tick. And that's the key around this place.[11]

The White House liaison staff came in for a good deal of criticism, much of it justified, during the first few months of the new administration. Some of this criticism came from members of Congress who found the new issue-oriented style of congressional relations quite incompatible with accepted ways of doing things, such as the White

House's traditional policy of not interfering with congressional prerogatives in regard to water projects. Within a month of taking
office in 1977, Carter proposed striking a number of Army Corps of
Engineers projects from the budget. Haynes Johnson recounted the
congressional reaction:

> Congress erupted. A private session with the president,
> demanded by some of the angriest senators, such as Russell
> Long and Gary Hart of Colorado, led to a scene—accounts
> of which quickly made the rounds. Long . . . stood up before
> a group of White House aides and, his voice dripping with
> sarcasm, introduced himself: "My name is Russell Long, and
> I am the chairman of the Senate Finance Committee." Long,
> whose state held five of the projects marked for extinction,
> proceeded to shout out his objections to Carter's decisions.[12]

At a more mundane level, members who wanted small favors
from the White House, such as autographed pictures of the president,
found it very difficult to obtain such benefits from liaison staffers
who wanted to talk about the crude-oil equalization tax. As one
congressional staffer put it:

> When Jerry Ford would sign a bill, he'd use nice metal pens
> with his name on them, and then he'd pass them out to the
> members who had worked on the bill. But Carter signs bills
> with a felt-tip pen, and then he puts the pen back into his
> pocket.

In addition, the liaison staffers were not seen as good transmitters of
messages between Capitol Hill and the White House. Unlike their
predecessors in both Republican and Democratic administrations,
they were perceived as being some distance from the president and
thus unable to pass information from Capitol Hill directly to him.
Carter's decision to house most of the liaison staffers in the East Wing
of the White House, where the social staff had its offices, rather than
in the West Wing, also hurt perceptions of the staff on Capitol Hill.

Carter did make some changes in his liaison staff, in both personnel and organization, about six months into his presidency. A number of the liaison staffers who came in at the beginning of the
administration were replaced, usually by individuals with more Washington experience. In particular, William H. Cable, who had been a
congressional staffer for more than ten years, was brought in to the
White House to direct the House lobbying effort, and Robert Thomson, former counsel to the Democratic Senatorial Campaign Committee, was hired to work on Senate liaison. Unlike most of their
colleagues in the liaison office, Cable's and Thomson's prior political

experience was entirely in Washington, not in Atlanta or on the Carter campaign.

At the same time, the issue based organization of the liaison staff was done away with. It was replaced by a system in which liaison aides specialized on either the House or the Senate, but in which there was to be no specialization for the various ideological and/or partisan blocs in those chambers.[13] Rather, members were assigned to lobbyists on a somewhat haphazard geographical basis. Cable described the organization of House lobbying in this way: "We do it on a geographic basis but don't make them from contiguous states. I don't want to find myself the lobbyist for the Northeast or the Southwest. This way makes us more responsible to Congress as a whole."[14]

In a departure from practice in previous Democratic administrations, the Carter White House's lobbyists devoted substantial efforts to Republican as well as Democratic members of Congress. This was especially the case on the Senate side, where there were quite a number of moderate Republicans during the Carter years.

Cooperative Lobbying as a Means of Accomplishing the Liaison Staff's Goals

The White House Office of Congressional Relations often has very few political resources available to it. The office has always been small, with fewer than ten professionals on the staff at any one time. The liaison personnel rarely have substantive expertise in any issue area. The congressional relations staff has usually had a rather limited role in the process of policy formulation.

How can the liaison staff overcome these disadvantages and assist the president in the passage of his legislative program? One means of doing so, exchanging benefits with members of Congress, is the subject of Charles Jones's chapter in this volume. Another means is to engage in cooperative lobbying efforts with those outside the White House who also support the president's programs. In this section of the chapter, I will discuss the relationships that have existed between the White House legislative liaison staff and three institutions that have often been of considerable assistance to that staff—department and agency liaison staffs, the congressional leadership of the president's party, and Washington representatives of interest groups.

OCR and Department and Agency Liaison Staffs. Each of the cabinet-level departments, and many of the independent agencies as well, has its own legislative liaison staff, usually headed by an official with the title of assistant secretary for legislation. There is one important difference in the functions of the White House and the departmental liaison staffs that should be noted at this point. At the White House, the liaison staff is only involved in the "political" process of attempting to obtain passage of the president's programs. A separate organization (the Domestic Council, the Domestic Policy Staff) is responsible for the development of the policy initiatives in the first place. At the departmental level, however, the same staff is responsible both for policy formulation and for legislative liaison. Thus, departmental legislative staffers are often hired for their substantive expertise as well as their political skills.

During the Johnson and Nixon administrations, the work of the departmental legislative staffs was closely coordinated from the White House. As I have already mentioned, most assistant secretaries for legislation were selected by the White House during these administrations, and regular weekly meetings took place between the OCR lobbyists and their departmental counterparts. At these meetings, the president's staff would continually stress the need for the departments and the White House to march in unison on Capitol Hill. As Lawrence O'Brien put it:

> . . . the emphasis constantly is on the President's program, that all elements of this program really in the final analysis are part of a single program, . . . The only man I'm aware of who has been elected to office is the President of the United States. And he has proposed to the people what he conceives his program to be. The people made a determination that he should be their President. Furthermore, you have the Democratic Party Platform, and it is, as we see it, a mandate for action.
>
> So by establishing this team and working very, very closely with these people in the departments and agencies, it gave us additional manpower, and it insured that our activities would be properly channeled for maximum results, and we would not have cross-wires and individuals going off in separate directions and working with the Congress.[15]

Another member of the Johnson OCR staff described the importance of the administration's being united on Capitol Hill:

> Johnson put a great deal of emphasis on the fact that the administration ought to speak with one voice. And if you speak with forked tongue on the Hill, your credibility, and therefore your influence, is going to be substantially lessened.

For the most part, during the Kennedy through Ford presidencies cooperative relationships were maintained between the Congressional Relations Office in the White House and the department and agency liaison personnel. Departmental lobbyists, as I have already noted, at times assisted the White House by working on legislation outside their own issue areas. This system of cooperation was beneficial to OCR because it enabled additional administration lobbying resources to be brought to bear on Capitol Hill. If Southern Democrats were having difficulty supporting a bill proposed by the Department of Health, Education, and Welfare, for example, those members could be contacted not only by HEW liaison personnel, but also by White House representatives and, still further, by Agriculture Department lobbyists, who might be expected to have close ties with the Southern Democrats. Similarly, HEW and Labor Department representatives could be brought in to talk to members from the cities about the reasons the farm program deserved support. Granted, extradepartmental work represented only a small portion of most liaison staffs' time, but it was of considerable help to OCR in its efforts to pass the presidents' bills.

Most of those who were department and agency lobbyists before 1977 believed that the organization and coordination of the liaison system by OCR was an effective means of interacting with Congress. These staffers knew that when their department faced a difficult legislative situation they could often call on the White House or on other departments for assistance in liaison. This assistance was particularly welcomed by departments such as State or Treasury, which historically had been weak in their relations with Congress. Some personnel at the secretarial level in the departments, however, were unhappy with the liaison system, since they believed that the White House was unjustifiably bypassing them and interacting directly with the department's legislative staff.[16]

The relationship between the White House and the departmental liaison staffs during the Carter administration was quite different from what it had been during earlier administrations.[17] At the beginning of his term of office, President Carter put great emphasis on the importance of reducing the influence of the White House within the executive branch and of devolving authority and responsibility to the departmental level. The practice during his administration was, therefore, for the secretary to appoint his or her own liaison officers without White House involvement.

This method of personnel selection occasionally led to the view (expressed at the Carter White House, at least by some among the liaison staff) that departmental lobbyists were working too much for their own department's positions, and not enough for the administration's or the White House's. Such questions about the loyalties of the department liaison staffs were not raised often. When they were raised, however, they were considered to be very serious. More often, though, the White House lobbyists perceived the departmental lobby-ists as their partners or assistants. Another White House liaison agent:

> [The department lobbyists] do almost all of the errand run-ning. If a congressman calls me up with a problem, I'll hand it off to Dick Warden [at HEW] or Harry Schwartz [at HUD] or whoever's responsible for it. Sometimes I'll tell the department person to get back to the member, and to tell him I told you to call him back. Other times, I'll ask the department to give me the answer, and I'll call the member back. It all depends how we stand with that member at the given time, and what he needs from us and we need from him soon.
>
> In addition to doing that, they can help us, and other departments, out on bills with members they have special relationships with. Jack Stempler [at Defense] may not care very much about [election day] voter registration, but if he calls up Congressman "Bombs Away" and tells him he thinks voter registration is a good thing, that Congressman's going to be very likely to vote for it. After all, this is Stempler from the Pentagon calling, not Joe Califano or Pat Harris. So we've asked each department to give us a list of ten members they have especially good relations with, members they can call on things outside their own depart-ment's business. This also knits the department liaison people closer together, and makes members see the adminis-tration as a team is behind a particular program.

It may be somewhat far-fetched to expect a member of Congress to vote in a particular way simply because he is contacted by a depart-mental lobbyist with whom he is sympathetic on departmental issues. Still, attempting to construct such cross-departmental lobbying alli-ances does mean a reduction in the amount of its own resources that the White House has to expend.

How did the departmental lobbyists view their White House counterparts? The answer also bears on cross-departmental lobbying. One departmental liaison staffer believed there should be more cross-departmental lobbying:

> [Cross-departmental lobbying] is done, but I would like to see more of it. Maybe what should be done is that the Pentagon guy and the HEW guy should go to see the mem-ber of the Armed Services Committee together. The Penta-

gon guy can hold the member's hand while the HEW guy talks substance.

The White House could ask us for more than they do. When I was on the Hill, I was Congressman ———'s AA. I worked on the energy issues, and I know the members of the Commerce Committee. . . . I told Schlesinger, if you ever need my help with the Commerce Committee don't hesitate to call. But they've never asked me for help.

While a majority of the departmental lobbyists believed in the utility of interdepartmental liaison efforts, some believed that they should not waste their own department's resources on lobbying for other departments' bills. The following is a typical sentiment expressed by such an assistant secretary:

So far, I've established good relationships with many members of Congress, but those relationships exist because I'm interested in ——— and those members are interested in ———. I don't think my calling up and saying you should vote against the Clinch River project is going to make any difference in terms of changing the way that member's going to vote. He'll still need me, and I'll still need him, for the Department's own business, regardless of how he votes on Clinch River.

Perceptions of the White House lobbying effort in general, and of the weekly meetings of the departmental lobbyists with the White House people, were also mixed. First, some assistant secretaries saw the White House liaison staff as too small and too concerned with "putting out fires" to be of much assistance in their long-term efforts to build majorities behind their own department's legislation:

. . . ninety percent of what's said at those meetings is of no interest to us at all.

We have very good ties with the people on the Domestic Policy Staff who work on this department's legislation. We actually don't have that much to do with the White House liaison staff. They have Friday afternoon meetings for all the liaison people, but it seems all that is discussed there are energy and dams. They simply don't have the time or the personnel to work on our legislative programs. . . .

The White House office is too small to be of much assistance to us. They don't know anything about the substance of this department's legislation. They have to handle the whole government. They can be useful working with the leadership and the committee chairmen on scheduling, but that's about it.

On the other hand, some departmental liaison officers spoke very highly of the White House lobbyists:

> I've never had any bad relations with them. Whenever we've asked them to help us out, they have, and the rest of the time, they've stayed out of our hair. For example, at the end of this week, the Senate committee is going to mark up the department's appropriations bill. There are a lot of very important issues raised in that bill, particularly after the House got through with it. So I sent a memo over to Moore, telling him what our problems were, who had to be called, and what had to be said to them. And they did everything I asked them to.

> I think very highly of the liaison people in the White House. . . . They've never turned us down when we asked for their help. . . . On a big bill we have to ask them to assist us. They did everything we asked them to on the ———— bill. . . . We have those Friday meetings in the Roosevelt Room, which Frank Moore chairs. . . . The meetings are useful, in that we can all see where the entire administration's legislative program is.

Still, the cooperative relationships between White House and departmental liaison personnel were undoubtedly less robust and less well developed under Carter than in earlier administrations. In earlier administrations, the liaison system was viewed as hierarchical, with the White House on top and the departments below. The Carter organization was perceived as being flatter. It was more difficult for the White House to get the departments to adhere to its wishes. The White House and the departmental lobbyists had to expend more of their resources on maintaining this rather amorphous structure, and fewer resources on actually communicating with Congress, than when a more hierarchical structure was used.

OCR and the Congressional Leadership. From the Eisenhower through the Ford administrations, the White House liaison staff was often successful in serving as a broker between the president and the congressional leadership of the president's party. This relationship was more fruitful under the Democratic presidents, because the congressional leadership with which they worked was the majority leadership, not the minority one.

The White House had to develop close relationships with the leadership, for no program could pass through Congress unless the leadership was willing to guide it through the legislative process. The opposition or even the indifference of the leadership could mean the defeat of the president's proposals. Moreover, the leadership determined whether the liaison staff could function on Capitol Hill. By not giving White House lobbyists access to their offices and their information networks (the whip organizations), the leadership could create a climate in which the White House lobbyists would not be welcome in Congress. The venerable Speaker Sam Rayburn was somewhat reluctant to work jointly with the White House at the beginning of the Kennedy administration in 1961. Lawrence O'Brien recounted the situation as follows:

> Well, of course first of all, this activity was all new to me. And we moved cautiously and carefully. We had to explore reaction. And the distinguished Speaker at that time, Speaker Rayburn, was of course a major point of contact. And I can remember in those early days and weeks as I went to the Hill (being somewhat concerned that we would be accepted, that we would have the freedom of movement in contact with the leadership and the members, that we would not step on someone's toes), and as I recall those early days, it was not unusual to have a considerable wait to see the Speaker. And I think I was always filled with a certain degree of concern, trepidation, if you will—I found as time went on that there was a warm relationship, one of the great periods of my time here has been in the association that I always remember with Speaker Rayburn. But I must say at the outset I don't know how the people felt about us, but I do know that we were very, very careful not to cross that barrier that we felt existed constitutionally. I don't think we ever have crossed it, but we have found out you can talk across it, if you will. You can get together quite easily. But the early days—it wasn't that the Speaker made it difficult—I think we were concerned, nervous about the whole thing, and perhaps the Speaker was wondering a little bit about us, because he hadn't had the experience as a leader up there of having that kind of continuing contact from the White House and the President on down.[18]

Throughout the period under discussion, however, the leaders of the president's party realized that the presence of White House liaison personnel on Capitol Hill would actually benefit them; the liaison staff could provide the leaders with information on members' voting intentions it would otherwise be difficult for them to obtain. The leadership therefore legitimized the liaison staff's presence as a group of full-time lobbyists on Capitol Hill and fostered an atmosphere in which members of their party were encouraged to cooperate with the

White House. Members who went along with the White House, and thus with their party's leadership, would be remembered when the leadership was distributing benefits such as office space, trips abroad, and committee assignments.

The information that the leadership received from the White House about the likely outcomes of roll calls was often useful. Sometimes it was even more accurate than that gathered by the leaders themselves. An example from the Kennedy-Johnson period illustrates the point.

Senate Majority Leader Mike Mansfield, not being interested in collecting power for his own account, did not believe that his office needed to serve as a central source of information about the Senate. Each senator, he felt, should be responsible for managing his own bills and for getting majority support for them; the leadership would merely coordinate the schedule. Thus, Mansfield did not conduct the painstaking head counts on key issues that his predecessor as majority leader, Lyndon Johnson, was always gathering. The White House filled this void in information about the preferences of senators. Since Mansfield would not conduct the head counts, the White House liaison staff did, working out of Mansfield's office. The intelligence collected by the White House was crucial to the Senate leadership. Without this information, the leadership would have been much less certain in making its decisions on matters such as when to bring a bill up for debate and when to call for a vote. While most congressional party leaders took a more active view of their jobs than Mansfield, the White House was often able to provide them with more information about the preferences of members than the whip offices alone would have been able to assemble.

The technique of establishing and maintaining good relations with the Democratic congressional leadership was used by the Carter White House less than by its predecessors. This was partly a consequence of the White House's slighting Speaker Thomas P. O'Neill (Democrat, Massachusetts) on several occasions at the beginning of the administration. The Speaker and his wife were assigned obscure seats for the inaugural gala; the administration appointed two Massachusetts Republicans, Evan Dobelle and Elliot Richardson, to senior positions without consulting the Speaker; and Carter withdrew his fifty-dollar-per-person tax rebate plan, which the Speaker had publicly supported, without consulting him. These and similar slights made it very difficult for the Speaker and his staff to work on a friendly basis with the White House liaison office, and to make their rooms in the Capitol available to the White House, even though most of these unfortunate events were not the doing of the OCR personnel, and even though O'Neill was basically sympathetic to Carter's legislative goals.

Snubs of the Speaker were not, however, the major reason for the Carter administration's being less able to work with the Democratic leadership to attain passage of its legislation. Both houses of Congress had new leaders in 1977, and these leaders perceived their roles differently from their predecessors. While Speaker O'Neill would have liked to facilitate the passage of White House legislative programs (as evidenced by his establishing a special committee to consider the president's energy legislation in 1977), he was constrained by the changes in the distribution of power in the House— changes that made power and responsibility available to a far larger proportion of the House members than in the past and thus made them less responsive to the Speaker's wishes. In addition, Senator Robert C. Byrd (Democrat, West Virginia), the new majority leader, emphasized defending the integrity of the Senate in the institutional sense, and keeping it moving in the procedural sense, rather than attaining substantive goals, whether or not they were in agreement with the president's.

These developments meant that the congressional leadership was less available to the White House for scheduling legislation and persuading members. O'Neill was more constrained by his rank and file in making decisions, and Byrd made the Senate less permeable to White House influence than it had been when Johnson was president and Mansfield majority leader. The consequence of these developments was that legislation was sometimes voted on before majorities could be assembled in support of it because the leadership could not or would not make the effort to secure the votes for passage. Because the White House liaison staff did not have complete information about members' preferences, OCR could not get the votes either. Thus, the Carter White House suffered some embarrassing defeats on the floors of both houses. These defeats, in turn, led to a perception of ineptness on Capitol Hill on the part of the Carter White House in general and the congressional liaison staff in particular. These perceptions of ineptness made it all the more difficult for the liaison staff to obtain votes subsequently.

OCR and Interest Groups. The White House congressional liaison office can frequently take advantage of the resources of certain interest groups. As in the case of the congressional leadership, the liaison staff can make an initial investment of its resources to establish close relationships with interest groups. As a result of these close relationships, both the White House and the groups are able to collect more legislative information, and to achieve more legislative successes, than if they had been working independently. At times, a trilateral relationship among the White House, the leadership, and the interest groups can work to the benefit of all three partners. Such was the case in 1964, when the Leadership Conference on Civil Rights, the Senate Democratic leadership, and the Johnson White House worked together to defeat the Southern filibuster on what became the Civil Rights Act of 1964.

The relationships between the OCR and interest groups have not always been harmonious. The liaison staff wants to see legislation passed because that legislation is part of the president's program. Although the liaison office works on several major pieces of legislation simultaneously, the interests of many group representatives are more narrowly focused on one or two pieces of legislation—for example, the Sierra Club on revisions to the Clean Air Act, or the Associated Milk Producers on the level of dairy price supports. Thus, there is always the possibility of conflict arising between the groups and the liaison staff. The groups can begin to believe that the White House is not devoting sufficient attention to their own particular programs, or that the content of the bills as proposed by the president does not include all of their demands.

The White House is less able to rely on the resources of interest groups than on those of the congressional leadership. Both the liaison staff and the leadership are usually concerned not only with the substance of policy but also, and to a greater extent, with protecting and enhancing their own power stakes in the legislative struggle. Both the liaison staff and the leadership place great emphasis on maintaining their reputations for power (and, in OCR's case, the reputation of their principal, the president) in a city where one's professional reputation is often as important as one's actual accomplishments.[19] With the interest groups, though, the situation is different, for the group lobbyists are primarily interested in the substance of programs, and in the substance of only a few programs at that. The perspectives toward the legislative process of the liaison staff and the interest groups are thus likely to be dissimilar.

For this reason, the liaison staffs have often attempted to ensure that contacts between the administration and single-purpose interest groups take place mainly at the level of the departments and agencies. The focus of the department and agency congressional liaison personnel, which is primarily on their own organization's programs, would more likely be congruent with that of most interest groups. The White House lobbyists prefer to cooperate with interest groups that are working for a broader legislative program, with contours more closely resembling the White House's. The OCR and other White House staffers must still monitor contacts between interest groups and the departments, however, to prevent such contacts from degenerating into mutually protective ones in which the groups and the departments together go to their allies on Capitol Hill in an attempt to make end runs around the president.

The best example in recent times of a cooperative relationship between the legislative liaison staff and a general-purpose interest group was that between the Kennedy-Johnson OCR and the AFL-CIO. During the 1960s, the AFL-CIO supported many social welfare programs—in education, health care, civil rights, and urban development. Much, if not most, of this legislation was part of the Kennedy-Johnson program, so the substantive content of the legislative packages being lobbied by the White House and the AFL-CIO differed very little. Effective exchanges of legislative intelligence were often arranged between the White House and labor. The OCR would concentrate its information-gathering efforts on Southern Democrats, while the labor lobbyists would devote their efforts to ascertaining the preferences of the Northern Democrats. By dividing up the work in this way, both the White House and labor could get a better sense of the likely outcome of a roll call than if each had attempted to count the members independently. This information could then be shared with the third partner in the relationship, the Democratic leaders on Capitol Hill.

It is difficult to point to other examples of such mutually reinforcing relationships between the White House liaison staff and an interest group. Such interactions have not usually been found during Republican administrations, for the business and other interest groups more sympathetic to Republican presidents usually have not had very wide-ranging legislative goals. In the contemporary period, interest groups are less important to the White House in governing because they are less important to presidential candidates in getting elected. Interest-group leaders no longer act as brokers at national party conventions, and recent changes in the campaign finance laws have virtually eliminated the need for candidates to obtain contributions from interest groups concerned with the policies they will put forward.

It should be noted, however, that on a number of occasions the Carter White House liaison team worked closely with the "public-interest" groups. The main concerns of these groups were usually governmental processes or environmental protection. Common Cause lobbyists, for example, worked with the White House in the effort to obtain passage of the Civil Service Reform Act of 1978. These groups, however, were often unable to provide much political support to the administration at the grass roots. In congressional constituencies, such groups had few supporters who held strong opinions about the issues on which the Washington staffs were lobbying.

The Congressional Liaison Staff and the Formulation of Public Policy

Under no recent president has the congressional liaison staff been active in formulating the administration's legislative program. Presidents Eisenhower, Kennedy, Johnson, and Ford did consult Congress when preparing their legislative packages. Presidents Nixon and Carter, however, did not. These varying patterns of presidential interaction with Congress in policy development are nicely illustrated by the contrasting styles of the Johnson and the Carter administrations.

Lyndon Johnson insisted that the legislative branch be consulted before major domestic policy initiatives were sent to Capitol Hill. His belief that Congress should be consulted was not derived from any abstract theory about the coequal position of Congress in the constitutional scheme. Rather, it was based on considerations of the benefits such actions could bring to the president.[20]

Johnson recalled that "the trick was to crack the wall of separation enough to give the Congress a feeling of participation in creating my bills without exposing my plans at the same time to advance Congressional opposition before they even saw the light of day. It meant taking risks, but the risks were worth it." LBJ noted that "when people have a hand in shaping projects, these projects are more likely to be successful than the ones simply handed down from the top."[21] One would think that the White House legislative liaison staff would have been the most logical unit to coordinate this process of prior consultation with members of Congress. Such, however, was not the case.

The process of domestic policy development in the Johnson administration began with the selection of a number of task forces in different issue areas. The task forces were working groups whose goal was the formulation of specific policy recommendations for the coming legislative year. Once the task forces submitted their reports, in the late fall of each year, Johnson's chief domestic aide, Joseph Califano, assembled from the reports the components of what he considered to be a substantively good, as well as politically feasible, legislative program. As part of this process, Califano and other domestic policy advisers consulted with members of the appropriate congressional committees. These consultations focused on the substance of the legislation, as well as on amendments and clarifications needed to give the proposals a better chance of being approved.

The liaison staffs were not brought in until after the basic outlines of each year's legislative program had been determined, and they did not usually participate in the consultations with committee members. Instead, the president's and Califano's discussions with the liaison office were concentrated solely on the means of presenting the legislative program to the Congress and on matters of communications and timing.

Johnson thus made it clear that the legislative staff was to be responsible for liaison only after the outlines of his legislative program had been determined. He believed that OCR staffers should not become extensively involved in policy planning, because their lack of substantive orientation would lead them to compromise away the substance of legislation too easily.[22] Yet, by insisting on advance congressional consultation through his domestic advisers, Johnson increased the likelihood that he would attain legislative success.

In the Carter White House, as in the Johnson White House, there was a distinct separation of roles between the Domestic Policy Staff, responsible for policy development and formulation, and the legislative liaison staff, responsible for presenting programs to Congress once they had been developed. Preliminary contacts with committee members and staff on the substance of proposed legislation were the responsibility of the Domestic Policy Staff. For example, preliminary discussions with the committees concerned with health legislation were the responsibility of the health specialists on the Domestic Policy Staff. The legislative liaison staff entered the picture only after programs had been formally introduced on Capitol Hill.[23]

Although the Johnson and Carter OCR staffs were similar in this respect, neither being extensively involved in the development of new policies, there were still some important differences between Johnson and Carter in how they consulted Congress in the preparation of legislative initiatives. As noted earlier, Johnson often went to great lengths to give committee chairmen and other leaders in Congress the impression that their views were being solicited as the administration's legislative program was being developed. Actually, of course, this consultation was undertaken as much to keep the congressional leaders "on the reservation," to co-opt them, as to incorporate their opinions into policy initiatives. It would be more difficult for a legislator to criticize a program to which he had allegedly made a contribution than one he had known nothing about until it was announced.

Furthermore, these sorts of consultative and cooperative activities were undertaken not only with the Congress, but with the interest groups as well. Again, Johnson's concern was twofold. First, he wanted to assemble a supporting coalition of important interest groups behind his proposals. Second, the interest groups' lobbying staffs could serve as sources of legislative intelligence during the process of passage. Johnson believed that the interest groups would be more forthcoming with this legislative intelligence, which could lessen the burden on the White House's own liaison staff, if they had been consulted while the policies were being developed.

In the Carter White House, there was much less of this concern with developing supportive political coalitions behind program proposals. Members of the Domestic Policy Staff did on occasion meet with individuals on Capitol Hill or in the Washington offices of interest groups. These meetings, however, were often more for the exchange of technical information among substantive experts than for the building of political support.[24] Likewise, when exchanging information with congressional policy makers, the White House staffers frequently met with congressional staffers rather than with members.

Especially during President Carter's first year in office, an attitude was expressed by many in the White House, an attitude perhaps emanating from the Oval Office itself, that the role of White House policy makers was to develop the best technical solution to a pressing policy problem. It was assumed that those in other institutions in Washington—Congress, the bureaucracy, and the interest groups—would rapidly reach a consensus on the superiority of this technical solution. Opposition to such policy proposals was seen as petty, parochial, and self-interested. It was opposition that would rapidly diminish once the president went over the heads of the Washington community and made a direct appeal to the public's sense of the national interest.

This attitude was perhaps best exemplified during the development of President Carter's first energy program (April 1977). This program was put together during the first ninety days of the president's term by James Schlesinger and a number of other technical experts on the White House staff. During this three-month period, consultation with Congress, the many interest groups that were concerned with energy policy, and the bureaucracies that would have to implement the program was almost nonexistent.[25]

The energy program also illustrates another aspect of policy formulation during the Carter presidency—the president's penchant for announcing deadlines in advance and insisting that policy proposals be made public before those deadlines. Carter believed that he had made a commitment to the public to introduce programs in many issue areas—energy, welfare reform, and taxation, to name only three—and that this commitment overrode the need to develop a technically well-thought-out (a somewhat different criterion from the technically best) and politically feasible legislative proposal.

These aspects of policy making in the Carter White House—little consultation with the representatives of other institutions in Washington, the belief that the technically best policy proposal was the only correct one, and the imposition of rigid public deadlines on policy planners—reflect much of the same attitude toward politics that was exhibited in Carter's initial decision to organize the legislative liaison office along issued-based lines. If the president believed that he had a nearly plebiscitary relationship with the people, then he did not have to concern himself with building coalitions with other Washington institutions, with making substantive compromises on policy, and with considering not only the formulation of policies but their implementation as well. All the president had to do, when faced with policy opposition, was to go on television and attack the institutional sources of that opposition, without giving much, if any, consideration to the substantive merits of the criticisms being offered.

The Carter case illustrates the importance of procedural as well as substantive factors as explanations for the amount of conflict between Congress and the White House. Even if members of Congress are inclined to support the president's programs on substantive grounds, they will be unwilling to take political risks on the president's behalf unless a feeling of trust and confidence between Congress and the White House has been developed in advance of the president's need for congressional support on a particular issue. Having a legislative liaison office organized with this goal in mind can thus be an advantage of no small importance to a president who seeks to be both active and successful on Capitol Hill.

Conclusions: Legislative Liaison in the 1980s

Ronald Reagan's legislative liaison staff is made up of people like those who were on the staffs of OCR in previous administrations (with the exception of the initial Carter staff). Reagan's first director of legislative liaison was Max L. Friedersdorf, former head of OCR for President Ford. The other members of the staff all had congressional or lobbying experience for several years before moving to the White House. The Reagan staff is somewhat larger than that of previous presidents, with four staffers assigned to the Senate on a regular basis, and five to the House of Representatives.[26]

In the first nine months of his administration, Reagan accomplished a good deal on Capitol Hill. Not only did he obtain passage of his budget blueprints basically unchanged, but he also put together what appeared at the time to be a new majority coalition in the House of Representatives—a working majority of Republicans and Southern Democrats which was able to defeat the Democratic leadership on important matters related to the Reagan economic program. Toward the end of 1981, however, as the president proposed even deeper cuts in the federal budget, the stability and permanence of the congressional alliance supporting him, particularly in the House, was increasingly open to question.

Nevertheless, two recent developments in congressional–executive relations should generally ease the task of the Reagan liaison staff in obtaining passage of the president's programs. The first is that many members of Congress believe they must support Reagan's programs because their constituents demand that they do so—the belief that the 1980 election was a mandate for conservative policies. Even though survey evidence calls into question the notion of a mandate (for example, majorities of those surveyed in November 1980 stated that the federal government was spending too little on health, education, and the environment),[27] members apparently perceive the 1980 presidential election as representing a public demand for policy changes in line with those put forward by the administration. In this situation, the liaison staff has an important political resource available to it. Members do not necessarily have to be convinced on the merits of issues; they merely have to be shown that it would be good politics back home for them to support the president. If that argument does not work, they can be threatened with political retaliation by the president, a threat that many members apparently take quite seriously.

The second recent development that should help the liaison office is that the period of institutional opposition between Congress and the president appears to be coming to an end. Partly as a consequence of Vietnam and Watergate, Congresses throughout the 1970s put great emphasis on protecting and defending the legislative branch's place as an independent policy-making institution. Members of Congress in this period resolved that they would not be pushed around by the president, as they had been by Johnson and Nixon. As memories of the Johnson and Nixon eras fade, both among the general public and among members of Congress, repre-

93

sentatives and senators are becoming willing once again to grant the White House the benefit of the doubt, to go along with the administration because it represents a public or party position. Perhaps the best recent example of this phenomenon was the approval in the House on June 25, 1981, of the so-called Gramm-Latta II substitute to the budget reconciliation bill—a substitute written in large part in the offices of Office of Management and Budget Director David Stockman, running to more than a hundred pages in the *Congressional Record,* and not made available to the members until just a few hours before the vote was taken.

In this environment of greater cooperation between the two ends of Pennsylvania Avenue, the liaison staffers will no longer be seen by many members of Congress as agents of a foreign power. This will make the job of OCR lobbyists more pleasant, but one must also wonder if Congress is returning to its supine days of the 1950s and the 1960s and if a more passive Congress will have unfortunate consequences for the American political system in the long run.

Notes

1. Stephen Hess, *Organizing the Presidency* (Washington, D.C.: Brookings, 1976), p. 33; Erwin C. Hargrove, *The Power of the Modern Presidency* (New York: Knopf, 1974), pp. 53-55.

2. James T. Patterson, *Congressional Conservatism and the New Deal* (Lexington: University of Kentucky Press, 1967).

3. Hess, *Organizing the Presidency,* p. 51; Abraham Holtzman, *Legislative Liaison: Executive Leadership in Congress* (Chicago: Rand McNally, 1970), pp. 231-34.

4. Hess, *Organizing the Presidency,* p. 51; Holtzman, *Legislative Liaison,* pp. 231-39.

5. Hess, *Organizing the Presidency,* p. 89; Holtzman, *Legislative Liaison,* pp. 230-45; Lawrence F. O'Brien, *No Final Victories: A Life in Politics from John F. Kennedy to Watergate* (New York: Ballantine, 1974), pp. 102-11; "Larry O'Brien Discusses White House Contacts with Capitol Hill," *Congressional Quarterly Weekly Report,* July 23, 1965, pp. 1434-36.

6. Eric L. Davis, "Building Presidential Coalitions in Congress: Legislative Liaison in the Johnson White House" (Ph.D. dissertation, Stanford University, 1977).

7. Eric L. Davis, "Legislative Liaison in the Carter Administration," *Political Science Quarterly* 95 (Summer 1979), pp. 287-302.

8. This and all other unattributed quotations in this chapter are drawn from the author's interviews with persons who were involved with the legislative liaison process between 1961 and 1980.

9. Some of the material in the following section is drawn from Congressional Quarterly, Inc., *The Washington Lobby*, 3d ed. (Washington, D.C., 1979), p. 30.

10. Nelson W. Polsby and Aaron Wildavsky, *Presidential Elections*, 5th ed. (New York: Scribner's, 1980).

11. Haynes Johnson, *In the Absence of Power: Governing America* (New York: Viking, 1980), p. 166.

12. Ibid., p. 159.

13. A limited form of issue-based organization was reinstituted later in Carter's term, when certain liaison staffers were assigned specifically to foreign policy issues.

14. Congressional Quarterly, Inc., *The Washington Lobby*, p. 30.

15. "Larry O'Brien Discusses White House Contacts," p. 1436.

16. Holtzman, *Legislative Liaison*, pp. 264-72.

17. Much of the material in the remainder of this section is drawn from Davis, "Legislative Liaison in the Carter Administration."

18. "Larry O'Brien Discusses White House Contacts," p. 1435-36.

19. Richard E. Neustadt, *Presidential Power: The Politics of Leadership from FDR to Carter* (New York: Wiley, 1980), pp. 44-63.

20. Doris Kearns, *Lyndon Johnson and the American Dream* (New York: Harper & Row, 1976), pp. 221-25.

21. Ibid., p. 222.

22. Interview with Joseph Califano, Washington, D.C., November 22, 1976.

23. *Congressional Quarterly Weekly Report*, October 6, 1979, pp. 2199-2204.

24. Anne Wexler's Office of Public Liaison was mainly concerned with building public, not congressional, support for Carter's programs.

25. Congressional Quarterly, Inc., *Energy Policy* (Washington, D.C., 1979), p. 34.

26. *Congressional Quarterly Weekly Report*, January 24, 1981, p. 174.

27. Everett Carll Ladd, "The Brittle Mandate: Electoral Dealignment and the 1980 Presidential Election," *Political Science Quarterly*, vol. 96 (Spring 1981), p. 22. Also recall that the turnout in 1980 was only 53 percent; thus, only 27 percent of all eligible Americans actually voted for Ronald Reagan.

4

Presidential Negotiation
with Congress

CHARLES O. JONES

In his book, *The Vantage Point,* Lyndon Johnson relates an important lesson taught to him by a Texas state senator, Alvin Wirtz. Senator Wirtz had arranged a meeting of private utility company owners, trying to persuade them to make electric power available to small farmers. Johnson got upset with one of the company presidents, "and in the course of our discussion I told the man that he could 'go to hell.'" Later Senator Wirtz called Johnson aside and said: "Listen, Lyndon, I've been around this business for a long time. . . . If I have learned anything at all in these years, it is this: You can *tell* a man to go to hell, but you can't *make* him go." That bit of advice was offered to Johnson in 1937. He never forgot it.

> I thought of that story many times during my Presidency.
> It seemed particularly apt when I found myself in a struggle
> with the House or the Senate. I would start to speak out,
> then I would think of Senator Wirtz and remember that
> no matter how many times I told the Congress to do some-
> thing, I could never force it to act.[1]

The Founding Fathers were determined that the president should not command Congress. Even the master congressional tactician, Lyndon Johnson, knew that success depended on his understanding the limits on the presidency. The two institutions have been described as being like "two gears, each whirling at its own rate of speed. It is not surprising that, on coming together, they often clash."[2]

This chapter will describe and analyze this coming together of the president with Congress. Normally the relationship tends to be

I am indebted to Bert A. Rockman, University of Pittsburgh; Norman J. Ornstein, Catholic University; and the editor of this volume, Anthony King, University of Essex, for their helpful comments.

activated by the president because he wants something. He is forced to acknowledge, however, that members of Congress also have needs. The trick is to make his wants mesh with their needs. Since theirs is a dependent relationship, the president and Congress negotiate. What is the nature of these negotiations? How do negotiating conditions vary from one administration to the next? What are the different styles and techniques of negotiation associated with recent presidents? Which are most successful and why? These are the questions to be treated here.

The Nature and Conditions of Negotiation

Negotiation is a process by which contending parties seek agreement on an issue of importance to each. It is characterized by various means of persuasion; those used typically depend on the resources available, including the estimates each side makes of the strength and capabilities of the other. Many social scientists use the term "bargaining" as synonymous with "negotiation." Strictly speaking, however, a bargain involves a transaction or trade—something for you in exchange for your giving something to me. It is good to remember, therefore, that presidents engage in a wide range of negotiating strategies in addition to the classic bargain—for example, those designed to convince the members of Congress that cooperation is in their own best interest or those based on an interpretation of what is good for the nation at a particular time.[3] Note that bargaining is typically a form of negotiation that brings the president in close contact with the members of Congress; other forms allow greater distance between the two. As we will see, presidents differ in their choice of and preferences for various negotiating strategies, as well as in their resources (including personal capabilities) for implementing preferred strategies.

Robert A. Dahl and Charles E. Lindblom are among those who define bargaining as more or less synonymous with negotiation. Nevertheless, their excellent analysis suits present purposes by stressing the importance of the classic bargain in American politics. For them, bargaining is "a form of reciprocal control among leaders."[4] It is characteristic of a society that wants to get something done but has distributed the power to do that something among a variety of groups in and out of government. Dahl and Lindblom argue, "Leaders bargain because they disagree and expect that further agreement is possible and will be profitable. . . . Hence bargaining takes place because it is necessary, possible, and thought to be profitable."[5]

The "human embodiment of a bargaining society" is the politician, "whose career depends upon successful negotiation of bargains."[6] The skill involved in successfully negotiating bargains tends to be more procedural than substantive. The politician may have substantive commitments, but these commitments are often compromised in the pursuit of a majority.

> Because he is a bargainer, a negotiator, the politician does not often give orders. He can rarely employ unilateral controls. Even as a chief executive or a cabinet official he soon discovers that his control depends on his skill in bargaining. . . . The role calls for actions such as compromise, renunciation, face-saving of oneself, which are morally ambiguous or even downright immoral to people with morally rigorous standards.[7]

Presidents uncomfortable with bargaining in its classic form are, according to this analysis, in a somewhat odd position.

Dahl and Lindblom observe that the U.S. Constitution established multiple conditions for bargaining. Vertical and horizontal controls and checks operate to prevent the realization of a national majority even if it exists. The result is often three- or four-dimensional bargaining within and between branches in program development, and bargaining may even carry over into program implementation. Congress and the president are at the center of this complex set of policy relationships. And as Nelson W. Polsby points out: "If the Constitution can be said to grant legitimacy to anything, surely it legitimizes conflict between Congress and the President."[8]

Saying that negotiation is ubiquitous in American politics is not to say that it always looks the same or is well managed. Three principal factors appear to condition presidential–congressional negotiations:

- The issues: Who wants what? How do decision makers in each branch define social, economic, and political needs? Who controls the agenda?
- The president: What does he want? What are his resources? How does he view the presidency? the Congress?
- The Congress: Which party is in the majority? What is the dominant congressional view of the presidency? of the role of Congress?

This list is brief, but one should not be misled into believing that the task of classification is thereby made simple. Even cursory reflection on the conditions reveals the challenge faced by scholars in seeking to generalize about presidents and Congresses. Perhaps we can do no more than characterize the relationships of each administration. Surely we are unlikely to do more, however, unless we specify significant conditions and identify applications.

Presidential–Congressional Conversation

Before making applications to four recent administrations, I need to say something general about what Anthony King refers to as "presidential–congressional conversation."[9] By this he means both the talk itself and the bargaining "counters" or "chips" that presidents rely on.

The talk itself appears to differ in amount, volume, and intensity, but not in type. That is, some presidents hardly make a move without congressional involvement; others find it almost unnatural to include members of Congress in their ordinary decisional discourse. Yet all presidents engage in formal and informal talk, which may be directly or indirectly targeted at Capitol Hill. Formal talk includes the State of the Union and other messages, press conferences, radio and television addresses, etc. Words on these occasions may be aimed directly at the members or filtered through others—the press, interest groups, or constituents. Informal talk includes the less public discourse of the president and his aides—the daily contact between the White House and members, or between the White House and those who may be expected to influence the members.

Formal and informal words on a topic do not always bear the same messages. The more public exhortations are typically expected to satisfy the expectations of diverse groups and thus must be prepared with great care and attention. Often members of Congress understand and are tolerant of the demands being met in formal talk, even when they are themselves the objects of criticism or ridicule. Their tolerance may be nurtured by simultaneous or subsequent informal conversation of a reassuring nature. As will be illustrated by the Nixon and Carter presidencies, these norms of conversation are not always accepted, in which case relations with Congress are strained.

What is behind the talk? What do presidents have to offer? And how do the offerings change? Much of this chapter is devoted to demonstrating that these questions are difficult to answer for all presidents. Conditions vary and what is, or is deemed to be, appropriate in one administration is judged inappropriate in another. Still, one can prepare a catalog of appeals and rewards, as George C. Edwards III has done in *Presidential Influence in Congress*.[10] The more positive inducements on the standard list for the president include knowledge of Capitol Hill, respect for the legislative process, persistence, public standing, interpretations of the national interest, projects and services, personal amenities, and political and campaign support. Negative appeals include threats, penalties, withholding political or campaign support, and excluding members from benefits enjoyed by others.

Beyond saying that the standard list is differentially applied across issues and through time, one can also observe that certain of these appeals are more associated with formal talk (for example, interpretations of the national interest, veto threats), others with informal talk (for example, projects, amenities, campaign support). Further, it appears that changes have occurred in what constitutes an acceptable trade between the president and Congress. As will unfold in the cases presented below, bargaining (in the narrow sense of trading) appears to have come into disrepute in recent years, either because the president wants less from Congress, as with Nixon, or because he personally eschews that form of negotiation, as with Carter. What the Reagan administration holds in store will be the subject of final comment. Suffice it to say at this point that he evidences a style not unlike a president he professes to admire—Franklin D. Roosevelt.

Four Administrations

It is instructive to examine different presidencies to illustrate the variation in negotiating conditions. My plan is to analyze the administrations of the four most recent presidents—Lyndon Johnson, Richard Nixon, Gerald Ford, and Jimmy Carter. They represent a remarkably diverse sample of conditions, styles, and techniques. In the course of preparing this chapter, I became convinced that political and personal *conditions* help to explain presidential *styles* of relating to Congress, and these styles, in turn, contribute to determining which *techniques* are used to get the legislative program enacted. I am quick to point out that I am not proposing anything so rigorous as a causal model. Rather, I have found it convenient in my own thinking to make these linkages between conditions, styles, and techniques.

Table 4–1 presents basic election information about the four presidents. Clearly Lyndon Johnson assumed office with great advantages—an impressive nationally based victory and a better than two-thirds Democratic majority in each house of Congress. Nixon had an equally impressive victory in 1972 but lacked the congres-

TABLE 4–1

ELECTION RESULTS AS POLITICAL CHARACTERISTICS OF FOUR ADMINISTRATIONS

Administra-tion	President			House		Senate	
	Popular vote	Electoral vote	Electoral base	Margin	Change[a]	Margin	Change[a]
Johnson							
1964	61.1%	90.3%	National (outside Deep South)	67.8%D	+ 8.5%	68%D	+ 1%
1966				56.8%D	−11.0%	64%D	− 4%
Nixon							
1968	43.4%	55.9%	Regional (West, Midwest, Border South)	55.9%D	+ 0.9%	57%D	+ 7%
1970				58.4%D	− 2.5%	54%D	+ 1%[b]
1972	60.7%	96.6%	National	54.9%D	+ 3.5%	56%D	− 2%
(Ford), 1974	[c]	[c]	[c]	66.9%D	−12.0%	60%D	− 4%
Carter							
1976	50.1%	55.2%	Regional (South, East)	67.1%D	+ 0.2%	61%D	+ 1%
1978				63.4%D	− 3.7%	58%D	− 3%

a. Refers to percentage change for president's party from previous Congress; D indicates the Democratic party.
b. Two senators were not in either of the major parties.
c. Nominated by Nixon in 1973 to be vice president; approved by the Senate, 92-3, and by the House, 387-5.

SOURCE: Compiled by the author from data in U.S. Bureau of the Census, *Statistical Abstract of the United States* (Washington, D.C., 1979), pp. 497–507.

sional advantage. His 1968 victory was much less impressive. Carter had a very narrow victory, but his party won sizable majorities in both houses of Congress. And Gerald Ford had to govern without electoral support and was faced with large Democratic majorities in Congress. The contrast between Johnson and Ford is particularly dramatic. As an official of the Office of Management and Budget (OMB) observed:

> You ought to think of the Presidency as an engine. Each President enters office facing the same model—the horse-power is generally stable and the gears are all there. What differs is the *fuel*. Different Presidents enter with different fuel. Lyndon Johnson entered office with a full tank, while Ford entered on empty.[11]

Political and personal advantages or limitations stem from more than election returns, however. Also involved are the factors mentioned earlier—the issues as well as presidential and congressional images of how the system ought to work. One of the more reliable inventories of issue priorities is the presidential State of the Union message. Table 4–2 displays the range of issues identified as important by the presidents in the years selected. Most obvious is the shift from foreign to domestic priorities (and back again in 1980). Less obvious, perhaps, is the fact that many of the domestic requests by Nixon, Ford, and Carter were reform measures seeking to reshape the structure and substance of programs enacted during the 1960s—a shift from issues requiring expansion of government to those demanding consolidation or even contraction of government.

The broad developments on issues are summarized in the first column of Table 4–3. Columns two and three provide general responses to the questions of how the president and Congress viewed their own responsibilities and those of the other branch. Thus, for example, compare the characteristics of the first Johnson administration with those of the Carter years. With Johnson, a full agenda of expansive domestic issues was aggressively presented by a president with impressive resources. Johnson had a "mixed-government" view of national policy making. For him both the president and Congress had legitimate authority to be involved. He got support from a Democratic majority, most of whom appeared to believe that the president should rule.

With Carter, on the other hand, a less comprehensive agenda contained many consolidative and even contractive proposals. Demands were being heard to coordinate existing government programs or to eliminate them altogether. Carter himself had fewer resources

TABLE 4–2

Issues Emphasized in Presidential State of the Union Messages for Selected Years, 1965–1980

Administrations	Major Issues	Other Important Issues
Johnson		
1965	Great Society programs	Foreign, defense policy
1966	Vietnam, foreign, defense policy	Poverty, taxes, crime, urban development, clean rivers, civil rights
1968	Vietnam, foreign, defense policy	Employment, cities, housing, health, consumer protection, crime
Nixon		
1970	Vietnam, foreign, defense policy	Environment, government reform, welfare reform, inflation, crime, cities/rural areas
1972	Foreign, defense policy	Economy (employment, inflation); (Congress urged to enact earlier requests)
1974	Energy	Health, revenue sharing, transportation, education, privacy, welfare reform, trade, veterans benefits
Ford		
1976	Economy (employment, inflation), energy	Health, social security, welfare reform, crime, national security
Carter		
1978	Energy, economy (employment, inflation)	Government reform, foreign and defense policy, Panama Canal
1980	Foreign, defense policy	Energy, economy (employment, inflation)

Source: Compiled by author from State of the Union messages and from reports on them in the *Congressional Quarterly Weekly Reports*.

and appeared to believe in an executive-centered government (a president working with an efficient bureaucracy). The Democrats were in the majority in Congress but were highly critical of the president and demanded at least equal involvement in the full range of activities associated with the policy process.

These impressive variations in the work to be done, the political resources available to do the work, and the impressions in each branch as to who should do what work, lead us to expect different behavior in presidential–congressional relations. But there is more. The personal background and qualities of the individual presidents may also be expected to have an effect. Politically Lyndon Johnson was born and raised in the U.S. Congress. He began his political career working on the staff of a member of the House in 1931 and was himself later elected to the House and then the Senate. He served as Senate Democratic whip and floor leader during the 1950s. Johnson's strength and resourcefulness in Congress and in the South led to his being selected as Kennedy's running mate in 1960. Not surprisingly, Johnson's style of dealing with Congress was that of the *majority leader as president*.

Richard Nixon also served in Congress but only briefly. He was elected twice to the House of Representatives and once to the Senate. He resigned his Senate seat after two years in office when he was elected vice-president. His total congressional service was just six years. Nixon's eight years as vice-president and his experience in running for president in 1960 contributed to an interest in foreign policy. Henry Kissinger reports that he was struck by Nixon's "perceptiveness and knowledge" of foreign policy when he first met him. At that meeting Nixon indicated that "he was determined to run foreign policy from the White House."[12] Nixon's interest in international affairs, and possibly the reasons the subject fascinated him, influenced his relations with Congress.[13] Perhaps it is not overstating the case to suggest that his style was that of the *foreign minister as president*.

Gerald Ford's career parallels that of Lyndon Johnson, but on the other side of the tracks. Ford was first elected to the House of Representatives in 1948 and became leader of the House Republicans in 1965. As Kennedy had selected Johnson, Nixon chose Ford to serve with him as vice-president in part because of Ford's knowledge of Capitol Hill and the respect he commanded there. We are safe, then, in identifying Ford's style of congressional relations as that of the *minority leader as president*.

Jimmy Carter had virtually no national political experience prior to his election as president. He served two terms in the Georgia

TABLE 4–3

CHARACTERISTICS OF FOUR ADMINISTRATIONS, 1964–1980

Administrations	Issues	Presidential Characteristics	Congressional Characteristics
Johnson			
1964–1966	Domestic, expansive	Full agenda, assertive, impressive resources, mixed government	Democratic majority, supportive, presidential government
1967–1968	Foreign, expansive	Reduced agenda, assertive, limited resources, presidential government	Democratic majority, critical, mixed government
Nixon			
1969–1972	Foreign, consolidative	Moderate agenda, moderately assertive, mixed resources, presidential government	Democratic majority, critical, mixed government
1973–1974	Domestic, consolidative	Moderate agenda, assertive, mixed to limited resources, presidential government	Democratic majority, aggressively critical, congressional government
Ford			
1974–1976	Domestic, consolidative	Moderate agenda, moderately assertive, limited resources, mixed government	Democratic majority, critical, congressional government
Carter			
1977–1980	Domestic, consolidative to contractive	Moderate agenda, less assertive, mixed resources, executive government	Democratic majority, critical, mixed government

SOURCE: Author.

State Senate (1963–1967), ran for and lost the governorship in 1966, ran again in 1970 and won. Interestingly, Carter was forty-six years old before he won major elective office, whereas Johnson was twenty-nine, Nixon was thirty-three, and Ford was thirty-five. Carter's 1976 nomination and election are explained in large part by his lack of Washington-based experience. Indeed, he campaigned on this theme, seeking to capitalize on the post-Watergate public mood of distrust of politics. Once in office, therefore, Carter's methods of dealing with Congress were those of the *political layman as president*.[14]

Before turning to an analysis of each of these presidents, I must reiterate that I cannot identify the precise relationship among these various political and personal factors. I do not really know, for example, whether our politics gives us Richard Nixon and Jimmy Carter or they give us our politics. I simply want to point out that the different blends of political and personal conditions are associated with different presidential bargaining styles and techniques on Capitol Hill.

Lyndon Johnson—Majority Leader as President

> If I were to name the one factor above all others that helped me in dealing with the Congress, I would say it was the genuine friendship and rapport I had with most Congressmen and Senators. I understood and respected men who dedicated their lives to elective office. Most politicians are men of principle dedicated to the national interest. I believed that I, as President, had the responsibility to appeal to that dedication, to outline what I considered the national interest required, to lay out the alternatives, and to hope that a reasonable man would understand and accept his duty.[15]

Winston Churchill once observed that he was a "child of the House of Commons." In like manner, Lyndon Johnson was a child of Congress. In several recent works on presidential–congressional relations, Johnson has received considerably more attention than any of the other presidents—often twice as much as the rest combined. One also finds in reading presidential memoirs that Johnson himself liked talking about how he dealt with Congress; other presidents in the modern era (including Ford) have little to say on the subject. Much of our current lore about presidential legislative style therefore comes from the Johnson administration, particularly from the first three years (1964–1966). It should be noted that Johnson's behavior also influenced expectations on Capitol Hill—setting the standard by which other presidents would be measured, regardless of changes in political conditions.

What was this "majority-leader style"? And what techniques were employed? Understanding the style, as exercised by Lyndon Johnson, begins with acknowledging a consummate interest in and knowledge of Congress. To like anything is to enjoy seeing it work. And Johnson liked to make Congress work. While serving as Democratic floor leader in the Senate, "he wanted the bills to become laws."[16] His move to the White House did not change this goal. Nothing about Congress seemed to bore Johnson. By all accounts, as president he wanted a daily accounting of Capitol Hill activities— particularly before the Vietnam War came to dominate and frustrate his political life.

Complementing this presidential desire for legislative production were the several favorable political conditions cited in table 4–1. Even before his landslide victory in 1964, Johnson was in a position to capitalize on the progressive mood of Congress following the tragedy of John F. Kennedy's assassination. Further, much preliminary work on developing social programs had been completed by the Democrats in the Eisenhower and Kennedy years. James L. Sundquist described the situation as follows:

During the early years of the period [1953–1956] . . . the problems were being identified and the initial forms of remedial action were being devised. In the middle years [1957–1961] . . . political support was being mobilized and the measures themselves were being refined in public debate. . .

The late years of the period [1962–1965] were a time of rounding out the program with additional proposals, of solidifying popular support, and of maneuvering the program through the policy-making institutions of government.[17]

Favorable political conditions, a full agenda, and a strongly motivated and interested president combined to produce "the Congress of fulfillment . . . of accomplished hopes . . . of realized dreams."[18] It is important to be reminded of this happy coincidence of factors when deciding whether to measure other presidents by the Johnson standard.

The various legislative strategies and techniques relied on by the Johnson administration during these early years follow from, in the sense of being logically derivative of, the developments above. And they tended to be positive in nature—after all, the president was trying to enact an extensive legislative program. "Many carrots and a few sticks, these were the tools of O'Brien's men" (Lawrence O'Brien headed Johnson's liaison office).[19] Based on several accounts of Johnson's relations with Congress, I have compiled the following list of techniques or strategies.

Know what is going on. Johnson wanted to know everything that affected or might potentially affect his legislative program. Not only was the knowledge itself important to him in judging what to do, how, and when, but he had a reputation to uphold. "The foundation of Johnson's involvement was intimate knowledge of Congress, knowledge that came from beyond even his own vast experience."[20] He wanted the members to think that he knew even more than he actually knew. The illusion of knowledge can be created by organization and activity. Anyone observing the amount of legislative-directed activity in the Johnson White House would draw the conclusion that the legislative liaison team (which included the president himself) must surely know everything about everyone. And that is exactly the impression Johnson wanted to create.

Know thyself. It is a commonplace that the national legislative process extends beyond the halls of Congress. Much of what happens in the executive branch affects legislation and legislators, either by design or by circumstance. Departments and agencies want existing programs authorized and funded. Many of these programs involve contracts, construction, projects of various kinds, services, etc., that will benefit the constituents of representatives and senators. And new programs proposed by the president or the departments and agencies require legislative approval. It was Johnson's style to adopt a congressional perspective in the preparation of programs for approval and in the administration of programs in the states and districts. He accomplished these goals by ensuring that "the liaison staff had a substantial involvement in the formulation of policy."[21] The staff used the Bureau of the Budget (now the Office of Management and Budget) to track legislation. And according to Stephen J. Wayne, "the agenda of every cabinet meeting included an item on legislative activities."[22] The president was also anxious to know about all appointments, contracts, and projects so that he and the appropriate members of Congress could take credit. Knowing thyself, then, is simply being aware of what is going on within the administration that is pertinent (1) to what you send to Capitol Hill for approval and (2) to what you do by way of administering programs that affect the members in their states and districts.

Act fast. Lyndon Johnson was extraordinarily anxious about moving quickly early in his term. He believed that a president's impact is very short-lived. Here is how he put it in his memoirs:

> The President and the Congress run on separate clocks. The occupant of the White House has a strict tenancy. . . .
> A President must always reckon that this mandate will proved short-lived. . . . For me, as for most active Presidents, popularity proved elusive.[23]

Paul C. Light offers evidence to support Johnson's conclusions. He identifies two important patterns associated with presidential relations with Congress—the cycle of decreasing influence and the cycle of increasing effectiveness.[24] The first cycle was well understood by Johnson and was the stimulus for fast action on his Great Society programs. The second cycle was less applicable to Johnson. Light states that "Presidents can be expected to learn over time."[25] But Johnson knew more than practically anyone else. That is not to say he had nothing to learn about Congress but rather that new information came in rather small increments.

Be persistent. Doris Kearns quotes Johnson as saying that:

> There is but one way for a President to deal with the Congress, and that is continuously, incessantly, and without interruption. If it's really going to work, the relationship between the President and the Congress has got to be almost incestuous. He's got to know them even better than they know themselves. And then, on the basis of this knowledge, he's got to build a system that stretches from the cradle to the grave, from the moment a bill is introduced to the moment it is officially enrolled as the law of the land.[26]

At least two forms of persistence are suggested in this quotation. First is that associated with a particular bill—making contact with members over time, not being discouraged by setbacks, maintaining continuous pursuit. Second is the more general persistence characterized by habitual communication and contact on Capitol Hill. Though this second brand of persistence is less focused, it supplies the foundation for more specific requests.

Set priorities. In his description of presidential lobbying by Kennedy and Johnson, John F. Manley speaks of "superintending the legislative process."[27] Surely a part of "superintending" is to be sensitive to the pace and workload of Congress. Johnson had an enormous legislative program, but he was aware that he should not overload the system.

He sent bills one by one rather than in a clump. . . . Also, he sent them when the agendas of the receiving committees were clear so that they could be considered right away, without time for opposition to develop and when the members most intensely concerned about the bills would be most likely to support them.[28]

One begins to understand the importance of Johnson's intimate knowledge of the workings of the Hill. Either a president must know about committee and subcommittee schedules or establish a mechanism for finding out. Johnson had both advantages—a sort of fail-safe system. As will be noted, Carter had neither.

Be accessible. Accessibility of the president to members of Congress must start with the president's inviting contact between himself and his own liaison people. He cannot possibly maintain close communication with all 535 members, but it is important that the members know that they can get to the president if they need to. Johnson's passionate interest in the legislative process once again led him quite naturally to establish means for two-way congressional contact. The liaison officers could make commitments for the president. "Johnson had even issued a standing order with the switchboard that any time O'Brien called, he was to be put through regardless of the hour. The calls went in both directions."[29]

Implicate the members. In describing Johnson's philosophy and approach to Senate floor leadership, Ralph K. Huitt observed that:

Johnson was a legislative pragmatist. He believed it possible to do anything that was worth the effort and the price, and *so considered every problem from the standpoint of what was necessary to achieve the desired objective, and whether the objective was worth the cost.* He learned early and never forgot the basic skill of the politician, the ability to divide any number by two and add one.[30]

Johnson carried this approach to the White House. He wanted the Congress to work on his bills, but he understood the importance of finding a basis for compromise. He employed the time-honored method of implicating the members through consultations, appointments to "secret task forces," and advance notice.[31] Such methods helped him build support but also informed him about the limits of his support.

Make party leaders look good. Polsby reminds us that there are forces encouraging cooperation between the president and Congress and "high on any list . . . would be the effects of party membership."[32] Not unexpectedly, it was Johnson's style to work with party leaders—almost incorporate them into his daily operations. Manley points out that the House and Senate Democratic party leaders "worked so closely with the White House during the 1960s that the system more resembled the parliamentary form of executive–legislative relations than the presidential."[33] The executive branch lobbyists conducted their own legislative head counts. These polls were combined with those of the party leadership to produce reliable information on probable outcomes. All of this activity was good business for the president, but it also made party leaders look good.

Go to the public last. "I sometimes felt that Congress was like a sensitive animal—if pushed gently it would go my way, but if pushed too hard it would balk." Lyndon Johnson "preferred to work from within, knowing that good legislation is the product not of public rhetoric but of private negotiations and compromise." But his objections to the public opinion route to Congress involved more than the immediate effect on a piece of legislation. He believed that taking an issue to the people typically involved picking "a fight with the Congress." It was not enough to state one's position on the issue. That would not get press or public attention. The president also had "to say mean words and show [his] temper."[34] Thus, there are possible long-run effects of going to the people—in essence going over the heads of the members of Congress, who, after all, also believe they represent the people. These views of Johnson illustrate the problems in managing continuity between formal and informal talk. Perhaps it goes without saying that Johnson also considered arm twisting a last resort.

Summary. These several guidelines to White House lobbying on Capitol Hill are all consistent with the majority-leader style of building coalitions. They worked extraordinarily well for enacting Johnson's domestic program, 1964–1966. Such complete management of congressional relations, however, demands a great deal of the president's time. It so happens that President Johnson wanted to use his time in this way. By 1966 the Vietnam War required his full attention, and from that point on the president had to concentrate on foreign and defense issues that were less familiar and more frustrating to him. His congressional relations deteriorated rapidly since he seemed to be incapable of applying to foreign issues the guidelines that worked so effectively for him on domestic programs. The 1968 presidential election brought to the White House a person with impressive interest and expertise in foreign and defense policy, and variable interest in domestic issues.

Richard Nixon—Foreign Minister as President

. . . Nixon had no more stomach for face-to-face confrontation with members of Congress than for those with any
one else. When he did invite a member into the Oval Office
to ask his help, the personal Nixon pressure was mild indeed—the antithesis of the insistent Johnson treatment.
"I know you have your problems with this," the President
would say, "and I will completely understand if you can't
come with me, but if you can I'd appreciate it." . . . Although no contest with Congress engaged Nixon so vis-
cerally as his humiliating failure in the spring of 1970 to
win Senate confirmation of Judge G. Harrold Carswell to
the Supreme Court, he never personally demanded or
pleaded for any senator's vote.[35]

It would be difficult to imagine a more striking contrast in congressional styles than that between Lyndon Johnson and Richard
Nixon. As noted earlier, the explanation lies in large part with personal and political factors. These were two very different men
belonging to different political parties and facing different sets of
issues. A review of the data on Nixon in tables 4–1 to 4–3 illustrates
some of the more important changes. Certainly most notable among
these was the fact that Nixon faced a Democratic Congress. But
this condition by no means explains the problems that developed.
Both Eisenhower and Ford also faced Democratic Congresses and yet
avoided the animosities that developed in the Nixon administration.
For reasons too complicated to explore here, Nixon came to question the
legitimacy and competency of Congress, particularly after his landslide
victory in 1972.[36] Therefore, whereas Johnson's interest in and
knowledge of Congress were the most important determinants of his
relations with that institution, Nixon's interest in nonlegislative issues
and his basic distrust of Congress were important in explaining his
approach to the institution.

This lack of motivation and involvement was reflected in the
organization of Nixon's legislative liaison arrangements. Most significantly, the legislative liaison staff "appeared to become distanced
from the president."[37] Bryce Harlow first headed the office. He
served in a similar post under Eisenhower and was very close to
Nixon. After Harlow changed jobs in early 1970, however, none of
the operational persons in the office had intimate, daily contact with
the president.

Nixon himself "seemed to lose interest in programs quickly and
was frequently upbraided in Congress for not trying to get his programs passed."[38] He was also not above publicly upbraiding Con-

gress—something that Johnson avoided if at all possible. Before delivering his State of the Union message in 1971, for example, he issued a statement criticizing the record of the previous Congress. Here is some of what he had to say:

> In the final month and weeks of 1970, especially in the Senate of the United States, the nation was presented with the spectacle of a legislative body that had seemingly lost the capacity to decide and the will to act. When the path was finally cleared, vital days had been lost, and major failures insured.
>
> In probably no month in recent memory did the reputation of the whole Congress suffer more in the eyes of the American people, than in the month of December, 1970. In these times when the need to build confidence in government is so transparent, that was good neither for the Congress nor the country. Let us hope that it never takes place again.[39]

That the president may have been right about his observations was even more reason not to make them public. It was unusual to have the president humiliate Congress just weeks before presenting his legislative program.

We begin our review of strategies or guidelines by noting that the Nixon agenda in the early years differed markedly from that of Johnson in his early years. First, of course, was the dominance of foreign and defense matters—a condition that suited Nixon and that could be used with good effect in dealing with Congress (that is, Vietnam created the priorities). Second, many of the most important domestic requests were designed to reform and reorganize the Great Society programs—a goal not likely to be warmly accepted by the members who had enacted these programs a few years earlier. We should not therefore be particularly surprised to find that many of the guidelines for congressional contact produced conflict rather than harmony. James David Barber argues that Nixon may have preferred it this way.

> With his remarkable flexibility regarding issues and ideologies, Nixon can be "defeated" any number of times on specific questions of policy without feeling personally threatened. His investment is not in values, not in standing fast for some principle . . . his investment is in himself, and Nixon's self is taken up with its management. As Margaret Mead has noted, "The President thrives on opposition. It is a form of stimulation for him." Thus he will court the

strains of political resistance, finding in them yet another confirmation of his virtue.[40]

Why then have we labeled his style as that of the foreign minister as president? Simply because a president faced with international crises is generally acknowledged to be performing a virtuous role. And in Nixon's case it gave him a legitimate excuse for rising above the fray—coping with problems more important than those associated with getting a legislative program through Congress. It also provided a basis for Nixon to criticize Congress. Surely legislators could be expected to cooperate at the domestic level if the president is ending wars and establishing communication (as with China) to prevent future wars. Now one can see how President Nixon believed himself justified in chastising the naughty Ninety-first Congress and admonishing them, like a scolding father: "Let us hope that it never takes place again."

The guidelines, too, become comprehensible even though they are antithetical to those espoused by President Johnson. For the fact is that they suited Nixon's evaluation of his political situation and the role he chose to play as a response. Here then are some of them.

Don't involve the president in lobbying. As indicated in the opening quotation, Nixon simply would not display his commitments in face-to-face encounters with members. He did not like the contact, and he would seldom ask, plead, or cajole in order to get a vote. This work was to be done by others. At the same time, however, Nixon made judgments about those who supported and opposed him, and he would reward his friends and seek reprisals against his opponents.

Reduce accessibility. If the president did not want to bargain personally with the members, he likewise did not want them to come to him. Stephen J. Wayne quotes a House Republican as saying that: "I pretty well concluded that there was almost no way to contact him except if you had a personal relationship."[41] This distance between the president and the members was lengthened as a result of the reduced role of the liaison people in White House decision making. Though Harlow had the ear of the president, his successor, William Timmons, did not—and neither was as close to Nixon as O'Brien was to Johnson.

Work with your friends. Although the Democrats were in the majority throughout Nixon's five and one-half years in office, there was surprisingly little reaching out to Democrats by the president. His personal contacts with members were with those he knew. His meetings with congressional leaders were not particularly productive. Naturally this separation and distance made the job of the liaison people especially difficult.

Steer the proper course. In his memoirs, Nixon states that:

> I was determined to be an activist President in domestic affairs. I had a definite agenda in mind, and I was prepared to knock heads together in order to get things done. . . . But it didn't take long to discover that enthusiasm and determination could not overcome the reality that I was still the first President in 120 years to begin his term with both houses of Congress controlled by the opposition party.[42]

Perhaps because of Democratic control of Congress, more likely because of his own demeanor, Nixon was never prepared "to knock heads together." It was more convenient for him personally to rely on the force of the idea and a steadiness in purpose. This is not to say that the White House staff did not engage in arm twisting—only that it was not the style of Nixon himself. He believed that: "If a President is sufficiently forceful, sufficiently sound in his policies and sure of his purpose, and able to take his argument persuasively to the people, Congress will go along a good deal of the time."[43]

Summary. In a manner of speaking, Nixon's style did not facilitate legislative lobbying at all. Rather it contributed a rationale for the distance he wanted between himself and Congress. And, of course, much of what he personally wanted the government to do could be accomplished with limited legislative involvement (at least as contrasted to Johnson). Interestingly enough, Nixon's separation from Congress and his own legislative liaison personnel apparently reduced the effect of Watergate on the president's legislative program. "Despite the awesome political and personal consequences of the congressional investigation and legal controversies, Timmons [successor to Harlow as head of legislative liaison] believed the effect of Watergate on pending legislation was minimal."[44]

Gerald Ford—Minority Leader as President

> I think the President has to accept the fact that he must spend more time personally with members of Congress, and he must work with the leaders of both parties to enhance their strength and influence. *Members of Congress are important.* The President cannot spend too much time with them. . . . I think a President has to give the leaders in the Congress and influential members of both parties an

open door to come and take part in policy decisions. He doesn't have to guarantee that he will do what they say, but at least they have to have the feeling that their views were considered before the fact, and not after.[45]

Gerald R. Ford served in the House of Representatives for twenty-five years before being nominated by Nixon to serve as the first vice-president selected under the procedures of the Twenty-fifth Amendment. During that long congressional service, he was in the majority for just two years—1953–1954, when the Republicans held a narrow eight-seat majority in the House. Thus for twenty-three of his twenty-five years in the House, Ford learned well the problems associated with minority status. As a member, chairman of the Republican conference (1963–1965), a senior member of the Committee on Appropriations, and Republican floor leader (1965–1973), Ford experienced the frustrations of trying to fashion majorities either in support of Republican initiatives or against Democratic programs. His rise to a leadership position was largely due to his capacity to work well with others—to make accommodations without losing a sense of purpose. When Ford defeated Charles Halleck for the floor leadership in 1965, Halleck commented: "It's the only election I've ever lost and it was because I got myself involved in a beauty contest."[46] Robert L. Peabody suggests that much more than "age and physical appearance" were at stake, however: ". . . the activists were able to convince a majority of their colleagues that Ford would project a more positive image to the nation and work toward more constructive alternative programs within the House of Representatives."[47]

As minority leader, Ford had to work with a Democratic administration for four years and Democratic party leaders in Congress for over eight years. He also had to coexist for four years with his counterpart in the Senate—Everett McKinley Dirksen. Sometimes working with Dirksen was as difficult as working with the Democrats. For example, when Ford tried to criticize President Johnson's handling of the Vietnam War, Dirksen rebuked him. "You don't demean the chief magistrate of your country at a time when a war is on."[48] The point is that Ford developed a style for coping with those likely to upstage him—either because they had the votes or because they commanded the audience. When Nixon entered the White House, Ford was also put in the position of having to lead under severely limiting conditions. During the Johnson administration at least he was not responsible for enacting the president's program, though, as noted, he had to be careful in his criticisms, given Dirksen's close association with the president. With a Republican in the White House, however, the situation changed, and Ford was made responsible for enacting the president's program. In the Ninety-first Congress, Republicans held 44 percent of the House seats; in the Ninety-second Congress, they held 41 percent of the seats. And in doing his job Ford could not depend on consistent and attentive support from the president.

The techniques relied on by Ford were very much like those used by Johnson, but accommodated to a set of political circumstances that were severely limiting. After all, Ford was an unelected president.[49] He was nominated because of his congressional experience, and he was approved by bipartisan votes in the House and Senate. By experience, personality, and means of selection, then, one expected Ford to develop close working relationships with Congress. But his agenda of government programs was much more limited than that of Johnson. He therefore did not approach Congress with the same urgency. His requests tended to be more consolidative in nature— adjustments in existing programs, management of the economy and energy resources, executive reorganization.

As president, Ford relied on the legislative style he had learned so well in the House of Representatives. He was accessible, he worked closely with party leaders on Capitol Hill, he implicated members in his legislative program, he invited close contact with his legislative liaison people. Here is what Ford himself had to say about congressional relations:

> In dealing with the Congress, Nixon and some of his aides
> had tended to work with individual Senators and Repre-
> sentatives who they felt were loyal to him instead of work-
> ing with the elected leadership. That strategy didn't help
> the legislation that Nixon was trying to push, and it in-
> furiated Hugh Scott and John Rhodes [minority floor leaders
> in the Senate and House respectively] because it undercut
> their authority as party leaders. I assured both men that
> I considered them leaders in fact as well as in name, and
> I promised to pull no end runs. Indeed, from the moment
> I became President, I set aside several hours a week for any
> member of Congress who wanted to come and see me
> privately.[50]

This sensitivity to and interest in the members of Congress makes Ford sound like a relaxed Lyndon Johnson. Thus, there is no point in providing a detailed description of the similar techniques each applied. Ford did successfully use one technique, however, that suited his political situation—a technique that Johnson used only as a last resort.

Threaten a veto. The veto is definitely helpful to a minority president—particularly one with a limited program—who wants to resist expansion of government. After all, sustaining a veto only requires getting either 146 votes in the House or 34 votes in the Senate. Awareness of this advantage on Capitol Hill makes the threat of a veto a highly useful weapon for minority-party presidents. Nixon used the veto more than his Democratic predecessors but much less than Eisenhower. Ford, on the other hand, relied heavily on the veto for getting what he wanted.

> In order to make the veto threat credible, the liaison staff had to be able to sustain presidential vetoes. This became the major strategic objective of the Ford liaison operation. The tactics used in this effort did not differ markedly from those employed in other legislative situations and by other administrations although the stakes from the president's point of view were higher.[51]

Summary. Ford's brief presidency was one of the most extraordinary in American history. Elected by Congress to the vice-presidency, Ford assumed office when the presidency itself had suffered incredible damage as a result of Watergate. His legislative experience in the minority served him well in restoring balance between the presidency and Congress. "Members of Congress are important"—President Ford could say this convincingly, confident that the members themselves knew he meant it.

Jimmy Carter—Political Layman as President

> I think I have found it is much easier for me in my own administration to evolve a very complex proposal for resolving a difficult issue than it is for Congress to pass legislation and to make that same decision.
> The energy legislation is one example. I never dreamed . . . when I proposed this matter to the Congress that a year later it still would not be resolved. I think I have got a growing understanding of the Congress, its limitations, and its capabilities and also its leadership, which was a new experience for me altogether, never having lived or served in the federal government in Washington.[52]

This statement by President Carter is remarkably candid and naive, but it is revealing of his approach to presidential–congressional relations. He seemed genuinely surprised and perplexed by the extent of congressional involvement in public policy making. One wonders where he had been in the decade before his election, when Congress had thwarted presidential foreign policy, reshaped much of its own structure, and forced a president out of office. Where, indeed, was President Carter during these years? And how did this experience influence his behavior once in office?

In 1966 Carter ran for governor of Georgia and ran third in a crowded field. In 1970 he ran again—this time against former Governor Carl Sanders. He won the nomination in a bitter runoff primary.

> Carter conducted what many observers said was reminiscent of the anti-desegregation campaign waged by former Gov. George C. Wallace . . . of Alabama. But Carter's record before the primary indicated he was moderate and conciliatory toward racial matters.[53]

Former Governor Lester Maddox ran for lieutenant governor at the same time as Carter, though not necessarily with him. Carter and Maddox both won.

Carter's own view of his relationships with the Georgia legislature was that he "had to start from scratch." Few legislators had supported him in his campaign for governor, but, as he noted, "I had a heavy mandate from the Georgia people."

> The fact that Lester Maddox was the lieutenant governor overly emphasized in the public's minds the disharmonies. In general, the major [policy] changes were made with complete cooperation between me and the legislature.[54]

And, however it was that he campaigned for the office, Carter made his position clear on racial issues in his inaugural address: "I say to you quite frankly, the time for racial discrimination is over."[55]

In 1974 the chairman of the Democratic National Committee, Robert Strauss, appointed Carter as campaign coordinator for the midterm elections. This opportunity permitted Carter to travel widely and no doubt encouraged him to try for the presidential nomination in 1976. Unable to succeed himself as governor, Carter campaigned constantly for president in 1975 and 1976. Having sampled the anti-Washington mood of the nation during his travels in 1974, Carter settled on his campaign theme. In accepting the nomination, Carter emphasized his distance from the federal government. "I have never met a Democratic president, but I've always been a Democrat." He emphasized that his campaign had been a "humbling experience, reminding us that ultimate political influence rests not with the powerbrokers, but with the people." "It's time for the people to run the government . . ." and, of course, he was the people's candidate.[56]

Just as with his campaign for governor in Georgia, Carter had little or no support from members of Congress in seeking the presidential nomination. If anything, they tended to ridicule his effort. But he won—systematically eliminating many senators and one very persistent representative (Morris Udall) along the way.

In a sense, Jimmy Carter profited at the polls from his own ignorance of Washington politics, and perhaps it is not too surprising that he was misled into formulating an unworkable model of presidential–congressional relations. Interestingly, when he discussed the subject in a preelection interview, he appeared to use all the right words. It is only when these words are read in the context of his own experience that one comprehends how he really meant to behave once in office. In discussing legislative liaison Carter said that:

> I think just a few personal moves on my part—treating Congress members as though they were Presidents themselves, returning their telephone calls, letting my staff members respect them thoroughly, dealing with the problems that they present to me, making my own presence felt in the Capitol building itself on occasion—would be contributions that might alleviate the present disharmony and total separation. . . .[57]

And at another point Carter emphasized the importance of getting members of Congress involved "in the initial stages of the preparation of major proposals" and in letting members take credit for programs that affected their districts. On these points, Carter did not sound too different from Lyndon Johnson.

At other points in the interview, however, it became clear that he expected Congress to follow his lead—in essence to be a reserved partner of a president elected from the nation as a whole. Here are excerpts supportive of this view:

> The Congress is looking for strong leadership in the White House to make major comprehensive proposals on welfare reform, tax reform, health care, government organization, and so forth, and then let the Congress in its legitimate constitutional authority dispose of those proposals as it sees fit, working harmoniously with the White House. . . .
>
> [As governor I learned] to remind the members of the legislative branch that, to the extent that my election was successful, the American people join me in those commitments. . . .
>
> We must be sure that when a proposal is made for a change in our domestic or foreign governmental life, that that proposal can be justified in an open debate, and the stripping away of secrecy that in the past has concealed the selfish influence of special interest groups. . . . Now, if after

all those emphases are consummated and my voice to the American people is heard clearly, if we have a difference of opinion in the Congress that I consider to be important, I would never hesitate to go directly to the American people with my side of the debate. . . . But that would only be a last resort. . . .

I don't want to dominate the Congress, or to have an undue influence, but I want them to know that we represent the same people.[58]

What techniques were in fact employed by the political layman as president? The list is nearly as long as that for Johnson, but would strike the Texan as very curious indeed. We begin with the fundamental point that apart from Frank Moore, Carter's director of congressional relations, the legislative liaison staff was perceived to be quite distant from the president—"even more distant, in fact, than was Nixon's liaison staff."[59] The liaison office was originally organized to suit presidential perspectives—not the pace and demands of congressional work. For the crucial first six months of his administration, the office was organized by issues. "Instead of having specialists for the Senate and for the various blocs within the House, there would be specialists for energy issues, foreign policy issues, health issues, environmental issues, and so on."[60] Unfortunately this system did not work. It was out of kilter with the multiple-issue demands on individual members of Congress. The office never fully recovered from this initial mistake.

The legislative strategies and techniques relied on by the Carter White House are perplexing if one believes that the president ought to try to work with Congress as it is. They evidence considerably more coherence, however, if one believes that national politics and policy making should be changed. Carter was said to have a " 'premeditated' purpose . . . to wean the country away from" traditional leadership.

Carter's purpose was "to try to get this country mature enough that people realize they're going to have to make decisions on their own and not listen to political leaders, because political leaders, under this Constitution, simply don't have the capacity to handle it all."[61]

The following techniques appear more rational if this view is correct.

Create a favorable climate. In his careful study of Carter's legislative liaison system, Eric L. Davis reports that the principal task of the White House team was to facilitate "the president's program, not so much by convincing members of Congress on the specific issues, but by creating a climate of favor conducive to the president and his ideas."[62] The president's senior assistant for public affairs, Anne Wexler, had the responsibility "to create an instant coalition for a specific presidential priority." She remarked in an interview: "Our job is to create lobbyists. We do that by educating people on the substance of the issues. We never ask a person to call a Congressman, but we will tell him when a vote is coming up or when a markup is due and give him a lot of information about it."[63] Unfortunately, effective coalition building among groups was not immediately translated into effective coalition building on Capitol Hill (though there were some notable successes in the last years of the Carter administration).[64]

Act fast; ask for a lot. Carter apparently believed with Johnson that a president needs to move quickly. He produced his complex energy proposal by April 1977. But he did not pace the proposals in sending them to the Hill and thus projected no sense of true priorities. Actually, with his penchant for hyperbole, everything was a priority. Either way, Congress was confused.

> The House Ways and Means Committee had, at the same time, the president's income tax, welfare, hospital cost control, and energy tax proposals. This legislative glut, it is said, has baffled Congress about his priorities and stretched his prestige too thin.[65]

Having made serious errors during his first year, Carter then encountered the cycle of decreasing influence. He did learn from early mistakes, but according to Paul Light, as his "information and expertise grew, his influence dropped."[66]

Do not consult or notify in advance. Carter acknowledged the need for involving members of Congress in the preparation of proposals in his preelection interview. Once in office he tended to go it alone. For example, none of the congressional committee chairmen who would have to facilitate passage of the energy program was included in its development. Nor were members systematically informed of legislation, patronage appointments, or projects affecting their states and districts. Some of these initial problems were corrected, but terrible impressions were created. Many members came to doubt Carter's earlier statements of respect for Congress (possibly for good reasons—see below).

Appeal on the merits. It seems apparent that Jimmy Carter believed the rhetoric of his campaign, "If I'm elected, it's going to be done, and you can depend on it." A man of impressive self-confidence,

Carter wanted and expected Congress to adopt his programs because he had developed them. According to Thomas Cronin:

> Carter in office often acted as if he had some direct mandates to reshape domestic and foreign policy. Although not a populist by any stretch of the imagination, he tried nonetheless to be assertive, innovative, and purposeful. . . . He gave the impression that he was the rational man and that Congress should deal with him and his programs completely on their merits.[67]

Pronounce first, compromise later. Consistent with the appeal to merits was a tendency by Carter to announce a program as meeting some great challenge, or declaring that a particular proposal was the centerpiece of a larger program, and then make major concessions—possibly even withdraw the proposal altogether. In part this behavior ignored Johnson's first principle: "Know what is going on." As Cronin points out, Carter failed to explore "the minefields to see what traps and opposition he would encounter."[68]

> When he discovered that he did not have the necessary support, he would have to back down in public. . . . His compromises . . . came later in the game after damage had been done to his political reputation and his relationship with politically powerful others.[69]

Ignore traditional congressional politics. It is consistent with the political layman's role for Carter to have eschewed the amenities, announcements, favors, projects, and appointments associated with congressional politics. What president would have begun his term by cutting out water projects believed by members to be so vital to their districts (and their own future political careers)?

Summary. "It was as if he didn't like politics, and yearned to be above both politics and politicians."[70] This review of Carter's style and techniques suggests that his first instincts were to try to make Washington less political. Failing that, he was forced to engage in the very behavior that upset him. It is understandable that problems developed for him—both in pursuing his natural instincts and in trying to be somebody else.

Presidential Negotiation with Congress

I began this inquiry by emphasizing the role of negotiation and bargaining in a democratic society. Absolutely crucial transactions in national policy making occur between the president and Congress. The precise nature of these transactions appears to depend heavily on the president. What this analysis of four presidents has shown, above all, is that a relationship dependent on the president is one subject to rather dramatic change (particularly in these times of high presidential turnover). Earlier I identified several forms of negotiation—from the classic bargain as an exchange, and characterized by close contact between the parties, to the more distant call for support associated with presidential interpretations of what is in the best interest of the members or the nation. Presidents Johnson and Ford understood and accepted classic bargaining (as defined by Dahl and Lindblom) but differed markedly in their political resources. Presidents Nixon and Carter were uncomfortable with the politics of exchange, depending instead on a form of persuasion that preserved distance between them and the members of Congress. Despite individual differences within this set of four presidents, at least we have spotted similarities among two pairs—Johnson and Ford accepting a partnership or inside model of congressional contact, Nixon and Carter preferring an independent or outside model.

Which model is the most successful? It is difficult to say because different measures of success may be employed for each. The partnership model is like a marriage. As Ralph K. Huitt describes it: ". . . two elements seem to be indispensable: that both parties want it to succeed and (what is not so obvious) that workable arrangements be established which make the crucial day-to-day lives flow together easily without letting every chore or responsibility become a possible confrontation."[71] These elements are not unlike those identified by Dahl and Lindblom as crucial for bargaining. They occur because people "disagree and expect that further agreement is possible and will be profitable."[72]

"But," as Huitt notes, "what if a president does not want a marriage with Congress?"[73] What if the president seriously doubts that "further agreement is possible and will be profitable"? Or what if the president disagrees with Congress but expects that further agreement will be profitable only on his terms or only if the members improve their politics? Clearly those accepting this more independent mode of behavior will rely on methods different from those above.

Now at least we are in a position to specify measures of success for each model. For the partnership model one naturally looks for successful bargains. Were the bills passed? Did the president get what he wanted? Was the partnership personally profitable—was the president reelected? Taking into account the vast difference in political resources available to Johnson and Ford, it is fair to say that both were reasonably successful in making the partnership work, measured by the legislation produced. Johnson's production in the early years was phenomenal; Ford's consistently exceeded expectations. Johnson, however, got distracted by the intractable set of problems associated with Vietnam and did not even seek reelection. And Ford was narrowly defeated for reelection, though it may fairly be said that there was victory in defeat given his minority-party status. Conclusion? It is difficult to survive in national politics today even if one records a reasonably successful partnership with Congress.

For the independent model the test would seem to be whether the president is able to produce on his own. Was he successful in doing those things to which he gave high priority? Before the Watergate debacle, Nixon scored quite well on this measure. He wanted relatively little from Congress. Above all he wanted to be free to participate imaginatively in international affairs. He was also devising means for acting without Congress on many domestic matters. What we will never know for certain is how Congress would have reacted to his behavior had it not been for Watergate. There was evidence that they were determined to reduce his independence and that he might, therefore, have been much more constrained in his final three years even without the scandal that forced him out of office.

Carter did want something from Congress, and he was notably unsuccessful in employing the independent model for getting it. Carter was never free to produce on his own, and he was an unwilling and clumsy bargainer. Nixon's independent style was congruent with his goals and, up to a point, with the authority of the office (particularly in regard to foreign policy). Carter's independent style was incongruent with his goals and with presidential authority. Was their independence personally profitable? Nixon was reelected by a landslide but was the first president in history forced to resign. Carter was defeated, also in a landslide.

The significant social, economic, and political changes in recent decades have resulted in highly unstable executive–legislative relations, which, in turn, have contributed to, if not caused, inconstancy in the national policy process. It is no doubt unfair to argue that this outcome is all the president's doing. Congress, too, has changed dramatically in recent years, sometimes in response to shifting presidential styles. My concluding point is not to judge who is to blame, but to express concern about the effects of dramatically different presidential styles. I was able to pair off the four presidents—two each accepting the partnership and independent models. Still, there are significant differences in the conditions, styles, techniques, and effects within each pair. Interestingly some of these differences may be attributable to political party. Note that I have paired off a Democrat with a Republican in each case.

Though much remains to be said on this important topic, I have gone as far as I can comfortably go on the basis of available research. I cannot end, however, without commenting on prospective relationships between President Ronald Reagan and Congress. There are signs even in the early months of his administration that he accepts the partnership model but is more prone than Johnson or Ford to rely on the full range of negotiating strategies—from classic bargaining to precise and resolute translations of the national interest.[74] Certainly Reagan's performance before Congress on April 28, 1981, in support of his economic program well illustrated the use of all available techniques. As Hedrick Smith of the *New York Times* observed, he employed "the carrot, stick, and a lot of follow-up."[75]

It may be prosaic but appropriate to refer to Reagan's style simply as that of *actor as president*. Other labels to consider are communicator, personator, agent, or proxy. It happens that this style reflects a role-playing capacity consistent with the demands of representative democracy. Placing oneself in the position of another, communicating both the substance and style of the character, "enlisting the will and movements of others" (see below), predicting and translating audience reaction—these are commonplace responses in the theater, which serve the values of political representation. I am not making a judgment now about whether Reagan is a good or bad actor as president (though the early reviews have been favorable). I am simply observing that the style comes naturally to him and is suited to some of the demands of the office.

Perhaps the president in this century whose style most closely resembles that of Reagan is Franklin D. Roosevelt. Again we have a pair drawn from the two parties and thus observe important differences in policy substance. But the emphasis on communication and role playing is surely there for both. In Roosevelt's case, the motivation for "acting by proxy" may have been his illness. Kenneth Burke persuasively makes this point:

> It is even conceivable that his illness contributed substantially as an important motive shaping the quality of his understanding, and thence the quality of his acts. For during the period of the attack and the slow recovery, he must have experienced most poignantly and forcibly a distinction between action and motion, since he could act only by proxy, through enlisting the will and movements of others. Thus, even down to the purely physiological level, he must have learned to make peace with a kind of dissociation between impulse and response rarely felt by men whose physical motions are in more spontaneous or naive relation

to their thinking. Hence, it is conceivable that from this dissociation could arise a more patient attitude towards motives outside one's direct control than other men would naturally have. And from this could arise a sharpening of the administrative sense, which is decidedly that of *acting by proxy*, and utilizing the differences among the agents through whom one acts.[76]

One is tempted to make something of the 1981 assassination attempt (or Reagan's age) at this point, but any such analysis takes us too far into so young an administration. It is enough for now to take note of the similarity in styles of the two men and to speculate about the striking differences in motivation.

Finally I am anxious to urge more research and analysis of presidential negotiation with Congress. Surely there are few better starting places for comprehending the political dynamics of recent decades. As Richard E. Neustadt concluded in 1960:

> The President's advantages are checked by the advantages of others. Continuing relationships will pull in both directions. These are relationships of mutual dependence. A President depends upon the men he would persuade; he has to reckon with his need or fear of them. They too will possess status, or authority, or both, else they would be of little use to him. Their vantage points confront his own; their power tempers his.[77]

Events of the last two decades have made this analysis even more appropriate today. Yet our understanding of the who, what, when, and how of presidential influence remains fragmentary at best.

Notes

1. Lyndon B. Johnson, *The Vantage Point* (New York: Holt, Rinehart and Winston, 1971), p. 461.
2. Nelson W. Polsby, *Congress and the Presidency* (Englewood Cliffs, N.J.: Prentice-Hall, 1976), p. 198.
3. I am indebted to the editor of this volume, Anthony King, for urging me to clarify the various forms of negotiation and bargaining.
4. Robert A. Dahl and Charles E. Lindblom, *Politics, Economics, and Welfare* (New York: Harper and Row, 1953), p. 324.
5. Ibid., p. 326.
6. Ibid., p. 333.
7. Ibid., pp. 333-34.
8. Polsby, *Congress and Presidency*, p. 191.
9. In comments on this chapter. Hugh Heclo uses similar terminology in chapter 2 of this volume.

10. George C. Edwards III, *Presidential Influence in Congress* (San Francisco: W.H. Freeman, 1980), chaps. 5-7.

11. Quoted in Paul C. Light, "The President's Agenda: Notes on the Timing of Domestic Choice," *Presidential Studies Quarterly*, vol. 11 (Winter 1981), p. 69.

12. Henry Kissinger, *White House Years* (Boston: Little, Brown, 1979), p. 11.

13. See James David Barber, *The Presidential Character* (Englewood Cliffs, N.J.: Prentice-Hall, 1972), p. 351, where Barber discusses Nixon's penchant for treating difficult, even impossible, problems or crises. Kissinger also discusses Nixon's capacity for detachment, which seemed suited to his interest in international affairs. But he also observes that: "Triumph seemed to fill Nixon with a premonition of ephemerality" (p. 1471). I should note that I first considered Nixon's style as that of "secretary of state as president." The rise in importance of the national security adviser led me to rethink that title in favor of "foreign minister." I think Nixon would approve.

14. I was tempted to characterize Carter's style as that of "political missionary as president," based on his rejection of standard congressional politics.

15. Johnson, *Vantage Point*, p. 459.

16. Ralph K. Huitt, "Democratic Party Leadership in the Senate," *American Political Science Review*, vol. 55 (June 1961), p. 3370.

17. James L. Sundquist, *Politics and Policy: The Eisenhower, Kennedy, and Johnson Years* (Washington, D.C.: Brookings, 1968), p. 506.

18. Statement by Speaker John W. McCormack as quoted in Sundquist, *Politics and Policy*, p. 3.

19. Doris Kearns, *Lyndon Johnson and the American Dream* (New York: Harper and Row, 1976), p. 236.

20. Edwards, *Presidential Influence*, p. 117.

21. Stephen J. Wayne, *The Legislative Presidency* (New York: Harper and Row, 1978), p. 149.

22. Ibid., p. 150.

23. Johnson, *Vantage Point*, pp. 441, 443. Johnson also said: "You've got just one year when they treat you right, and before they start worrying about themselves." Harry McPherson, *A Political Education* (Boston: Little, Brown, 1972), p. 268.

24. Light, "President's Agenda," pp. 70-72.

25. Ibid., p. 71.

26. Kearns, *Johnson*, pp. 236-37.

27. John F. Manley, "Presidential Power and White House Lobbying," *Political Science Quarterly*, vol. 93 (Summer 1978), p. 264.

28. Edwards, *Presidential Influence*, p. 119.

29. Wayne, *Legislative Presidency*, p. 148.

30. Huitt, "Democratic Leadership," p. 337. Emphasis added.

31. Edwards, *Presidential Influence,* p. 119.

32. Polsby, *Congress and Presidency,* p. 195.

33. Manley, "Presidential Power," p. 266.

34. All quotations from Johnson, taken from *Vantage Point,* pp. 450-51.

35. Rowland Evans, Jr., and Robert D. Novak, *Nixon in the White House: The Frustration of Power* (New York: Random House, 1971), p. 107.

36. For details see my "Congress and the Presidency," in Thomas Mann and Norman Ornstein, eds., *The New Congress* (Washington, D.C.: American Enterprise Institute, 1981), chap. 8.

37. Wayne, *Legislative Presidency,* p. 156.

38. Edwards, *Presidential Influence,* p. 139.

39. Reprinted in Congressional Quarterly, Inc., *Nixon: The Third Year of His Presidency* (Washington, D.C., 1972), p. 5A.

40. Barber, *Presidential Character,* pp. 441-42.

41. Wayne, *Legislative Presidency,* p. 161.

42. Richard M. Nixon, *RN: The Memoirs of Richard Nixon,* vol. 1 (New York: Warner Books, 1978), p. 512.

43. Richard M. Nixon, "Needed: Clarity of Purpose," *Time,* vol. 116 (November 10, 1980), p. 32.

44. Wayne, *Legislative Presidency,* p. 163.

45. Gerald R. Ford, "Imperiled, Not Imperial," *Time,* vol. 116 (November 10, 1980), p. 31. Emphasis added.

46. Quoted in Robert L. Peabody, *Leadership in Congress* (Boston: Little, Brown, 1976), p. 137.

47. Ibid., p. 137.

48. Quoted in Neil MacNeil, *Dirksen: Portrait of a Public Man* (New York: World Publishing Co., 1970), p. 291.

49. It is relevant that Ford was not Nixon's first choice. Ford reports that John Connally "had been Nixon's first choice." Rockefeller and Reagan were also considered but were rejected as possibly splitting the party. "That left me as the 'safest' choice." Gerald R. Ford, *A Time to Heal: The Autobiography of Gerald R. Ford* (New York: Harper and Row, 1979), p. 107.

50. Ibid., p. 140.

51. Wayne, *Legislative Presidency,* p. 159.

52. Congressional Quarterly, Inc., *President Carter—1978* (Washington, D.C., 1979), p. 92A.

53. "Election 1970: The South," *Congressional Quarterly Weekly Report,* October 23, 1970, p. 2592.

54. Donald Smith, "Carter Sees Ford as 'Not Leading Congress,'" *Congressional Quarterly Weekly Report,* September 4, 1976, p. 2382.

55. Al Gordon, "Carter: Full-Time Campaign Shows Results," *Congressional Quarterly Weekly Report,* November 29, 1975, p. 2615.

56. Acceptance speech reprinted in *Congressional Quarterly Weekly Report,* July 17, 1976, pp. 1933-35.

57. Smith, "Carter Sees Ford," p. 2383.

58. Ibid., pp. 2382-83.

59. Eric L. Davis, "Legislative Liaison in the Carter Administration," *Political Science Quarterly*, vol. 94 (Summer 1979), p. 292.

60. Ibid., p. 289. See also chapter 3 in this volume.

61. Evan Dobelle, a Carter campaign aide, quoted in David S. Broder, *Changing of the Guard: Power and Leadership in America* (New York: Simon and Schuster, 1980), p. 128. It was evidence like this that tempted me to use the "missionary" label for Carter.

62. Davis, "Legislative Liaison," p. 290.

63. Dom Bonafede, "To Anne Wexler, All the World Is a Potential Lobbyist," *National Journal*, September 8, 1979, pp. 1476, 1478.

64. See Dom Bonafede, "The Tough Job of Normalizing Relations with Capitol Hill," *National Journal*, January 13, 1979, pp. 54-57.

65. Edwards, *Presidential Influence*, p. 175.

66. Light, "President's Agenda," p. 72.

67. Thomas E. Cronin, *The State of the Presidency*, 2d ed. (Boston: Little, Brown, 1980), p. 215.

68. Ibid., p. 174.

69. Statement by Betty Glad quoted in ibid., p. 174.

70. Ibid., p. 216. Another useful review of Carter and Congress is that by Randall B. Ripley in Steven A. Shull and Lance T. LeLoup, eds., *The Presidency: Studies in Policy Making* (Brunswick, Ohio: Kings Court, 1979), pp. 65-82.

71. Ralph K. Huitt, "White House Channels to the Hill," in Harvey C. Mansfield, Sr., ed., *Congress against the President* (New York: Praeger, 1975), p. 71.

72. Dahl and Lindblom, *Politics*, p. 326.

73. Huitt, "White House Channels," p. 76.

74. For early reports and appraisals of Reagan's congressional liaison operations, led by Max L. Friedersdorf, see Judith Miller, "Reagan's Liaison Chief on Capitol Hill to Focus on Harmony as His Priority," *New York Times*, January 6, 1981, p. B8; and Helen Dewar and Lee Lescaze, "Reagan Hill Team Gets Rave Reviews," *Washington Post*, March 17, 1981, p. A5.

75. On "Washington Week in Review," WETA-TV, Washington, D.C., May 1, 1981.

76. Kenneth Burke, *A Grammar of Motives* (Englewood Cliffs, N.J.: Prentice-Hall, 1952), p. 391. Emphasis added.

77. Richard E. Neustadt, *Presidential Power* (New York: John Wiley, 1960), pp. 35-36.

5

The President and His Party

AUSTIN RANNEY

Any discussion of the relations between the president and Congress should keep in mind that the men who wrote the Constitution of the United States believed that those relations should consist mainly of checks and balances, not of cooperation and certainly not of presidential leadership.

They proceeded from three basic convictions: that government is a necessary evil required by people's tendency to pursue their particular interests by methods and to lengths excessively damaging to the interests of others; that swift and concerted government action is likely to advance the interests of some groups at the expense of others; and that it is therefore better for government to do little or nothing than to do something over the strong objections of any of the nation's significant groups.

The authors of the Constitution sought to implement these convictions in two main ways. First, they fragmented and dispersed governmental jurisdiction between the nation and the states. Second, they fragmented and dispersed the power of the national government mainly between the president and Congress, with a bit left over for the Supreme Court.

The central concern of this book is the current condition of the various devices by which American presidents and other politicians have tried to join together, for purposes of getting the government to work, what the Constitution so successfully put asunder. Most of these devices fall under the general heading of "presidential leadership of Congress." The ideas underlying all of them are that America, like every other country, must sometimes take swift, coherent, and purposive action; that Congress is an assembly of independent ambassadors from semisovereign states and districts and therefore cannot by itself initiate such action; that the president, who has the enormous advantages of being one person and of being the only public official elected by all the people, is the only official who can take the lead;

and that the basic problem of American government is finding and perfecting institutions that will enable the president to lead Congress with maximum effectiveness.

In the opinion of many analysts over the years, one of the most promising devices stems from the fact that every president since George Washington has been a member of the political party to which many members of Congress—ideally majorities in both chambers—also belong. Moreover, the president is not just an ordinary member of his party. He is its leader, and he can and should use his party leadership as a way—perhaps the most effective way—of inducing Congress to adopt his programs.

The most forceful presentation of those ideas was made by Woodrow Wilson in his *Constitutional Government in the United States*, published in 1908 when he was still an academic political scientist. As Wilson summed it up:

> [The president] is the party nominee and the only party nominee for whom the whole nation votes. . . . He can dominate his party by being spokesman for the real sentiment and purpose of the country, by giving direction to opinion, by giving the country at once the information and the statements of policy which will enable it to form its judgments alike of parties and of men. . . . He may be both the leader of his party and the leader of the nation, or he may be one or the other. If he can lead the nation, his party can hardly resist him.[1]

In this chapter I consider how well Woodrow Wilson's description fits the presidencies of Ronald Reagan and his immediate predecessors. I then outline the extent to which recent presidents' copartisans in Congress have been faithful followers of presidential leadership. I conclude by trying to estimate how important the president's role as head of his party is in his efforts to lead the government.

The President as the Leader of His Party

Senses in Which He Is the Leader. According to the *Oxford English Dictionary*, a leader is "one who guides others in action and opinion; one who takes the lead in any business, enterprise, or movement; one who is followed by disciples or adherents. The foremost or most eminent member."[2] Clearly, the president's party leadership has some of these qualities more than others. Let us briefly examine each.

The party's most eminent member. The president of the United States is clearly the country's most eminent citizen. He holds its highest public office, which combines the symbolic and ceremonial functions of chief of state and the political and administrative powers of head of government. He is the first political object that children perceive as they begin to learn about government; for a while he is just about the only part of government they perceive clearly, and most adults know more about him and what he does than they know about any congressman or Supreme Court justice.

The president is also a partisan, even if, like Dwight Eisenhower, he has had little previous public association with his party. He has fought through the state primaries, caucuses, and conventions of the party; he has been nominated for the office by its national convention; he has appeared before the convention to accept the nomination; and he participates often in a variety of party affairs—speaking at fund-raising dinners, campaigning on behalf of party candidates for other offices, meeting with the party's national chairman and committee, and so on.

Accordingly, since the president is clearly the country's most eminent citizen and equally clearly a member of a political party, he is, by definition, that party's most eminent member. If he is widely regarded as an especially good president, he adds luster to the party's name as well, as Franklin Roosevelt did in the 1930s. By the same token, if he is seen to be an especially corrupt president, as Richard Nixon was in the early 1970s, or an especially weak one, as Jimmy Carter was in the late 1970s, some of the tarnish on him can rub off on his party. For this reason, if for no other, all his fellow partisans hope that their president's reputation will prosper.

Leader of the national committee. The president has no formal role in his party's national committee. Yet his informal control over its leaders and activities is nearly total. At any time from the moment he wins his party's nomination to the day he leaves office he need only pass the word about whom he wants as national chairman to the national committee, and the committee will promptly elect his choice, usually without dissent. Moreover, presidents typically want the chairman to be the president's man rather than the committee's man with a constituency of his own.

Two recent examples illustrate the point. In 1975 Robert Strauss, one of the most successful and popular Democratic national chairmen of recent times, appointed the Commission on the Role and Future of the Presidential Primaries, a small group chaired by Morley Winograd, Democratic state chairman of Michigan, and charged it with studying the causes and consequences of the proliferation of presidential primaries since 1968. On January 6, 1977, Jimmy Carter "recommended" that Kenneth W. Curtis, the former governor of Maine, replace Strauss, and the Democratic National Committee duly ratified the president's choice on January 21. The committee also renamed the Winograd Commission the Commission on Presidential Nomination and Party Structure, nearly doubled its membership, and appointed faithful Carter supporters, including Rick Hutcheson, a White House aide, and Pat Caddell, Carter's pollster, to the new slots. The whole point was to make sure that the commission did not exercise its enlarged mandate to review the party's national convention delegate selection rules in any way that might make Carter's renomination more difficult in 1980, and the commission's report, published in 1978, showed that the administration's strategy had worked splendidly. Nevertheless, rumors persisted that the White House felt that Curtis's leadership could have been a good deal more vigorous, and on December 7 Curtis announced his intention to resign from what he described as "this lousy job." On December 28 Carter "recommended" John C. White, his deputy secretary of agriculture, for the job, and on January 27, 1978, the national committee ratified the choice.

In many respects the Republican case is even more striking. On January 14, 1977, with Gerald Ford about to leave the White House, the Republican National Committee conducted one of the most open and hotly contested elections for a national chairman in its history. The two leading contenders (there were five in all) were Bill Brock, the former senator from Tennessee who had lost his seat in the 1976 election, and Richard Richards, the Republican state chairman of Utah. Brock had supported Ford in the close and sometimes bitter contest for the party's 1976 presidential nomination, and Richards had supported Ronald Reagan. Hence Ford's supporters now backed Brock for the chairmanship, and Reagan's supporters backed Richards. After three ballots Brock won a close victory.

In the next three years Brock became one of the most active, successful, and respected national chairmen in history. This is not the place to recount his achievements in detail, but they included the active recruitment of promising candidates for Congress and state legislatures, the conduct of "schools" on campaign organization and techniques for those candidates, the support of their campaigns in 1978 and 1980 with money and materials, national party provision of and financial support for directors of organizational development in the state parties, the development of REPNET (a national program of computer services, including mailing lists of potential donors, political targeting, survey processing, and the like, all made available to state parties at a minimum charge), a Local Elections Campaign Division devoted to winning more state legislative seats, and a lively new journal of ideas called *Common Sense*. Most observers gave Brock's leadership a great deal of the credit for the party's gains in the 1978 and 1980 elections for Congress and for the state legislatures.[3]

Despite Brock's achievements, however, many of Ronald Reagan's inner circle of advisers still considered that his 1976 opposition to Reagan and his moderate policy views showed that he was not a true Reagan man. In June 1980, a month before the Republican convention but well after Reagan had the nomination locked up, these advisers urged Reagan to ask Brock to step down immediately. Reagan finally decided against this move, but the convention adopted a new rule providing that "the chairman, co-chairman and all other officers except the chairman should be elected immediately following the National Convention 1980, and *in January of each odd numbered year thereafter*."[4] Brock was duly reelected in July—though Drew Lewis, Reagan's campaign chairman in Pennsylvania and later secretary of transportation, was also elected as deputy chairman and "chief operating officer." And in January 1981 Reagan gave his backing to Richard Richards, who was duly elected by the national committee. (As a reward for his past services, Brock was named to a post formerly held by Robert Strauss—U.S. trade representative, with the rank of ambassador.) There could hardly be a clearer example of the president's dominance over his party's national committee and the choice of the national chairman. He takes the lead. He calls the tune.

Initiation of the party's policies. American political parties have two kinds of party policies, and the president or the presidential candidate takes the lead in initiating both kinds. One kind consists of the policies advocated by an incumbent president. By simple virtue of the fact that they are his policies, they are generally referred to in the news media and in political conversation as his party's policies. This does not mean, of course, that all his party's members in Congress—or, for that matter, in the national committee and in the state and local party organizations—support the president's policies. It only means that there is no other party official or agency that claims to have a voice in setting the party's policies that is equal or superior to the president's. The party out of power, as we shall observe below, is in quite a different position.

The other kind of policies that American parties are said to have are those set forth in the platforms they adopt at their quadrennial conventions. Some commentators dismiss the platforms as collections of ritual endorsements of policies on which nearly everyone agrees and paperings-over of issues on which there is widespread and bitter dispute. The fact is, however, that most convention delegates and party leaders—including presidents running for reelection—take the platforms quite seriously, for they perform two significant functions. The first is the external function of appealing to as many voters, and offending as few, as possible. The second—and, in recent years, more important—is the internal function of helping to unite the party's various factions behind the ticket so that they will support it enthusiastically.

Any incumbent president who, like Richard Nixon in 1972 or Jimmy Carter in 1980, has the nomination clearly in hand also has to control what goes into and what is excluded from the party platform. In both parties the platform-writing process is administered by the national committee, and in 1980 most members of the Democratic platform committee held their first hearings in March, five months before the national convention assembled. They finished the first draft of the platform in mid-June, two months before the convention. Since the president dominates the national committee, he is bound to dominate the writing of the platform. But if he faces a disgruntled minority whose support he badly needs to win reelection, as Jimmy Carter did with the Edward Kennedy faction in 1980, then he is well advised to do what Carter did: let them have their way over almost anything in the platform about which they feel strongly, barring only direct and explicit repudiations of policies his administration has pursued or the endorsement of policies (in this case wage and price controls) to which he is unalterably opposed. In 1980 the Democratic convention adopted a new rule, backed by the Kennedy forces, to the effect that, after the platform has been adopted, all the presidential candidates must state in writing what differences they have with it and must pledge to carry it out despite those differences. But Carter finessed the matter by issuing a statement that neither flatly rejected nor explicitly embraced the Kennedy amendments that had been added to the Carter-dominated platform. The upshot is that a Republican president's control over his party's platform is as strong as ever and, although a Democratic president's control may not be quite as strong, he retains most of the initiative in its drafting and a substantial if not absolute veto over its contents.

It is arguable, of course, that American political parties do not have party policies in the sense that parties in most other democratic countries do—that is, a series of proposals for government action that are (1) developed by party agencies, (2) set forth in official party pronouncements, and (3) supported by nearly all of the party's elected public officials nearly all of the time. Both the president's policies and the presidential-candidate-dominated party platforms satisfy the first two conditions, but the third condition raises the most serious questions about what it means to say that the president is the leader of his party.

Senses in Which He Is Not the Leader. *The separation of party organizations.* When we speak of Jimmy Carter as leader of the Democratic party or Ronald Reagan as leader of the Republican party, we speak as though each party were, like most parties in other democratic countries, a single organizational entity with a hierarchical structure headed by the president. American parties, however, are not like that. Organizationally speaking, the "presidential parties" are quite separate from the "congressional parties," a separation which stems from and fully reflects the constitutional separation of powers between the two branches of government. The core of each party's presidential party is its national committee and national convention, and the Democratic party charter adopted in 1974 adds a few auxiliary agencies, such as a midterm delegate conference, a judicial council, a national finance council, and a national education and training council. As we have seen, the president certainly leads his party's presidential party.

Each party also has a full party organization in each house of Congress, the principal agencies being a party conference or caucus, a policy or steering committee, a research organization or committee, a campaign committee, a whip, a floor leader, and, in the majority party only, a Speaker of the House and a president pro tempore of the Senate.

The congressional parties play a number of important roles, especially in the appointment of committee and subcommittee chairmen and members and in the organization and allocation of the two chambers' time. But the president of the United States certainly does not take the lead in their affairs, and in many important respects he stands entirely outside them.

Most important, the president plays no role in the selection of his party's candidates for either house of Congress. They are all chosen in their districts or states by direct primary elections. The president may on rare occasions encourage someone to run in a particular primary, but he cannot prevent anyone else from running; he rarely supports one candidate over another; and, even when presidents have done so, presidentially supported candidates have lost more often than they have won.[5] Unlike the leaders of most democratic parties, then, the president has no power to ensure the nomination of a particularly desirable candidate for the House or Senate or to veto the nomination of a particularly undesirable candidate.

It works the other way as well. Congressmen and senators in both parties from 1972 to 1980 had almost no influence on the presidential nominating process. About 74 percent of the delegates to the national conventions were chosen in state presidential primaries. Congressional endorsements had little or no effect on the outcome of those primaries, and no presidential nominee bothered much to seek such endorsements. Congressmen and senators had lost the automatic delegate slots that used to be reserved for many of them at the national convention, and only very small fractions of the congressional parties even bothered to attend the conventions.

After 1980 the Democratic party made some effort to alter this situation. The new national chairman, Charles Manatt, appointed a commission, chaired by Governor James B. Hunt, Jr. of North Carolina, to recommend changes in the rules for selecting national convention delegates. In 1982 the Hunt commission recommended, among other things, that up to two-thirds of the party's senators and representatives, chosen by their respective congressional caucuses, be made delegates to the 1984 convention without being required to pledge in advance their support for a particular presidential aspirant.

This may restore some congressional voice in the selection of Democratic presidential candidates, but it will not materially improve congressmen's chances of winning the nomination. The special requirements of the presidential nominating process will still demand full-time campaigning for two years or more before the election year, especially in preparation for the early and crucial Iowa caucuses and New Hampshire primary; no prominent or conscientious senator or representative can afford so much time, and the failure of Representative Morris Udall and Senator Henry Jackson in 1976 and of Senator Howard Baker and Senator Edward Kennedy in 1980 suggests that Congress is no longer a desirable—or perhaps even a viable—base from which to run for president.[6] In short, members of Congress have about as little power over whom their party nominates for the presidency as the president has over whom his party nominates for the House and Senate. The consequences that Richard Neustadt pointed out in 1960 are even stronger and clearer in the 1980s:

> What the Constitution separates our political parties do not combine. The parties are themselves composed of separated organizations sharing public authority. The authority consists of nominating powers. Our national parties are confederations of state and local party institutions, with a headquarters that represents the White House, more or less, if the party has a President in office. These confederacies manage presidential nominations. All other public offices

138

depend upon electorates confined within the states. All other nominations are controlled within the states. The President and congressmen who bear one party's label are divided by dependence upon different sets of voters. The differences are sharpest at the stage of nomination. The White House has too small a share in nominating congressmen, and Congress has too little weight in nominating Presidents for party to erase their constitutional separation. Party links are stronger than is frequently supposed, but nominating processes assure the separation.[7]

After a president is elected, he has little to say about, and even less influence on, the selection of his party's leaders in Congress. I am unable to find any verified instance in which a president has tried to get a Speaker or floor leader or whip removed. Occasionally a president or a president-elect has expressed support for a congressional party leader whose position is in some jeopardy, but even that is rare, and congressmen strongly resent such outside interference in their affairs. Shortly after his election in 1980, Ronald Reagan announced that he endorsed the reelection of Howard Baker (Republican, Tennessee), who was under some fire for being too moderate, as Republican leader in the Senate, but also announced that his old friend and campaign chairman Senator Paul Laxalt (Republican, Nevada) would be the only member of Congress to be included in his "supercabinet"—his inner circle of advisers. That promised to make for a novel and instructive set of relations among the three men.

The threadbare coattails. There was a time when observers believed that many of the presidential party's representatives and senators would follow the president's lead because they hoped to "ride his coattails" to reelection. They knew, so the argument ran, that most voters voted straight party tickets, with the result that congressmen's electoral destinies depended largely on the popularity of the man at the head of the ticket. It was therefore very much in the congressmen's interests to help the president make the kind of record in office that would sweep the whole ticket to victory. A smart president could convert this feeling into a powerful weapon in several ways. For one, he could threaten to withhold his endorsement from any fellow partisan in Congress who failed to support his programs. For another, he could make the argument that he and his fellow party members were all in the same electoral boat and would sink or sail together, so it behooved Democrats (or Republicans) at both ends of Pennsylvania Avenue to build a party legislative record that would carry them all to victory.

A number of political scientists have studied this presumed "coattail effect," some by using sample survey techniques and others by analyzing comparative election returns. They have generally concluded that, whether or not presidential coattails were ever important in reelecting congressmen, they had little or no significance in the 1970s and are likely to have even less in the 1980s. There appear to be many reasons for the unraveling of the coattails, but those mentioned most often are the decreasing number of competitive districts and the increasing campaigning resources and electoral security of incumbent representatives (senators appear to be a different matter). In short, a president running for reelection these days leads his party's ticket only in the sense that he is its best-known candidate, not in the sense that the electoral fate of his party's congressional candidates depends heavily on how well or how badly he does.[8]

Moreover, presidents in the 1980s control almost no party resources that congressmen count on in their campaigns for reelection. Because of the low ceilings imposed upon the expenditures of presidential campaign organizations by the Federal Campaign Finance Act amendments of 1974, most presidents are now reluctant to campaign jointly with their party's congressional candidates lest some of the latters' activities and expenditures be charged against the presidential campaign's limits. The national committees' limited campaign funds are spent mainly on the presidential campaigns, although in 1980 the Republican committee spent a lot on a general campaign for the party's presidential *and* congressional candidates: "Vote Republican —for a Change!" Indeed, the national committees' historical focus on presidential campaigns was the main reason for the creation of the two parties' congressional and senatorial campaign committees in 1866, and it has continued to sustain their independence from the national committees ever since.

The fact that the president now controls so few of the resources needed by congressmen leads one to ask, Does it really matter to most congressmen whether the president is of their party? The answer appears to be, Yes, but not as much as it used to. For one thing, most congressmen still have some sense of belonging to one of two teams engaged in a continuing series of contests, and their team loyalties generally make them prefer their man to win over the other team's. For another thing, their party's candidate is likely to have more policy positions similar to their own than the other party's candidate. For still another, senatorial courtesy—the de facto power of a state's senior senator to have a controlling voice in the selection of federal judges and other federal appointees to serve in his state—

operates only with a president of one's own party, not with an opposition president. But most congressmen now feel, as they did not a generation ago, that their own electoral fortunes depend little or not at all on how well or how badly their party's presidential candidate does at the polls.

Leadership of the Opposition. *The Westminster model.* To American eyes, one of the most wondrous of all the institutions that make the British version of democratic government so different from the American is the position of the leader of Her Majesty's loyal opposition. The position was established by an act of Parliament; it is always occupied by the leader of the largest nongovernment party in the House of Commons; and it carries an annual salary comparable to that of a junior minister in the government (in 1981 it was £27,000 per year), paid out of regular treasury funds. Equally remarkable to American eyes is the fact that, especially when the Conservatives are the opposition party, the leader of the opposition is just as much the official and acknowledged chief spokesperson and organizational leader of the opposition party as the prime minister is of the governing party.[9]

The Washington model. In Washington, by contrast, one speaks not of "the government" or "the opposition," each with its clear leader, but of the "in-party" (the party whose label the current president bears) and the "out-party" (the other party). We have been canvassing the senses in which the president is and is not the leader of the in-party, but we should note here that the only time in which the out-party has any single, generally acknowledged leader is in the period between the nomination of its presidential candidate and the November election. For the next four years the news media, and sometimes the party itself, turn to various officials to serve as the out-party's spokesman; but everyone knows that whoever is chosen is no leader even in the limited senses in which the incumbent president is leader of the in-party.

The news media, for example, sometimes refer to the defeated presidential candidate as the out-party's "titular leader";[10] but everyone quite correctly understands that phrase to refer to a title without authority. Some out-parties' national chairmen have been strong leaders in revivifying their parties' organizational structures after crushing national defeats—for example, Ray Bliss (1965–1969) and Bill Brock (1977–1981) for the Republicans and Paul Butler (1957–1961) for the Democrats. But they have rarely spoken on issues of public policy, and, when they have, no one has taken what they said

141

as in any way an authoritative pronouncement of the party's stand on those issues. The out-party's leaders in Congress are, of course, constantly making pronouncements on public issues. Sometimes the television and radio networks have even given them periods of free air time in which to reply to especially "political" broadcasts by the president. Again, however, everyone recognizes that their authority to speak for the out-party comes from only one segment of the party—its organizations in the two houses of Congress—and from the networks, not at all from the national convention or the state parties.

Both national committees have, when their parties were out of the White House, established special committees to formulate and announce stands on policy questions—the Democratic Advisory Council (1956–1960), the Democratic Party Council (1969–1976), and the Republican Coordinating Committee (1964–1968). In each case the main purpose was to keep the parties' congressional leaders from monopolizing the attention of the news media and the public as sole spokesmen for the out-party. And in each case, while the council or the conference did succeed in drawing some attention away from the congressional leaders, no one regarded it as a kind of collective leadership of the loyal opposition. It is clear that the American out-party has no person, committee, or council that plays any such role.[11]

Building Presidential Coalitions. What does it matter if the out-party has no leader even in the limited respects in which the president is the in-party's leader? Its main consequence is that, unlike every new British prime minister, a new American president brings to office no well-established working coalition of interest groups and party leaders in Congress, the national committee, and state and local party organizations that has been built during a period in which he was leader of the opposition. He becomes the leader of his party only when he wins its presidential nomination, and he continues only if he wins the election. As president he can try to cobble together a different coalition for each issue that comes along, and even the most ineffective presidents can manage a few such coalitions. But things are likely to go much better on many more issues if he can somehow build a relatively strong and enduring coalition that will provide him with ideas and support for most of the problems he must face.

Before the 1970s many presidents of both parties began to build their governing coalitions in the course of winning their party's nomination. They and their lieutenants met with a number of congressmen, governors, mayors, state chairmen, and other state and local party leaders who had the power to appoint significant numbers of delegates to the national conventions and therefore the power to "deliver" their votes to whichever presidential aspirant they chose. In "cutting deals" with these leaders for their support, presidential aspirants had to make promises—cabinet appointments and lesser patronage appointments to persons named by the party leaders, pledges to press for certain policies and oppose others, even commitment to a particular person as the vice-presidential nominee. The main object of these negotiations was to win delegate votes, but they also had a side benefit: the president-to-be got to know well many of the people who would be important to him when he took office, and consequently the process of building his nominating coalition was an important foundation for the subsequent process by which he built his governing coalition.

That is no longer the case. The "reforms" of the presidential nominating process since 1968 were intended mainly to strip party "bosses" and "power brokers" of their power to name delegates, and they succeeded brilliantly. By 1980 about 74 percent of the delegates to the conventions were chosen by presidential primaries, not by party leaders. Moreover, almost all of those delegates were chosen because they supported a presidential candidate who had done well in their state's primary, not because of their personal service to or eminence in the party and certainly not because they had been hand-picked by some state or local party leader. In addition, each party's elected public officials have been largely cut out of the presidential nominating process, and few of them now even attend the national conventions or serve as delegates (the proposals of the Hunt commission, noted above, may change this for the Democrats).

The net effect of these changes has been to separate completely the process of building the coalition needed for nomination from the process of building the coalition needed for governing. In the 1980s presidential nominations are not won by making a series of deals with powerful state and local party leaders and congressmen; indeed, an aspirant is actually handicapped by being known as the bosses' candidate, even though the bosses no longer have power to advance the cause of any candidate. Presidential nominations are instead won by tireless personal campaigning by the candidate in the smaller caucus/ convention and primary states and by elaborate television campaigns in the larger primary states. The winner has little or no contact with his party's leaders in Congress and owes them nothing for his victory. By the same token, they owe him nothing. Accordingly, when a president takes office in the 1980s, he has to build his governing coalition from scratch, for nothing in the way he has won either the nomination

THE PRESIDENT AND HIS PARTY

AVERAGE PRESIDENTIAL SUPPORT SCORES BY PARTY, 1953–1978

Percentage of Roll-Call Votes
Supporting the President's Position

Chamber	Democrats	Republicans
With Democratic presidents in office		
House	69	40
Senate	62	45
With Republican presidents in office		
House	46	64
Senate	44	66

SOURCE: Edwards, *Presidential Influence*, pp. 61-62.

or the election has created a network of mutual obligations with his party's leaders and organizations in Congress and in the states on which he can base his new coalition. Hence his effectiveness as a leader of his fellow party members in Congress depends on their willingness to follow—and that is quite a different matter.

Congressional Following of the President's Lead

Presidential Support Scores. Since the early 1950s the *Congressional Quarterly* has been keeping track of "presidential support" scores expressing the extent to which the various members of Congress have supported the president on those roll-call votes in which he has indicated a clear preference for a particular vote. The average scores from 1953 to 1978 are summarized in table 5–1. They show clearly that each party's members in each house of Congress have supported presidents of their own party about two-thirds of the time and presidents of the opposing party less than half the time.

These data, however, are not conclusive evidence that members of Congress follow their president's lead most of the time, for they might merely indicate that the congressmen are voting their own convictions, which often happen to agree with those of their parties' presidents. Several studies have attempted to overcome this difficulty by seeing whether congressmen's policy stands change noticeably when a president of the opposite party is replaced by one of their own party. They have found that to some degree such changes do take place. For example, about one-fifth of the Republicans in both

144

chambers who had been voting consistently against foreign-aid bills proposed by Democratic presidents shifted to support similar bills when they were proposed by Republican presidents—and about the same proportion of the Democrats in both chambers shifted their votes in the opposite direction. Another study found that Republican congressmen support activist federal domestic policies more often when they are proposed by Republican presidents than when they are proposed by Democratic presidents, while Democratic congressmen's support of such policies remains about the same regardless of whether the president is a Democrat or a Republican.[12]

Presidential Party Leadership in Competition with Other Factors in Congressional Voting. Students of Congress generally agree that a number of factors influence congressional voting. One is the congressman's own convictions. Another is his perceptions of the needs of his constituency and the views of his constituents. And a third, often overlooked but still of considerable importance, is his identification with his party and his desire to support it whenever he can. As Randall Ripley says of members of the House:

> Most members . . . think of party before they think of anything else, particularly at the stage of voting on the floor. Even if a member often votes against his party, he is still concerned with retaining the good will of the leaders and members. His friends are likely to be in his own party, and he knows that he can jeopardize his standing with some of them unless he is willing to stretch a point and occasionally help the party, even though he may feel somewhat differently about the issue. Only a handful act almost independently of party. Their friends are few—usually other mavericks. . . . What the leaders do, in a variety of ways, is to appeal both to the sense of solidarity that the member is likely to feel with his party and to the fear of possible ostracism, which means the immediate loss of psychological preferment and a possible future loss of tangible preferment.[13]

Ripley is speaking here of the party leaders in the House—the Speaker, the floor leader, and the whip. Where does the president come in? The answer is that by far the most effective way for the president to appeal to his fellow partisans in Congress is to enlist the help of his party's leaders in each chamber to appeal to their followers. A direct presidential appeal to members over their leaders' heads is not only likely to fail; it is likely to stir up resentment in both the leaders and the rank and file, which will make it more difficult for the

145

president to get what he wants next time. In short, while a presidential candidate may find it useful, even necessary, to campaign for his own nomination and election with frequent attacks on "the Washington establishment, he cannot make much use of his party leadership" in Congress unless he works with and through his party's congressional establishment.

It is not difficult to do, especially in the House. As Ripley points out:

> Since the beginning of Franklin Roosevelt's administration, the House leaders of the President's party have, in effect, acted as lieutenants of the President, accepting virtually his whole legislative package and working for its adoption. . . . It is now assumed that if the President proposes a bill, they will support it.[14]

This is considerably less true for some committee and subcommittee chairmen in the House than for the floor leaders and whips and somewhat less true for the Senate than for the House, but in both chambers the leaders of the president's party start from a strong desire to work with him.

There are several reasons for that desire. We have already noted that, despite the often-mentioned weakness of their party ties, most congressmen still have a lively sense of belonging to one or the other of two great competing teams, and their team loyalty impels most of them to vote as a president of their party asks, except where such a vote would clearly go against what they perceive to be their constituents' interests or wishes. The leaders of the president's party in Congress not only have these same team loyalties but, as leaders of the congressional part of the team, also have a considerable stake in moving the president's program along as swiftly and smoothly as possible. Professionally speaking, his legislative success is their success, and poor relations and meager results may harm their reputations as much as they harm the president's or more.

The main instruments for cooperation between the two branches of the president's party are communication and consultation. Since the late 1950s every president has held regular meetings with his party's congressional leaders (and less regular but frequent meetings with the leaders of the opposing party). The meetings usually take place once a week over breakfast at the White House,[15] and the agenda usually has several items: the president tells the congressional leaders what new pieces of legislation he plans to send to the Hill and when and how he feels about the progress of the legislation he has already sent. Sometimes he even asks their advice about legislation he is considering for the future.[16] The congressional leaders, in turn, tell the president what is happening to his legislation, why, and how he might help it along.

Like any institutional arrangement conducted by human beings, these meetings depend for their success to a great degree upon the meshing of the experience, skills, and personalities of the people involved. Most observers believe that Lyndon Johnson and Gerald Ford, for example, had excellent relations with the congressional leaders of their parties, in part because they themselves had been such leaders before they became president (Johnson as Senate majority leader and Ford as House minority leader); both of them understood the ways of Congress, enjoyed the company of congressmen, and got on well with the leaders of Congress after they became president. In contrast, John Kennedy and Richard Nixon, although they had been congressmen and senators, had never held leadership positions in Congress. Moreover, neither had particularly enjoyed the congressional life, and neither was a particularly prominent member of his congressional party. As presidents, their relations with their parties' congressional leaders were markedly less warm and successful than those of Johnson and Ford. Franklin Roosevelt had never served in Congress, but he understood and liked congressmen; his relations with the Democratic congressional leaders were excellent. Dwight Eisenhower was much more of a stranger to the ways of Congress, and his relations with congressional Republican leaders, especially Senator William Knowland, were never better than correct.[17] Jimmy Carter came to the presidency with no previous congressional experience—indeed, with no Washington experience of any kind. Moreover, according to one of his chief speech writers,

> his skin crawled at the thought of the time-consuming consultations and persuasion that might be required to bring a legislator around. He did not know how congressmen talked, worked, and thought, how to pressure them without being a bully or flatter them without seeming a fool. He needed help from someone who knew all those things, who had spent time absorbing that culture. But for his congressional liaison he chose a Georgian named Frank Moore, a man whose general aptitude was difficult for anyone outside the first circle to detect, and who had barely laid eyes upon the Capitol before Inauguration Day.[18]

Ronald Reagan and Jimmy Carter are the only two presidents in the twentieth century to take office with no previous Washington experience whatever. But Reagan, unlike Carter, began with a special effort to cultivate good relations with congressmen in general and

Republican congressional leaders in particular. He visited the Hill right after his election and several times in his first months in office. He resisted all efforts of his more conservative advisers to persuade him to oppose the reelection of the moderate Howard Baker as Senate Republican leader; indeed, he persuaded his closest friend on the Hill, Senator Paul Laxalt (Republican, Nevada), to nominate Baker for reelection. He appointed as head of his congressional liaison office Max Friedersdorf, who had served on the Nixon and Ford liaison staffs and was well known and liked by congressmen of both parties in both houses. As a result, there was general agreement that in the early days of his administration Reagan's relations with the Republican leaders in Congress were much better than Carter's had been with the Democratic leaders during his term of office.[19]

No matter how well or how badly one or another has managed it, however, every president since Franklin Roosevelt has used regular meetings with—and occasional advice from—his party's congressional leaders as one of his more important instruments for persuading Congress to enact his legislative program.

How Partisan Are American Presidents?

Some Rankings. Let us imagine a presidential partisanship scale. At one extreme (let us set it, as it should be set in all good scales, at 100) is the most partisan president we can imagine: one who has been active in party affairs at all levels for many years; who both says and believes that all wisdom and most patriotism reside in his party; who believes that any candidate of his party for any office should be elected over any candidate of the opposition party, and who regularly and intensively campaigns for his party's ticket from top to bottom; who takes a strong and active interest in his national committee's activities, insists that it be well led, well staffed, and well financed; who makes past party service and party loyalty prime criteria in making all his major and minor appointments; who works closely with his party's leaders in Congress in developing his programs and considers the party one of his most important instruments of leadership; and who places high priority on leaving his party in the best possible condition to win elections after he has left the White House.

At the other extreme (let us score it 0) is the least partisan president we can imagine: one whose acceptance of a party's nomination is his first official association with it; who campaigns strictly for himself and his policies and never mentions his party or its other candidates; who has no interest in his party's national committee or other organizational affairs except when they threaten to cause him embarrassment; who treats with the leaders and members of Congress entirely on a nonpartisan basis and never makes any special appeals to his nominal fellow partisans or does special favors for them; who pays no attention whatever to partisan affiliation in making his appointments; and who has no concern whatever for the state of his party after he has left office.

In my highly subjective judgment, the only presidents in the twentieth century who would score close to 50 on such a scale would be Woodrow Wilson and Franklin D. Roosevelt, with Wilson ranking a notch above Roosevelt. (A few early signs suggest that Ronald Reagan may rank among the high-partisanship presidents, but at the present writing it is too early to say so with confidence.) Ranking the lowest would probably be Warren Harding, Calvin Coolidge, Herbert Hoover, and Jimmy Carter. And the average score for all fifteen twentieth-century presidents would be, say, 33.3.[20]

Why Are American Presidents So Unpartisan? Such an average score would surely be far lower than any we would assign to the head of government in any other modern democratic country. Why is it so low for American presidents? No doubt there are too many reasons to be covered in detail here, but let me briefly outline a few of the most important.

Weak congressional parties. Most of the time, especially in the twentieth century, American political parties have been too weak and uncohesive to constitute an agency capable of providing a president with the votes he needs to get his programs adopted. He can and often does work closely with his party leaders in both chambers, as we have seen; but their powers over their rank and file are those of scheduling the business and trying to persuade the members to support the president. They certainly do not include any power to order the members to get behind the president or to expel them if they oppose him. Given the parties' weakness, what is remarkable about the fact that the president usually gets the support of about two-thirds of his congressional party is that he gets so much, not that he gets so little.

The need for support from the opposition party. Given that on almost any issue before Congress a president will lose from a quarter to more than half of his own party, there are very few issues on which he will not need at least some support from members of the opposition party, and not infrequently he will need quite substantial support from them. Such support has, of course, been crucial for all Republican presidents since Herbert Hoover; for in the total of twenty years in which they held office from 1929 to 1977, in only four years (1929–1931 and 1953–1955) did any of them enjoy a Congress with Republican majorities in both houses. (Ronald Reagan, dealing with a Republican senate and a Democratic house, was better off than most Republican presidents.) Democratic presidents have been much better situated in this regard; even so, in order to get most of the important parts of their programs through Congress, most of them have needed at least some Republican votes to make up for defecting Democrats. Hence no president has felt that he could afford to be so completely partisan in word and deed that he would offend all the members of the opposition party so much that they would never support him on anything.

The increasing irrelevance of party to presidential politics. We noted earlier that party organizations and leaders at all levels have been largely stripped of their once-considerable power to select national convention delegates and deliver them to one candidate or another. Hence no presidential aspirant today bothers much with the party organizations in his drive for the nomination; indeed it may be most effective, as it certainly was for Jimmy Carter in 1974–1976, to run for the nomination as the candidate who is not in any way involved with or supported by the "party bosses."

The increasing antiparty tone of American political culture. I have argued elsewhere that from the nation's beginnings most ordinary Americans have had a poor opinion of political parties in general, as institutions—though most of them have most of the time "identified" with one party over the other.[21] Since the mid-1960s, however, even these party identifications have weakened substantially; there are more independents now than there have been for a long time, and party has a worse name than ever.[22] Most Americans evidently want to weaken parties still further, not strengthen them.[23]

The antipolitician bias of network television. These traditionally strong antiparty strains in American political culture have been considerably reinforced in recent years by the manner in which the television networks have portrayed American politics. In America, as in all other modern democratic countries, most people get most of their information about politics from television; but, unlike many other democracies, America has no party-controlled broadcasts, except for a few thirty-second "commercials" shown in election years. Hence most broadcasting about politics emanates from the local stations' news programs, the three national commercial networks' news programs, and an occasional longer documentary on a particular issue or person. For a variety of reasons—including the nonparty backgrounds and attitudes of most correspondents and producers and the antiestablishment, adversary posture of the broadcasting profession—political parties do not fare well in these broadcasts. Being collectivities, they are much harder to portray in dramatic pictures than personalities. Being such ancient features of the political landscape (the Republicans go back to 1854 and the Democrats to 1792), they are not novel or exciting in the way that a new issue or a new personality is. Worst of all, they are composed entirely of politicians, and everyone—certainly every network correspondent—is sure that politicians are by nature tricky, deceitful, and often dishonest characters who do what they do entirely because they want to be reelected, not because they have any sincere concern for the public interest.[24]

The President's Objectives. For all these reasons, any president is likely to pay a considerable price for appearing to be a strong party man. If he acts—or is portrayed—too much as Mr. Democrat or Mr. Republican, he is almost certain to lose some of the support from the opposition party that he needs in Congress. He will also present a very large target for the networks' tireless snipers. Worst of all, he will deeply offend a good many ordinary people who believe he should be "president of all the people," not an all-out leader of some gang of self-seeking politicians.

If the president were to set as one of his prime objectives strengthening his party organizationally, financially, and in public esteem so that it would go on to even greater success after he had left office, then these prices might be well worth paying. But most presidents give the highest priority to making a presidential record that will secure them a high position in history; and being a strong partisan and strong leader of a party has struck most presidents in this century as a poor way of winning good notices from contemporary or future historians.

There is no reason to suppose that Ronald Reagan and his successors will see things differently.

Notes

1. *Constitutional Government in the United States* (New York: Columbia University Press, 1908), pp. 67-69.

2. *Oxford English Dictionary*, vol. 1, compact ed. (London: Oxford University Press, 1971), p. 1589.

3. Cf. Cornelius P. Cotter and John F. Bibby, "Institutional Development of Parties and the Thesis of Party Decline," *Political Science Quarterly*, vol. 95 (Spring 1980), pp. 1-27.

4. Rule 25, paragraph (b), *Rules Adopted by the 1980 Republican National Convention* (Washington, D.C.: Republican National Committee, 1980), p. 10, italics added.

5. For a brief account of the few efforts by presidents to support or oppose the nomination of particular candidates in 1910, 1918, 1930, 1946, and 1980—and especially for Franklin Roosevelt's failure to "purge" anti–New Deal Democratic congressmen in the 1938 primaries—see Austin Ranney and Willmoore Kendall, *Democracy and the American Party System* (Westport, Conn.: Greenwood Press, Publishers, 1956, reprinted in 1974), pp. 286-98.

6. For a more complete discussion of how the new presidential nominating process has substantially reduced the role of congressmen, see Jeane J. Kirkpatrick, Michael J. Malbin, Thomas E. Mann, Howard R. Penniman, and Austin Ranney, *The Presidential Nominating Process: Can It Be Improved?* (Washington, D.C.: American Enterprise Institute, 1980).

7. Richard E. Neustadt, *Presidential Power* (New York: John Wiley Sons, 1960), pp. 33-34.

8. For a useful summary of the studies on and current skepticism about the "coattail effect," see George C. Edwards III, *Presidential Influence in Congress* (San Francisco: W. H. Freeman and Company, 1980), pp. 70-78.

9. For a brief description of the nature and role of the office of leader of the opposition, see Anthony H. Birch, *The British System of Government*, 4th ed. (London: George Allen & Unwin, 1980), pp. 157-61.

10. A venerable variation on this theme is that he is more accurately called the out-party's "hind-titular leader."

11. For more detailed discussions of this point, see Cornelius P. Cotter and Bernard C. Hennessy, *Politics Without Power: The National Party Committees* (New York: Atherton Press, 1964), especially pp. 94-105; and Frank J. Sorauf, *Party Politics in America*, 3d ed. (Boston: Little, Brown and Company, 1976), pp. 127-31.

12. The findings of the various studies are summarized in more detail in Edwards, *Presidential Influence*, pp. 61-66.

13. Randall B. Ripley, *Party Leaders in the House of Representatives* (Washington, D.C.: Brookings Institution, 1967), pp. 158-59. John Kingdon is probably correct in arguing that the party tie is less important to congressmen today than it was when Ripley wrote his book in the 1960s: *Congressmen's Voting Decisions* (New York: Harper and Row, 1973). Nevertheless, it remains one of the most important forces affecting most congressmen's votes.

14. Ripley, *Party Leaders*, p. 3.

15. This can have its problems. At the very first meeting between Jimmy Carter and the Democratic congressional leaders in 1977, for example, only coffee and rolls were served. Speaker Thomas "Tip" O'Neill complained about the poor treatment, and at the next meeting a full breakfast was served—but each congressman was billed for the full cost of his

breakfast. That touched off another round of complaints, and finally the White House decided that good congressional relations justified paying for a few breakfasts. Some of the people involved, however, still mention the episode as a typical example of Carter's ineptness in dealing with Congress.

16. If the president consistently fails to ask for congressional advice on legislation in its formative stage, his relations with the congressional leaders will soon sour. Just three months after he had taken office in 1977, for example, Jimmy Carter presented to Congress his mammoth and complex energy program. Right from the start many congressional Democrats strongly objected to the fact that the program had been prepared in secret by presidential adviser James Schlesinger (later secretary of energy) and other White House aides without asking any advice from congressional leaders or giving them any information. It took over two years for Congress to enact the full program (much of it in substantially altered form), and many observers felt that Carter's failure to keep congressional leaders informed while the program was being developed had a good deal to do with its subsequent tortuous passage through Congress.

17. Cf. the evaluations of various presidents' congressional relations in Randall B. Ripley, *Congress: Process and Policy*, 2d ed. (New York: W. W. Norton and Company, 1978), pp. 297-98.

18. James Fallows, "The Passionless Presidency," *Atlantic* (May 1979), pp. 33-46, at p. 41.

19. Cf. Dick Kirschten, "The Pennsylvania Avenue Connection—Making Peace on Capitol Hill," *National Journal*, March 7, 1981, pp. 384-87.

20. For somewhat similar rankings using somewhat similar criteria, see Ripley, *Congress*, pp. 308-23.

21. Cf. Austin Ranney, *Curing the Mischiefs of Faction: Party Reform in America* (Berkeley: University of California Press, 1975), chap. 2.

22. In 1964, for example, a Gallup poll reported that 49 percent of the people called themselves Democrats, 27 percent Republicans, and 24 percent independents. In 1980 Gallup reported 47 percent Democrats, 32 percent independents, and 21 percent Republicans.

23. In 1980 a Gallup poll reported 66 percent of the people in favor of abolishing the national party conventions entirely and replacing them with a one-day national primary; 24 percent opposed the idea, and 10 percent were undecided.

24. The most careful and convincing analysis of network television's antipolitician bias is Edward Jay Epstein, *News from Nowhere* (New York: Random House, Vintage Books, 1974).

6

Politics through Law:
Congressional Limitations on
Executive Discretion

ALLEN SCHICK

Ronald Reagan launched his presidency more encumbered by legal constraints than was Jimmy Carter. Carter was more limited by law than was Gerald Ford. Ford was more limited than was Richard Nixon. The 1970s was a boom period for the enactment of limitations on executive power. The most prominent limitations were the War Powers Resolution (1973), which sought to restrict the president's authority to commit U.S. forces abroad, and the Congressional Budget and Impoundment Control Act (1974), which circumscribed the president's power to withhold appropriated funds from expenditure. During the decade, Congress enacted more than a hundred legislative vetoes—provisions of law enabling it, the House or the Senate, or designated committees to block certain executive actions. Congress turned increasingly to temporary (annual or multi-year) authorizations, which subjected many federal agencies and programs to recurring legislative scrutiny and gave Congress fresh opportunities to curb executive discretion. Congress also wrote numerous limitations into appropriations measures, a practice spurred by increases in floor amendments and roll-call votes. The president's power of appointment was constrained by subjecting some positions (such as the director of the Office of Management and Budget) to Senate confirmation and placing others (such as a special prosecutor) beyond the president's reach. The march of restriction also affected executive procedure as Congress prescribed sunshine rules and freedom of information standards for federal agencies.

Congress did more than merely legislate new restrictions; it also established procedures to monitor or to enforce executive compliance. As might be expected, the potency of these procedures was uneven,

154

ranging from recourse to the courts in some areas to simple reporting requirements in others. But armies of congressional aides on the staffs of members or committees, plus thousands more working for congressional support agencies, kept watch over executive actions. In some instances, Congress assigned enforcement responsibilities to legislative officials. Thus, the Impoundment Control Act directed the comptroller general to notify Congress of presidential failures to report impoundments, to revise the classification of reported impoundments, and to sue for the release of impounded funds. The General Accounting Office broadened its review of agency activities during the 1970s, and it became more active and aggressive as an investigatory arm of Congress.[1] In an extraordinary effort to enforce its will, Congress in 1979 (through Public Law 96-151) directed the Veterans Administration to study the health effects of certain chemicals on Vietnam veterans in accord with a protocol approved by the director of the Office of Technology Assessment.

The enactment of statutory limitations rarely ends ambiguity over the respective powers of the legislative and executive branches. Only if one of the branches were completely vanquished could the boundaries be demarcated clearly and finally. The constitutional structure of the United States bars this outcome and requires instead that the relationship be governed by political considerations. Without denying the legal effect of congressional limitations on executive power, these actions represent efforts by Congress to bolster its political strength in relation to the executive branch. The political terms of accommodation between the two branches can be affected by statutory restrictions levied by one on the other. Legal curbs in an environment where power is both separated and shared should be seen as the conduct of politics by other means—not as an end to bickering between the two rivals but as a potential for change in the balance of power. To the extent that political conditions change, so too will the practical effect of many of the legal restrictions. If the 1980s turns out to be a different decade politically from the 1970s, then the riders, veto powers, limitations, and other curbs still on the books will operate quite differently from the way they did when first enacted.

This political relationship is not simply a two-sided affair; it involves not only Congress and the president but executive agencies as well. In fact, few of the restrictions enacted by Congress have been directly imposed on the president or his office. Most of the legislative vetoes, appropriations limitations, and authorizations enacted by Congress deal with specific programs or agencies. It would be erroneous to assume that presidential and agency interests always converge or that Congress intends to restrict the president when it limits a particular agency or activity. Nevertheless, there is an affinity in the way Congress relates to the White House and to federal agencies. In the 1970s, Congress generally acted similarly toward the president and executive agencies; it tried to restrict both. Moreover, as chief executive, the president serves as the principal guardian of executive branch prerogatives, and he cannot be indifferent to limitations imposed on particular agencies. Although targeted against a particular agency, a legal restriction can weaken the president's executive authority and invite further congressional encroachment. Jimmy Carter recognized that the status of his office was intertwined with that of executive agencies when he tried to block the 1979 legislation that gave director of the Office of Technology Assessment (a congressional officer) a veto over the study by the Veterans Administration of chemicals used in the Vietnam War. This chapter recognizes the linkage of presidential and executive power, but it should not be assumed that every statutory constraint impairs the president's freedom to act.

Legislature versus Executive

Because they came after almost half a century of presidential imperium, the limitations enacted in the 1970s can easily be seen as trespasses on the legitimate power of the executive. But from the perspective of American history, the contemporary striving of Congress for control is only the latest chapter in a 200-year contest for supremacy in the national government. Congress once was actively involved in the execution of national policy, and its role was regarded as legitimate.

The relationship between the two branches was inaugurated under the influence of executive power. The Federalists wanted a national government that "left substantial freedom of action to high officials and kept Congress out of most administrative details."[2] With the Federalists in charge, the First Congress established executive departments under broad enabling statutes, leaving the implementing details to executive discretion. Congress willingly entrusted "the great bulk of administrative authority in the President . . . by placing him in a position to direct the affairs of every subordinate officer."[3] Furthermore, under Alexander Hamilton's influence, Congress made appropriations in broad categories, allowing the new departments wide latitude in the expenditure of funds. Hamilton vigorously lobbied for the passage of legislation he had prepared, and the House became so compliant to his demands that it operated without a Committee on Ways and Means. The young executive branch soon paid a high price for Hamilton's overreaching as Congress became more vigilant in guarding its independence and initiative in legislation.

The Jeffersonians who came to power in 1800 were, as Leonard White's administrative history shows, "more energetic in their effort to control administration than had been their predecessors. . . . They emphasized the responsibility of the executive branch and the administrative system to Congress."[4] His presidential office notwithstanding, Thomas Jefferson advocated tight legislative control over public funds. He urged that appropriations be made in specific sums to "every purpose susceptible of definition," and that Congress disallow transfers of money "varying from the appropriation in object or transcending it in amount." Jefferson also asked that contingent funds be reduced, "thereby circumscribing discretionary power over money."[5] This restrictive policy drew a sharp protest from Hamilton who (in his Julius Crassus letters) warned that "the business of government would be stagnated by the injudicious and absurd impediments of an overdriven caution."[6]

Line-item versus lump-sum appropriations was but one of the issues that vexed legislative–executive relations in the nineteenth century. Conflict also raged over congressional involvement in executive appointments, legislative investigations, and the specificity of legislation. These early conflicts set a pattern that has generally continued to the present. The executive seeks broad discretion; Congress seeks to control the particulars. The relationship tends to run in cycles. The president and other executive officials try to stretch the authority given them by Congress more broadly than might have been intended. Congress responds by narrowing executive discretion. But the new restrictions hobble executive performance and lead to demands for relaxation. When Congress limits, it usually does so piecemeal, by restricting particular activities rather than by writing general rules.

Congress was the dominant branch through most of the nineteenth century (wartime was the main exception) as its increasingly powerful and specialized committees imposed their preferences on the White House and executive agencies. In those years, Congress initiated and drafted most legislation—the president's role as "chief legislator" was not fully developed until the New Deal—and it often legislated in very great detail. Individual positions and their salaries were itemized in law; post roads were plotted by Congress; tariff schedules were enacted for hundreds of imported goods; pensions were voted for designated soldiers and their survivors. In the context of contemporary legislation, it is hard to imagine the extent to which Congress got involved in administrative matters; it would be a worthwhile exercise to read the laws enacted a century ago to get a sense of the role Congress once played. Congress could penetrate at will to the smallest administrative detail, giving the affected agency no course other than to follow its dictates. These legislative practices alarmed a young scholar—Woodrow Wilson—who in his influential 1885 book, *Congressional Government*, charged that Congress "has entered more and more into the details of administration until it has virtually taken into its own hands all the substantial powers of government."[7]

For almost a century, Wilson's phrase—"the details of administration"—has been used against Congress in order to place administrative matters off limits. As formulated by generations of public administrators and other reformers, it has meant that Congress should confine itself to making policy while entrusting all of the particulars to those who execute the laws. In practice, it has impelled and legitimized the withdrawal of Congress from numerous areas in which it was once involved. Nevertheless, Congress has realized that the essence of law lies in its implementation, and it has been reluctant to allow federal executives a free rein.

Congress has not, however, always felt that it has a real choice in the matter. Government expansion and the emergence of the United States as a world power bolstered the executive's claim of independence from detailed control and weakened the ability of Congress to control the executive by legislating the details. Perhaps the most decisive factor in the loosening of legislative constraints was the growth of the national government and its administrative structure. Civilian employment doubled from 50,000 to 100,000 in the 1870s and increased to more than 550,000 by the 1920s. During that half century, federal expenditures soared from less than $300 million to more than $3 billion.[8] As the number of expense items grew, the individual line items receded in importance; as the number of administrative appointments increased, congressional involvement diminished; as international trade expanded, it became steadily more difficult to decide all tariff rates in law; as the number of pensioners and their claims multiplied, Congress sought relief from pressure for special acts.

Congress justified its retreat from administration as necessary for improving the efficiency of the public service.[9] Congress could not satisfy this objective by dictating precisely how administrative activities were to be carried out or by getting involved in implementing details. So Congress decided to delegate more and to limit less. But this arrangement was not satisfactory to Congress, which viewed federal agencies as spendthrifts that consumed all of their appropriation before the fiscal year was over and then coerced it to make up the deficiency. If Congress could not control agencies by legislating restrictively, neither did it believe that it could solve the problem merely by unshackling them. As agencies and their budgets expanded, Congress became convinced that new controls were needed.

Congress's solution has had profound consequences for executive–legislative relations and for presidential power. Congress in effect empowered the president to act as its agent of control. This critical step was taken in the Budget and Accounting Act of 1921. President William Howard Taft had called for a national budget in 1912, but Congress rebuffed his initiative and insisted on the usual estimates from federal agencies. World War I, however, brought sharp increases in federal spending (from $700 million in 1916 to $18 billion three years later) and convinced Congress that a presidential budget was necessary to control federal spending. After the war, without prodding from the White House, Congress willingly turned the financial controls over to the president.

The Budget and Accounting Act sought to control federal agencies by barring them from going directly to Congress with requests for funds. Instead, they were required to prepare estimates for the president, who would submit a comprehensive budget to Congress. In retrospect, it is apparent that the budget process broadened the president's power at the expense of Congress, but at the outset the budget operated as an effective instrument of legislative control. In accord with congressional objectives, federal taxes, outlays, and the public debt were all reduced during the first decade of presidential budgeting. That these reductions were achieved by the vigorous intervention of the president's new Budget Bureau into agency operations did not disturb Congress. The budget had been brought under control, and Congress had good reason to believe that, through presidential action, its own power had been strengthened.

This approach was fully in accord with canons of public administration that advocated the concentration of administrative responsibility in the chief executive; only the chief executive could be responsible for the government as a whole. Only he, therefore, could prepare a budget covering all the activities of government. But while subscribing to this conception of public administration, Congress (and most American legislatures) refused to adopt arrangements that would have explicitly curtailed its powers. Thus, Congress did not adopt the proposal that it bar itself from appropriating more than the amounts recommended in the president's budget.

The president willingly served Congress because his interests were closer to those of the legislative branch than to those of the executive agencies. No less than Congress, the White House felt helpless in the face of agency expansion. With hardly any staff of their own, presidents in the nineteenth and early twentieth centuries were unable to direct the growth of government. Expenditures seemed as much out of control to occupants of the White House as they did to members of Congress. By taking command of the budget, presidents in the 1920s served their own interests as well as those of Congress.

The New Deal and World War II changed the relationship between the executive and legislative branches and made the president chief executive in his own right, not merely as the agent of Congress. These critical events fueled an enormous expansion of the federal government and a redistribution of power between the two branches. From the New Deal to World War II, the number of federal employees doubled, while expenditures (which had stabilized in the $3 billion range throughout the 1920s) tripled. The war brought steeper increases, as 2 million people were added to the employment rolls and $90 billion to federal expenditures.

Even before the war, Franklin Roosevelt realized that an enlarged federal government was likely to be a permanent condition, not an interim measure until economic normalcy returned. He therefore moved to equip the presidential office with the resources and capacity to formulate and to execute national policy. Through his Committee on Administrative Management, chaired by Louis Brownlow, Roosevelt institutionalized presidential leadership of the executive branch and in the process gained for his office dominion over Congress as well. The conversion of the budget from a financial-control process into a presidential policy-making tool illustrates the manner in which the White House took command of the national government.

A staff report prepared for the Brownlow committee in 1937 conceived of the budget as a means of handling public funds, and it therefore recommended that the Bureau of the Budget remain in the Treasury Department (where it had been placed by the 1921 act) and be closely linked to the Treasury's other financial responsibilities.[10] But this arrangement would not have achieved the Brownlow committee's main objective, to strengthen the president's control of the government. The committee opted instead for the Budget Bureau to become "the right arm of the President for the central fiscal management of the vast administrative machine."[11] It urged that the bureau's staff be expanded (it numbered only about forty-five at the time) "to aid the President in the exercise of overall control."[12] In a recommendation expressly designed to broaden the president's legislative power, it advocated that the bureau's clearance process "be applied to all legislation proposed by the executive departments and agencies and should not be limited to fiscal considerations."[13]

The Brownlow committee succeeded in augmenting the president's budget powers. The Budget Bureau, with a tenfold increase in staff, became the principal agency in the new Executive Office of the President. The budget became a statement of presidential policy (including legislative proposals), and the clearance process was extended to ensure that agency submissions to Congress were in accord with the president's program.

The president gained more than the institutional wherewithal to conduct the business of government; no longer was presidential leadership seen as a usurpation of congressional power but as an appropriate and expected role. The "textbook presidency" (in Thomas E. Cronin's apt phrase) became the embodiment of national political leadership and benevolence. In the international sphere, congressional assertiveness was subdued by hot and cold wars and by the spell of bipartisanship. Checks and balances were weakened by pervasive confidence that executive power would be beneficently applied in the national interest. Congress embraced the view that it should follow the president's lead and not meddle in foreign affairs. Because of its protracted duration, the cold war ensured that presidential dominance would not subside even though the shooting had stopped. From the Truman Doctrine in the 1940s through the Gulf of Tonkin resolution in the 1960s, Congress followed the president's lead in the international arena. At the command of the White House, it produced "blank-check" resolutions authorizing presidential actions in the name of the national interest.

Congressional initiative also withered in the domestic sphere. The New Deal spawned the expectation that government would provide tangible benefits for the people. Interest groups lobbied Congress to grant agencies discretion to perform public good in their behalf, and they often received a favorable hearing from legislative committees. As massive federal bureaucracies dispensed benefits to their clients, Congress was compelled to give them a clear field to do their job. Legislative controls would have been costly hindrances to the work of these agencies.

General Rules and Administrative Discretion

When Congress controls, it legislates the particulars; when Congress withdraws, it legislates in general terms. Before the Classification Act of 1923, Congress appropriated funds for designated positions and specified in law the salary for each. The Classification Act authorized the Personnel Classification Board to make all necessary rules and regulations . . . [and provide] such title and definitions as it may deem necessary according to the kind and difficulty of the work."[14] The change in legislative practice was swift and dramatic. The fiscal 1922 appropriation for the Office of the Commissioner of Internal Revenue listed the salaries of 527 officers and employees. It provided, for example, $900 each for 50 mail messengers, $840 each for 48 messengers, and $720 each for 21 assistant messengers. The fiscal 1926 appropriation for the same office provided a lump sum of $810,000 for "personal services in accordance with the Classification Act of 1923."

More dramatic yet was the withdrawal of Congress from tariff setting, an activity that had roiled it for more than a century. The ill-fated Smoot-Hawley Act of 1930 covered 170 pages in the *Statutes;* the Reciprocal Trade Agreements Act of 1934, authorizing the president to reduce tariffs as "required or appropriate to carry out any foreign trade agreement that the president has entered into," took up only two pages.[15]

By what authority does Congress transfer its vast legislative power to executive hands? When Congress withdraws, what remains of its legislative power? These are legal questions, but the answers, even when they are wrapped in the mythology of constitutional interpretation, are political. Congressional withdrawal is a fact against which no legal reasoning can prevail. The facts speak for themselves, and ultimately the courts speak for the facts.

"That the legislative power of Congress cannot be delegated is, of course, clear," the Supreme Court declared in a 1932 case upholding the delegation at issue.[16] The legal gymnastics required to reach these contradictory conclusions are not at all complicated. Since Congress may not delegate its legislative power, it does not delegate when it empowers executive officials to make policy; it simply lets them "fill up the details."[17] In this way, the courts preserve the doctrine of nondelegability while political realities are accommodated.

It was but a short step from the legal argument that Congress *may* let others handle the details to the political argument that Congress *should* assign the details to administrators. Thus, only eight years after barring delegation, the Supreme Court held that "delegation by Congress has long been recognized as necessary in order that the exertion of legislative power does not become a futility."[18] This line of reasoning has been embraced by Congress. Legislative debate on the 1934 reciprocal trade bill revealed that the belief was widespread that Congress does more damage by legislating the details than by ceding authority over them to administrators. Representative John Martin spoke for the majority when he pleaded that "Congress, overwhelmed as it is . . . could no longer deal with the vast intricacies and complexities of tariff legislation." But this was not an isolated case:

> And what is true of the tariff is true of transportation, communication, of the banking and monetary systems, of internal revenue, of internal improvements, of the entire recovery program, and of every major national policy. The utmost that the Congress can do, and do intelligently, is to lay down policies and define limits, and it is difficult even to find time to do this.[19]

The solution suggested by Martin was one already endorsed by the courts. "Congress cannot delegate any part of its legislative power," read a 1931 Supreme Court decision, "except under a limitation of a prescribed standard."[20] But the courts and Congress have been willing to accept any legislative statement as sufficient constraint on executive discretion. The standards set by Congress can be as broad and vague as "just and reasonable," "excessive profits," or "public interest, convenience or necessity," and the courts will uphold them.[21]

In recognition of the vagueness of substantive standards, Congress and the courts sought procedural safeguards for the exercise of delegated power. The 1934 reciprocal trade legislation, for example, required the president to "provide reasonable public notice" and to consult with various federal agencies before concluding a trade agreement with another country. Over the years, Congress has standardized procedural requirements in legislation such as the Federal Register Act (1935), the Administrative Procedure Act (1946), and the Federal Advisory Committee Act (1972). A leading treatise on constitutional law concludes that "the Court does not really require much in the way of standards from Congress. . . . It may well be, then, . . . that the requirement of legislative standards is being shifted to a requirement of administrative standards and safeguards."[22]

Due process, however, was a poor substitute for substantive legislation. Reliance on a procedural test encouraged further legislative withdrawal from the administrative sphere and legitimized loose and overly broad legislation.[23] Moreover, a due-process standard excluded Congress from participation in the making of policy. Congressional committees and members could participate in administrative proceedings without impairing the procedural rights to which other parties were entitled. Thus, Congress removed itself from the policy-making process when it abandoned substantive standards in favor of procedural ones. As we shall see below, devices such as the legislative veto are attempts by Congress to reclaim a role in the administrative process.

Legislative Oversight: Evaluation or Control?

When courts rule on legislative delegation, they examine the issue from the perspective of the government agency exercising power. Their central concern is whether the agency exceeded its authority, not whether Congress relinquished its own. What does Congress retain when it delegates? The standard answer is that Congress is responsible for overseeing the performance of executive agencies. For almost a century, legislative oversight has been promoted as the means by which Congress can ensure that executive power is wielded properly and in accord with legislative expectations. Although legislative oversight first appeared as a justification for broad delegation, in recent times it has been embraced by Congress as a means by which it can regain its lost powers.

A consideration of legislative oversight is hobbled by disagreement over its meaning. Joseph Harris limits it to "review after the fact"; Morris Ogul includes any legislative behavior "which results in an impact, intended or not, on bureaucratic behavior." Joel Aberbach takes a middle course, defining oversight "as congressional review of the actions of the federal departments, agencies, and commissions and of the programs and policies they administer."[24] The problem in definition arises out of a fundamental change in the purpose of oversight. Where it was once conceived as a substitute for congressional intervention in administrative matters, oversight has become a powerful form of intervention. Harris's definition reflects the traditional view of oversight in which legislators examine the performance of administrators after they are done. Ogul takes a contemporary view in which Congress is actively involved during the execution of policy.

Woodrow Wilson, one of the first to use the term, saw oversight as a counter to excessively detailed legislation. "There is no similar legislature in business," he argued in *Congressional Government*, "which is so shut up to the one business of lawmaking as is our Congress."[25] In terms of administrative freedom to act, oversight had a critical advantage over legislation: law constrains administrative discretion in advance, oversight allows it full scope, subject to later legislative review. Oversight legitimates administrative discretion by making administrators accountable to legislative authority.

Later formulations made it clear that Congress should intervene less and oversee more. While acknowledging that "the need for such oversight increases with executive initiatives in policy and the delegation of discretion under the broad terms of statutes," Arthur Macmahon in an influential article complained that "Congress seeks in sundry ways to claim what it gave; it asserts the right of continuous intervention."[26] The trade-off between oversight and legislative intervention was made explicit by Samuel Huntington, who argued that acceptance by Congress

> of the idea that legislation was not its primary function would, in large part, simply be recognition of the direction which change has already been taking. It would legitimize and expand the functions of constituent service and administrative oversight which, in practice, already constitute the principal work of most congressmen.[27]

Congress has been willing to make oversight one of its activities, but not at the expense of its law-making role. The Legislative Reorganization Act of 1946 charged each standing committee "to exercise continuous watchfulness of the execution by the administrative agencies concerned of any laws, the subject matter of which is within the jurisdiction of such committee."[28] In 1970, Congress recast oversight into a form of program review and directed most committees to submit biennial reports on their review activities. Four years later, the House provided for the establishment of oversight subcommittees and ordered its committees to prepare oversight plans at the start of each Congress.[29]

As measured by the number of hearings, investigations, and other review activities, Congress conducted much more oversight in the 1970s than it had previously. Moreover, with thousands of staff added to committee and member rolls during the decade, Congress was better able to monitor executive actions and to follow through on its concerns. Yet, the prevailing view, held by members and observers alike, is that Congress does not actually engage in much oversight. John F. Bibby's comment in 1968 that oversight is Congress's neglected function remains the consensus about oversight on Capitol Hill.[30] Why is this so? Why have perceptions about oversight failed to take account of real changes in congressional activity? Morris Ogul's dismal conclusion about the prospects for oversight provides some useful clues.

> No amount of congressional dedication and energy, no conceivable increase in the size of committee staffs, and no extraordinary boost in committee budgets will enable the

165

Congress to carry out its oversight obligations in a comprehensive and systematic manner. The job is too large for any combination of members and staff to master completely.[31]

Two themes merge here. Congress oversees more but influences less; and it does not conduct oversight in a comprehensive and systematic manner. Clearly, Congress cannot oversee everything done by the administrative branch. Congress has, however, adjusted to this obvious limitation by overseeing in the same way that it legislates, in a disorderly, fragmented manner. It oversees by exception, focusing on the matters that attract its attention while permitting most administrative activites to escape scrutiny. Likewise, Congress oversees in the same way that it once intervened in administrative details, by attending to the particulars, not by writing broad rules. This is a rational adaptation for an institution more interested in control than in evaluation. The key issue for Congress is not administrative performance but its ability to influence agency actions. Congress is interested in performance, but it expresses this interest by seeking dominion over agencies. The distribution of political power between the legislative and executive branches, not simply (or even mainly) the quality of programs, is at stake.

It is from this perspective that members of Congress find oversight wanting. They sit at more hearings, commission more audits and studies, have access to more data, but do not feel that they really control what happens downtown. This frustration has led Congress to devise stronger means of control and legal restrictions on executive agencies.

The New Congressional Assertiveness

Before the instruments of control applied by Congress in the 1970s are examined, it will be useful to consider why Congress was no longer content with the followership role it had practiced for decades. There is nothing automatic about the adjustments that occur in executive–legislative relations. They do not come at fixed intervals, nor can they be foreseen by examining changes in political control of the White House and Capitol Hill. Congress and the president are not locked into a closed system, responding only to each other. Congress is an open institution, exposed to outside currents and pressures. When the posture of Congress vis-à-vis the executive branch changes, the root causes are likely to be found in political conditions.

Vietnam and Watergate seem to offer sufficient explanations for the resurgence of Congress. The former broke the hold of non-partisanship on congressional loyalties; the latter depreciated the president's claim of inherent powers. In addition to these traumas, mini-shocks added to congressional disenchantment with a political arrangement that legitimized executive dominance. President Nixon overreached into the constitutional gray areas between the two branches, casting aside legislative priorities by impounding appropriated funds and shielding himself from legislative scrutiny by claiming executive privilege. Congress responded by narrowing executive discretion in these and other areas.

News headlines and open confrontations do not provide a full explanation, however. The new assertiveness of Congress also stems from fundamental changes in political moods and expectations. For years, Congress gave the executive branch free rein because, as noted earlier, it had faith in the virtues of a strong presidency and because it was confident that executive power would be used for the public good. Neither of these conditions prevailed in the 1970s.

The pluralist harmony that had prevailed in the postwar era was impaired in the 1970s. Pluralism's confident promise was that everyone would gain from government programs. An expanding economy would enable government to distribute its largess without disadvantaging any interest. Politics could be practiced as "who gets what," with government giving, not taking. With abundance, the political system could be compartmentalized into separate sectors, with each major interest having its own federal program, agency, and congressional committee. The iron triangle formed the links of politics, not its shackles.

This arrangement simplified the legislative process and made the production of new laws a pleasant task for members of Congress. With each interest getting its own, there was no need for them to compete with one another, nor much incentive to inquire into the costs—dollar or otherwise—of legislation. Congress practiced distributive politics, looking only at the benefit side of the issue, as if there were no losers. In this environment, Congress was encouraged to write legislation in general terms, attaching few strings and allowing administrators to implement programs according to their judgment.

Whether only in perception or in reality as well, American politics was transformed in the 1970s from affluence to scarcity. As a consequence, there was a new awareness of the redistributive consequences of government policies. Regulations were recognized to have costs, not just benefits; programs that helped some groups were seen to injure others. One community got its new highway, another got increased pollution; workers got added protection against job-related hazards, employers were made to bear the costs. This recognition broke down the compartments that had made pluralist politics so comfortable and assuring and opened up an era of adversary politics.

Legislating is not as easy or as comfortable as it once was. Adversary politics has escalated conflict within Congress as well as between branches. The losers (actual or political) want to be heard, and they are often as organized and vigilant as the beneficiaries. Congress has responded to these cross-pressures by being more active but less productive, by passing more limitations in law but fewer laws. A few statistics on the workload of Congress demonstrate that its legislative behavior has undergone remarkable changes. Despite an increase in reauthorizing legislation, there has been a sharp decline in the enactment of laws. From the early years of nationhood until the 1950s, the number of laws steadily increased; since then, however, there has been a sharp drop in the number of new laws. In fact, the average Congress produced 300 fewer laws during the 1970s than during the 1950s.

This decline in enactments has been accompanied by a steep rise in congressional activity. The House of Representatives now spends many more hours in session and has many more roll calls than in the past. The Ninetieth to Ninety-fifth Congresses averaged 1,652 hours in session, compared with 1,206 hours in the Eightieth to Eighty-ninth Congresses. There has been an even greater increase in the number of roll-call votes. These tripled from an average of 216 in the Eightieth to Eighty-ninth Congresses to 642 in the Ninetieth to Ninety-fifth Congresses. There was a comparable increase in committee activity, with a substantial rise in hearings and other meetings.

If, despite the decline in the number of new laws, the legislative agenda is overloaded, it is because of conflict over legislation. In an era of adversary politics, it takes more exertion to clear a bill because conflicting interests have to be reconciled. Committees must hold more hearings because divergent parties insist on being heard and because members insist on offering amendments during markup. Much the same happens on the floor, where there has been an enormous increase in the number of amendments.

There is a direct link between committee and floor actions in Congress and relations between the two branches. Where members are willing to entrust the fate of their policies to administrators, they are apt to legislate in broad terms. The law can be brief, with little bickering among members over the details. Not so, however, when members are skeptical about whether executive agencies will perform according to their expectations. Rather than provide broad mandates, they hedge legislation with limitations. There are more amendments because more details are settled in legislative chambers rather than in executive suites.

The rules of the House and Senate adjusted to the adversary relationship between the branches. When the relationship was cozy, committees were dominated by chairmen who controlled rank-and-file access to staff and information. Bills were marked up behind closed doors, often with the text of the legislation distributed only at the last minute. When the bill came to the floor, formal and informal constraints limited the offering or endorsement of amendments. In the 1970s, however, Congress became a more fragmented and open institution. Power shifted to subcommittees, which proliferated in number and crossed established jurisdictional lines. Chairmen lost control as staff and information were widely dispersed. Committee meetings were made open to the public under sunshine rules. In the House, recorded votes were permitted in the Committee of the Whole. Institutional norms encouraging specialization and apprenticeship were eroded.

As a consequence, Congress not only worked harder and produced less, but passed legislation of a different character than it had in the past. Members and interest-group representatives scanned the legislative calendar to identify "vehicles" onto which limiting amendments could be added. In this process, proponents got their bills and adversaries got their limitations. Often acceptance of limitations was the price floor managers had to pay for moving their legislation through the House or Senate. With limitations offered as the quid pro quo for passage, it was hard to find anyone in Congress to speak for the executive branch; often it was hard to find anyone in the executive branch to stand up for its prerogatives. Rather than make an issue of every offensive clause, agencies settled for limitations as the best deal they could get.

Significantly, the White House tended to be more protective of agency interests than the agencies themselves. Since restrictions were usually packaged into legislation giving agencies some benefits (such as more money or expanded authority), agencies were willing to take the bad with the good, especially since they expected Congress's enforcement of its restrictions to be spotty. Few of the benefits, however, accrued to the president, so he had little reason to accede to congressional restrictions. But the White House could not possibly monitor the hundreds of legislative baronies, nor could it effectively intervene in the thousands of private negotiations among members or between congressional agents and executive agencies. Moreover, the administration was often blind sided by floor amendments after it had reached an understanding with legislative leaders. Frequently the administration learned about limitations after the legislation had passed and was awaiting the president's action, too late to reopen the issue and (especially in the case of "must" legislation) too late for it to influence legislative action by threatening to exercise the veto power.

The Instruments of Control

In the 1970s, Congress sought to impose new limitations on executive discretion, but in most instances it chose not to return to the types of detailed legislation that had been written in the nineteenth and early twentieth centuries. The same factors that impelled Congress to cede broad power to executives in earlier decades continued to influence congressional behavior. Congress solved this problem by combining limitations and delegation in the same measure. The three principal instruments for congressional control were limitations in appropriation bills, temporary authorizations, and legislative vetoes. Each of these is considered in turn.

Limitations in Appropriation Bills. Although the rules of the House of Representatives bar legislation in appropriation bills (the Senate has a much weaker prohibition), the House's precedents allow limitations to be incorporated in such bills on the grounds that the power to withhold funds is inherent in the power to appropriate. Although the line between legislation and limitation is fuzzy, if restrictive language imposes new duties or requirements, it is likely to be ruled out of order; if it merely limits the use of funds, it is likely to be sustained.[32] Limiting provisions are thus cast in negative form; in the usual case, they do not establish policies or program direction, but place certain activities beyond the affected agency's reach. Members of Congress, however, have become adept in drafting limitations that change substantive laws, thereby satisfying the rules of the House while achieving their objectives.

There has definitely been an increase in the number of riders attached to appropriation bills. Table 6–1 compares the number of general provisions in the regular appropriation bills for the 1975 and 1979 fiscal years. In this brief interval, the number of such provisions rose from 172 to 207, a 20 percent increase. Table 6–2 shows a significant increase in the number of limitation amendments offered during House consideration of annual appropriation bills. In the 1972–1980 period, an average of thirty-nine such amendments were offered each year, compared with an annual average of only fifteen between 1963 and 1971. Moreover, more than 50 percent of the

TABLE 6–1

General Provisions in Appropriation Acts,
Fiscal Years 1975 and 1979

Agency	Fiscal 1975	Fiscal 1979
Department of Agriculture	10	11
Department of Commerce	4	4
Department of Defense (military)	61	76
Department of Defense (civil)	0	0
Department of Health, Education, and Welfare	9	21
Department of Housing and Urban Development	6	8
Department of the Interior	19	18
Department of Justice	9	7
Department of Labor	12	9
Department of State	9	10
Department of Transportation	15	24
Department of the Treasury	9	9
Department of Energy [a]	2	7
Environmental Protection Agency	2	0
General Services Administration	4	3
National Aeronautics and Space Administration	1	0
Veterans Administration	0	0
Total	172	207

a. In 1975, the Energy Research and Development Administration.
Source: *The Budget of the United States Government, Appendix, Fiscal Year 1976* and *Fiscal Year 1980.*

proposed limitations were adopted by the House in the 1972–1980 period compared with less than 30 percent in the preceding nine years.

There is an obvious advantage in using the appropriations process to limit agency discretion. Appropriation bills are "must" legislation, and neither the president nor Congress can afford to shut off funds for regular programs and agencies. Examples of limitations enacted under the wing of appropriation bills include the anti-abortion riders attached to recent appropriation measures, restrictions on the regulation of small businesses by the Occupational Safety and Health Administration (OSHA), and limitations on the regulatory activities of the Federal Trade Commission. Despite strong opposition in the Senate, limitations on the use of federal funds for abortions have been enacted because of the need to continue the programs and operations of key federal agencies. A restriction on OSHA was attached to 1978 legislation for the Small Business Administration, but failed to be adopted when the president vetoed the measure. A similar provision inserted in the appropriation bill was, however, signed into law.

When does Congress resort to limitations in appropriation bills? It appears that limitations are provoked by a number of factors:

• Limitations often are a direct response to recent or pending executive action. The appropriations for the Defense Department, for example, prohibit the consolidation or realignment of Navy pilot-training squadrons. This provision blocked a reorganization planned by the department. Once inserted in an appropriation, the limitation was retained in subsequent years. Often limitations remain legislative boilerplate long after the original reason for them has passed.

• Some limitations emanate from fundamental conflict over national policy. The restriction on abortion funding fits this category, as did those imposed by Congress on U.S. military activity in Cambodia.

• Conflict between the authorizing and appropriations committees sometimes leads to limitations. The House Education and Labor Committee's consideration of proposals to include agricultural workers under the jurisdiction of the National Labor Relations Board spurred the adoption of an appropriations rider preventing any such move.

• An appropriations measure is often seen as the only available vehicle to limit a federal agency. A provision inserted in the 1979 appropriation for the Department of Transportation barred it from using its funds "to implement or enforce any standard or regulation which requires any motor vehicle to be equipped with an occupant restraint system (other than a seat belt)." During floor consideration of this restriction, one proponent argued that the appropriation bill "is the only vehicle left for Members to express themselves on an issue affecting the lives and pocketbooks of millions of Americans."[33]

Placing limitations in appropriation bills is a tactic anyone can use. Liberals used it in the early 1970s to halt the bombing of Cambodia; conservatives exploited it later in the decade to impose their views on school busing and abortion. Members who rail against the practice when they oppose a particular limitation eagerly employ it when it suits their preferences. The appropriations committees complain about limitations added as the result of floor amendments, but they have no problem with the ones adopted in committee. These

TABLE 6–2

LIMITATION AMENDMENTS IN APPROPRIATION BILLS, 1963–1980

Year	Total No. of Floor Amendments Offered	No. of Limitation Riders Offered	No. of Limitation Riders Adopted	Percentage of Limitation Riders Adopted
1963	47	17	7	41
1964	27	11	2	18
1965	26	11	1	9
1966	56	8	1	12
1967	70	16	4	25
1968	75	20	7	35
1969	89	20	10	50
1970	51	13	1	8
1971	83	23	7	30
1972	89	26	5	19
1973	99	31	12	39
1974	109	34	15	44
1975	106	34	12	35
1976	122	33	13	39
1977	107	44	24	55
1978	140	38	23	61
1979	156	43	26	60
1980[a]	165	67	50	75

a. Covers amendments offered up to September 26, 1980.

SOURCES: For 1963-1977, see Democratic Study Group, "The Appropriation Rider Controversy" (February 14, 1978); for 1978-1980, see Daniel P. Strickland, "Limitation Amendments Offered on the Floor of the House, 1978, 1979, 1980" (Congressional Research Service, October 1980).

double standards make it very difficult to marshal support for changing the rules to inhibit limitations.

Yet Congress is not completely unrestrained in inserting limitations. One powerful restraint follows from the "must" characteristic of appropriations. If substantive limitations became a routine practice, it would be difficult for Congress to provide funds for government agencies. (Clearly the slowdown in the enactment of appropriations owes a great deal to this practice.) Many limitations adopted by the House or Senate are jettisoned in conference in order to expedite the appropriation's passage. Authorizing committees also constrain the excessive use of limitations: they do not want their legislative jurisdiction circumvented in the appropriations process. In 1980, for example, the chairmen of seventeen House committees protested the inclusion of legislation in appropriation bills.[34] Significantly, however, they did not ask for cessation of the practice, only for sequential referral of bills with legislative provisions to their committees for review. Perhaps these chairmen recognized that the practice is used so extensively that it would be futile to call for a halt; perhaps they also saw advantage in employing the appropriations process for this purpose.

Temporary Authorizations. At one time, permanent authorizations were standard practice; by the end of the 1970s, however, more than 40 percent of the budget required periodic reauthorization by Congress.[35] There were only about a dozen annual authorizations in the Ninety-first Congress (1969–1970) but more than thirty in the Ninety-fifth (1977–1978).[36] In a typical session, more than one-quarter of Congress's legislative output provides for the renewal of expiring authorizations. If comprehensive sunset legislation (requiring the periodic termination and review of all federal programs) were enacted,[37] the proportion of congressional work given to reauthorizations would inevitably increase.

Although the shift to temporary authorizations stems from diverse motives, in most cases Congress is seeking to strengthen its control over a particular program or policy. The temptation to "go annual" is particularly strong when Congress feels that executive performance is unsatisfactory. In the aftermath of Vietnam, the State Department was placed on annual authorization; in the aftermath of Watergate, so was the Justice Department. The intelligence operations of federal agencies were likewise made subject to annual review following congressional discontent with covert activities. In 1980, Congress responded to concern over the military preparedness of U.S. forces by extending annual authorization to the operations and maintenance accounts of the Defense Department.

The authorizations process is a reserved power. When Congress is satisfied with the operation of a program, the reauthorization is likely to be a pro forma exercise, with little floor debate and few restrictions on agency activities. In the House, many routine authorizations are considered under suspension of the rules, with limited time for debate and no opportunity for floor amendments. In the Senate, many noncontroversial reauthorizations are rushed through under unanimous consent agreements with little or no debate.

When controversy over a particular issue subsides, Congress sometimes lengthens the period of authorization. Thus, by the end of the 1970s the passions that had led to annual authorizations for the State Department had subsided, and Congress voted a two-year

174

authorization for the 1980 and 1981 fiscal years. When an issue is still alive, however, Congress will insist on annual review as a means of maximizing its control. An effort by the House Foreign Affairs Committee to convert foreign assistance to a two-year authorization was rebuffed by a floor amendment retaining the one-year period. "Why tie our hands now?" Representative Dan Lungren (Republican, California) asked in speaking for the one-year authorization:

> That gives us the option of assuring that next year's foreign aid program will be approved by this Congress, using all our efforts and taking advantage of all our opportunities to make the decisions that our constituents sent us here to make.[38]

Congress uses annual authorization as an opportunity to write specific dos and don'ts into reauthorizing legislation. The limitations tend to outnumber the positive policy directives, and they can relate to overall agency activities or to particular concerns. Virtually anything on the mind of Congress can be inserted into an authorization bill as a limitation on agency discretion. The fiscal 1980 authorization for the Justice Department, for example, prohibited the conversion of the federal penitentiary in Atlanta into a state or local prison, required the department to notify relevant House and Senate committees before any reprogramming of funds, established an independent special investigator for the Immigration and Naturalization Service, and directed the attorney general to notify Congress when he decided not to enforce a law because he deemed it unconstitutional.

Limited-term authorizations are a mixed blessing for Congress; they enable it to spell out administrative details in law, but they also add to congressional workloads. Thus, Congress faces the same dilemma with respect to these measures that it confronted when it wrote detailed laws. What is good for individual committees or members may not be good for Congress as a whole. Congress has been able to cope with its authorization workload because almost 60 percent of federal authorizations are permanent. If Congress were to adopt a sunset requirement, many of these permanent programs would be subject to periodic review. One cannot be certain, however, that increased legislative activity would bring more legislative control. Congress might find itself compelled to rubber stamp programs, or it might move away from annual authorizations and give federal programs a longer lease. Concern over excessive workload has been a powerful impediment to the enactment of sunset provisions, and while the trend to temporary authorizations has not been reversed, Congress prefers to apply this control selectively, not across the board.

Legislative Vetoes. The legislative veto has been the most conspicuous and controversial instrument of congressional control in recent times. Since 1932, when this procedure was introduced, Congress has adopted more than 250 veto provisions; of these, more than half were enacted during the 1970s. The legislative veto is a central feature in the War Powers Resolution and the Impoundment Control Act. Congressional interest in this method of control reached a peak between 1975 and 1978, when more than eighty veto provisions were incorporated into federal statutes.[39] More than half the members of the House have sponsored legislation that would extend veto procedures to the rule-making functions of regulatory agencies, but this proposal has not been approved by Congress.

The legislative veto is a statutory provision that authorizes Congress, or one or both of its houses, or one or more committees to disapprove of executive actions. The veto is usually coupled to a waiting period during which the executive action is held in abeyance and Congress can express its disapproval.

There are many variations of the legislative veto. Most require the president or the affected agency to notify Congress of the pending action. Some merely authorize review by Congress without providing for disapproval of the action. Others contain expedited procedures to ensure an opportunity for disapproval within the waiting period. Almost all of the disapprovals are by simple or concurrent resolutions, measures not presented to the president for his signature or veto.

The congressional power to disapprove of or to defer an administrative action rests on the argument that Congress can set the terms and conditions under which it delegates authority to federal agencies. This view has been challenged by a succession of presidents and attorneys general, but the Supreme Court has never directly ruled on the issue.[40] The issue came before the Court in the early 1980s in a case involving congressional review of immigration decisions, but a Supreme Court ruling dealing with a particular set of circumstances might not conclusively settle the matter. Not all legislative vetoes have the same legal purpose or effect. Some vetoes restore the situation to what it was before the administrative action was taken—these might be found constitutionally acceptable—while instances in which new conditions are established by congressional disapproval might be suspect. Some legislative vetoes pertain to adjudicatory actions, others to broad policy. These might be treated differently in law.

The critical issue in appraising the legislative veto is political, not legal. This was recognized by Attorney General Griffin Bell in a 1977 opinion that declared the legislative veto constitutional only for reorganization plans. This form of action, he argued, "carries the potential for shifting the balance of power to Congress and thus permitting the legislative branch to dominate the executive."[41] This line of reasoning suggests that presidents will accept the legislative veto when they gain more in political power than they surrender to Congress. Thus barely a year after his attorney general advised him that vetoes of this kind were unconstitutional, President Carter signed the Nuclear Non-Proliferation Act into law even though it contained nine separate veto provisions. Carter approved it despite his "reservations about the numerous provisions in this act which state that Congress may invalidate or approve executive branch action by concurrent resolution . . . because of its overwhelming importance to our nonproliferation policy."[42]

The actual effects of veto procedures on legislative–executive relations depend on how they are applied by the two branches. Delegation of power by Congress to the executive can vastly expand the authority of the president (or other executive officials) to act without advance legislative approval; the veto process offers Congress an expeditious means of intervening in and overruling executive decisions. The veto is part of a political package that both grants power to executives and reserves to Congress the authority to review the exercise of that power. The War Powers Resolution of 1973 recognized presidential authority to engage U.S. forces in military action without a declaration of war by Congress, but the resolution also provided for Congress to order the removal of U.S. forces from foreign hostilities by concurrent resolution. The 1974 Impoundment Control Act recognized the power of the president to defer or to propose the rescission of appropriated funds, but the act also provided for disapproval of deferrals by simple resolution of the House or Senate and for the release of funds withheld for rescission if Congress did not approve a rescission bill within forty-five days. If Congress were barred from exercising a veto, it would probably be reluctant to grant broad authority to the executive branch, and it might seek to accomplish its control objectives by writing detailed limitations and prescriptions into the law. Thus, the executive may be better served by an arrangement that encourages delegation than by a situation in which Congress's only option is to withhold authority in the first place.

Congress is in fact quite restrained in its use of the veto. From 1960 to 1978, only eighty-one veto resolutions became effective, and forty-nine of these—60 percent—were resolutions disapproving the impoundment of funds.[43] During these eighteen years, most legislative veto provisions did not even generate the introduction of a disapproval resolution, and only one in nine of the resolutions introduced in the House or Senate was adopted.

Congressional disapproval of agency actions provides an incomplete measure of the effectiveness of the legislative veto, because the device offers members and staff of Congress an opportunity to participate in the formulation of administrative decisions and to influence outcomes. By threatening to review regulations or other proposals, Congress can deter administrators from acting without actually wielding its veto power. This conclusion emerges from an incisive and careful study by Harold H. Bruff and Ernest Gellhorn of the effects of legislative vetoes on five federal programs: campaign finance regulations; public access to the Nixon papers and tapes; price and allocation controls on petroleum products; family contribution schedules set by the Office of Education; and rules issued by the Department of Health, Education, and Welfare. Bruff and Gellhorn found that Congress was active and influential in shaping agency rules and regulations before they were proposed for public comment:

> The veto power gave rise to negotiation and compromise over the substance of rules between the agencies and the congressional oversight committees. Significant negotiation occurred in all five programs despite their disparate natures, and it was often intense. . . . Since the agencies demonstrated varying abilities to resist congressional demands for changes in the substance of rules, it cannot be said that the committee staffs dictated changes to the agencies. . . . Still the negotiation process between the committees and the agencies always resulted in some compromise, if not agreement.
>
> One reason for compromise may have been doubts concerning the constitutionality of veto provisions, which deterred Congress from issuing ultimatums to the agencies. The major determinant of the substantive effect of the veto provisions, however, seems to have been the amount of bargaining power the particular agency had with Congress. The fact that the strength of federal agencies vis-à-vis Congress varies suggests that a general veto provision might have a greater substantive impact on some agencies than on others and that this impact might depend partly on factors extrinsic to the veto process.[44]

One of the weaknesses of legislative oversight is that it occurs only after a decision has been made to act in a particular way. The legislative veto compensates for this by injecting Congress directly into the policy debate. It therefore has the effect of bolstering the political power of Congress in relation to the affected government agency. But the influence of Congress comes through political means, not legal action. Congress bargains, negotiates, threatens, uses its political resources. It is able to do so because the legislative veto de facto makes it a party to the decision. Where it is appropriate for political judgments to influence the outcome, such as in decisions concerning U.S. relations with other countries or the expenditure of funds, the fact that the legislative veto strengthens the relative power of Congress does not violate the essentially political relationship between the two branches. But not all government decisions are grist for the political mill. Some involve the legal right and obligations of parties to an administrative action. When Congress uses its legislative veto to intervene in these cases, it converts a quasi-judicial process into a political one. If the drive for a legislative veto over administrative rules were successful, this device would have its broadest application in an area for which it is manifestly ill-suited.

The Limits of Control

The limits on the executive enacted by Congress have affected administrative behavior and government policy. Through limitations in law, Congress brought the bombing of Cambodia to a halt, curtailed the impoundment of funds, blocked the closing of military installations, inhibited covert intelligence activities, regulated the reprogramming of funds, and in myriad other ways affected policy outcomes. In the realm of foreign policy, Thomas Franck and Edward Weisband argue that executive dominance has been replaced by a system of policy codetermination in which power is shared between the two branches.[45] Congress has in addition reclaimed a sizable piece of the money power, writing its priorities into the federal budget and protecting them against presidential impoundment.[46]

Yet it would be a mistake to conclude that the presidency has been totally shackled by congressional fetters. The presidency is not an imperiled institution, bullied into docility by an aggressive and overreaching Congress. It has proven to be, as Thomas Cronin concludes, "an indestructible office, tough and resilient."[47] Nowadays presidents and executives have to rely more on negotiation and persuasion to get what they want from Congress; command and intimidation no longer suffice. In foreign policy, the president is still the dominant actor, though his actions have been tempered by congressional activism. In the domestic sphere, the relationship is more nearly balanced, but even Jimmy Carter managed to have most of his programs adopted.

If the president remains strong, it is because his power is not based solely on legal authority but owes a great deal to his political position. Curbing the president's legal position does not in itself reduce his political reach. Franck and Weisband term the congressional revolution in foreign policy "the defeat of politics by law."[48] But it was politics, not law, that enabled Gerald Ford to prevail in the *Mayaguez* incident, politics not law that enabled Jimmy Carter to thwart a veto of the shipment of nuclear material to India, politics not law that got the Panama Canal treaties through Congress, politics not law that stalled the agreement on strategic arms limitation in the Senate. Politics does not cease when law takes over; law merely redefines the avenues available to the parties and the resources at their command.

Limitations in law cannot end politics because they cannot so clearly demarcate the respective boundaries between the two branches as to end bickering and misunderstanding. Louis Fisher advises Congress when it has strong misgivings about an issue to "resolve the matter by relying on language in a public law, not by informal misunderstandings with executive officials."[49] But the record offers little support for the proposition that misunderstandings can be legislated away. Each international incident opens fresh debate over the president's war powers; the Impoundment Control Act generated a storm of controversy over presidential actions.

Precisely because legal limitations allow the political contest to continue, they are resolved in the political arena rather than in the courts.[50] The War Powers Resolution and the Impoundment Control Act did not resolve basic constitutional questions of executive–legislative relations, but they provided a method for settling disputes between the two branches without addressing more contentious issues. Congress has been able to deter the president from a massive commitment of U.S. forces abroad and from unilaterally withholding funds, but the president has been able to conduct foreign relations and the executive branch has been able to manage its financial affairs without undue difficulty.

Over the years, legislative–executive relations have been tranquil only when Congress has been compliant. When Congress goes along, the relationship is peaceful; when it intervenes, it is castigated as an interloper. The words commonly applied to congressional action have a pejorative tone: Congress intervenes, meddles, interferes, trespasses. When it functions as a check on the executive, Congress tarnishes its public image. It rises in public esteem when it bows to executive pressure and produces legislation with dispatch. During FDR's Hundred Days and LBJ's Great Society, Congress was seen as a responsive institution, not as the rubber stamp that it really was. But when it constrains executive ambitions, Congress is portrayed as

petty, indecisive, and obstructive. In the 1970s, congressional independence was not rewarded with public acclaim. Quite the opposite
occurred. Congress reached a new nadir in the public opinion polls,
sinking below the credibility level accorded a discredited White
House. It is the misfortune of Congress to be unappreciated when it
guards against abuses in executive power. This adverse public opinion
is a powerful deterrent against congressional encroachment on the
executive.

Legitimacy is the most elusive and yet most important determi-
nant of congressional or presidential power. When Harry Truman
dispatched U.S. troops to a "police action" in Korea without obtaining a congressional declaration of war, he was deemed to be doing
what was necessary to protect American security. When Congress,
a quarter of a century later, tried to set conditions for the commitment of U.S. forces, it too was generally considered to be doing the
right thing. It is hard for the disadvantaged branch to resist aggrandizement by the other when the action is taken for the public
good. But the court of political opinion never renders a final verdict
and, as perceptions of what is right and proper change, so, too, do the
actions of the two branches.

The way Congress relates to the president also turns on how the
chief executive is perceived in other quarters. A president who
dominates domestic politics or the international scene is not likely
to be subdued by an assertive Congress. But the loss of U.S. esteem
and potency abroad have compromised the president's relationship
with Congress. The limitations placed by Congress on the president's
authority to dispatch American troops overseas, to negotiate arms
sales, and to conduct foreign policy mirrored the real limitations
facing the president on the world scene.

Congress and the president are "two on a seesaw," with the
ascendance of one usually matched by the descendance of the other.
It would be naive to regard political power as sufficiently elastic to
accommodate the competing ambitions of the two branches. If Congress controls, the executive is constrained; if the executive is
dominant, Congress is docile. The exceptions occur when Congress
and the president make common cause against a third party, such as
happened in the 1920s when presidential budgeting was inaugurated.

The seesaw never comes to a complete rest; the dominance of
one branch is never complete. The subordinated branch has a reserve
of political and legal resources to give it some independence. Even
during the heyday of executive power, Congress frequently intruded
on matters deemed by executive officials to be within their legitimate
sphere of action.

The seesaw is beginning to tilt again toward executive ascendancy. One useful bit of evidence is the extent to which the term "the imperial Congress" has entered political discourse. Congress can be expected to write fewer limitations on executive power in the Reagan era than it did when Carter was in office. But Congress will not willingly give the White House a blank check. It will return neither to detailed lawmaking nor to unbounded discretion. Somewhere between, president and Congress will find sufficient common interest for the business of government to proceed.

Notes

1. In addition to its legislative role, the General Accounting Office (GAO) performs a number of executive and judicial functions. According to its estimates, GAO devotes approximately one-quarter of its staff to serving congressional committees and members of Congress.

2. Leonard D. White, *The Federalists* (New York: Macmillan Company, 1948), p. 512.

3. Ibid., p. 18.

4. Leonard D. White, *The Jeffersonians* (New York: Macmillan Company, 1951), p. 552.

5. P. Ford, ed., *The Writings of Thomas Jefferson*, vol. 8, pp. 120–21.

6. Quoted in Lucius Wilmerding, Jr., *The Spending Power* (New Haven, Conn.: Yale University Press, 1943), p. 53.

7. Woodrow Wilson, *Congressional Government* (New York: Meridian Books, 1956), p. 49.

8. As noted later, federal spending reached $18 billion during World War I but receded to the $3 billion level after the war.

9. The new discipline of public administration that developed along with the growth of government placed efficiency above all other values. See Luther Gulick and Lyndall Urwick, eds., *Papers on the Science of Administration* (New York: Institute of Public Administration, 1937).

10. A. E. Buck, "Financial Control and Accountability," in President's Committee on Administrative Management, *Report with Special Studies* (Washington, D.C., 1937), p. 142.

11. Ibid., p. 16.

12. Ibid., p. 17.

13. Ibid., p. 20.

14. 42 *Stat.* 1489.

15. The Smoot-Hawley Tariff Act of 1930 is in 46 *Stat.* 590-763; the Reciprocal Trade Agreements Act is in 48 *Stat.* 943-45.

16. U.S. v. Shreveport Grain & Elevator Co., 287 U.S. 85 (1932). This section benefits from *The Constitution of the United States of America: Analysis and Interpretation* (Washington, D.C., 1972), pp. 63-79.

17. The phrase is from the ruling of the Supreme Court in Wayman v.

Southard, 10 Wheat. 41 (1825). The Court distinguished between important subjects "which must be entirely regulated by the legislature itself" and subjects "of less interest, in which a general provision may be made, and power given to those who are to act under such general provisions, to fill up the details."

18. Sunshine Anthracite Coal Co. v. Adkins, 310 U.S. 398 (1940).

19. *Congressional Record*, vol. 78 (March 26, 1934), p. 5456.

20. U.S. v. Chicago, Milwaukee, St. Paul & Pacific, 282 U.S. 324 (1931).

21. Twice in 1935, the Supreme Court found delegation to be so unbounded as to violate constitutional precepts, but it abandoned this course in later cases.

22. *Constitution: Analysis and Interpretation*, p. 73.

23. One is reminded of Kenneth Culp Davis's comment that much contemporary legislation implies that "we the Congress don't know what the problems are; find them and deal with them." Quoted in Theodore J. Lowi, *The End of Liberalism* (New York: W. W. Norton & Co., 1969), p. 303.

24. Joel D. Aberbach, "Changes in Congressional Oversight," *American Behavioral Scientist*, vol. 22 (1979), p. 494.

25. Wilson, *Congressional Government*, p. 195.

26. Arthur Macmahon, "Congressional Oversight of Administration: The Power of the Purse," *Political Science Quarterly*, vol. 58 (1943), pp. 161-63.

27. Samuel P. Huntington, "Congressional Responses to the Twentieth Century," in David B. Truman, ed., *The Congress and America's Future* (Englewood Cliffs, N.J.: Prentice-Hall, 1965), p. 30.

28. 60 *Stat.* 832.

29. 84 *Stat.* 1156.

30. Only 17 percent (29 out of 168) of the House members responding to a 1979 survey thought that House committees were doing an adequate oversight job. See U.S. Congress, House Select Committee on Committees, *Final Report*, II. Rept. No. 96-866 (April 1, 1980), p. 280.

31. Morris S. Ogul, *Congress Oversees the Bureaucracy* (Pittsburgh: University of Pittsburgh Press, 1976), p. 5.

32. *Deschler's Procedure* (the authoritative manual on the rules and precedents of the House) devotes more space to the difference between legislation and limitations than to any other issue (U.S. Government Printing Office). See chaps. 25 and 26.

33. *Congressional Record*, vol. 124 (June 12, 1978), p. H3508, remarks of Representative Bud Shuster.

34. *Final Report*, pp. 387-89.

35. This estimate is based on a study by the Congressional Budget Office which identified 978 provisions of law that required periodic reauthorization. See Congressional Budget Office, "Congressional Control of the Budget and Authorizations" (unpublished staff analysis, July 26, 1979).

36. See Congressional Budget Office, "Annual Authorizations," (unpublished staff analysis, May 1979).

37. In 1978, the Senate passed a sunset bill (S. 2) which would have mandated the automatic expiration of authorizations every ten years. The House, however, did not act on this measure. Congressional interest in sunset legislation appears to have diminished since then.

38. *Congressional Record,* vol. 125 (April 5, 1979), p. H2005.

39. See the following reports by Clark F. Norton and issued by the Congressional Research Service: "Congressional Review, Deferral, and Disapproval of Executive Actions: A Summary and an Inventory of Statutory Authority" (April 30, 1976); "1976-77 Congressional Acts Authorizing Prior Review, Approval or Disapproval of Proposed Executive Actions" (May 25, 1978); and "Congressional Acts Authorizing Congressional Approval or Disapproval of Proposed Executive Actions" (February 12, 1979).

40. On December 22, 1980, the U.S. Court of Appeals for the Ninth Circuit ruled that a House resolution overturning a decision of the Immigration and Naturalization Service was a "prohibited legislative intrusion upon the executive and judicial branches." The case probably will lead to a Supreme Court ruling on the legislative veto.

41. Letter from Attorney General Griffin Bell to President Jimmy Carter, January 31, 1977.

42. *Public Papers of the Presidents: Jimmy Carter,* vol. 1 (Washington, D.C., 1979), p. 502.

43. These data are adapted from an unpublished report by Clark Norton of the Congressional Research Service.

44. Harold H. Bruff and Ernest Gellhorn, "Congressional Control of Administrative Regulation: A Study of Legislative Vetoes," *Harvard Law Review,* vol. 90 (May 1977), pp. 1410-11.

45. Thomas M. Franck and Edward Weisband, *Foreign Policy by Congress* (New York: Oxford University Press, 1979).

46. See Allen Schick, *Congress and Money: Budgeting, Spending, and Taxing* (Washington, D.C.: Urban Institute, 1980).

47. Thomas E. Cronin, "A Resurgent Congress and the Imperial Presidency," *Political Science Quarterly,* vol. 95 (Summer 1980), p. 234.

48. Franck and Weisband, *Foreign Policy,* p. 155.

49. Louis Fisher, *The Constitution Between Friends* (New York: St. Martin's Press, 1978), p. 249.

50. For example, there were fewer impoundment suits but more impoundments in the period immediately following enactment of the Impoundment Control Act than there were before.

7

The Open Congress
Meets the President

NORMAN J. ORNSTEIN

It is January 1980. Imagine Sam Rayburn materializing suddenly on
Capitol Hill, nineteen years after he last set foot on it. He first has
considerable trouble getting his bearings. There is the familiar old
Capitol, and the Cannon and Longworth Buildings. But what are all
these other new buildings and parking lots, not to mention once
familiar hotels and apartments that seem to be office buildings now?
And look at the bottom of the hill at that monstrosity that bears his
name! He enters his Capitol and feels a little better, although it is
awfully crowded; the mere handful of members, staff, and lobbyists
that he remembers are surrounded by hundreds of unknown people
milling around, dashing down the corridors and in and out of the
chamber. Entering the chamber, he feels still more comfortable—it
looks pretty much the same as it did when he last saw it, and with
Tip O'Neill in the speaker's chair the Democrats are obviously still
in control. Rayburn smiles contentedly. "Tip's a good man," he says
to himself. "He learned a lot from me." He positively grins when he
sees that good ol' Jim Wright of Fort Worth is the majority leader.
So the venerable Boston–Austin connection in the leadership is still
there.

A young, unfamiliar member is managing a bill; Rayburn sidles
up to an old colleague and learns to his shock that the bill manager
is in his second term in the House. Not only that, the bill and the
manager are from the Ways and Means Committee! Rayburn feels a
bit better when he sees Tip O'Neill get up on the floor and warmly

A small portion of this paper was adapted from a presentation delivered at a
conference on the presidency and Congress at the White Burkitt Miller Center
for Public Affairs, University of Virginia, January 24-25, 1980. The author is
grateful to Michael Malbin, John Kessel, Austin Ranney, Tom Mann, and
Anthony King for helpful comments.

endorse the bill. But he is horrified again as he witnesses a succession of young Democrats get up and denounce, in blunt language, O'Neill, the Ways and Means chairman, and the Democratic president. He watches, stunned, as the bill goes down in flames, largely on the votes of Democrats. A second-termer managing a bill? From Ways and Means? Supported by the Speaker, the committee, and the president? And it gets rolled on the floor? What's going on here, anyhow? But then again, Rayburn can remember times when he and a young Democratic president had been humiliated, too—also with the help of Democrats. But it usually did not happen so openly, so publicly on the floor!

Rayburn's mortification is compounded by his confusion at the vote. Not only does no clerk call out the roll, but members are not calling out aye or nay. They seem instead to be sticking pieces of plastic in fancy machines, and, suddenly, the familiar House chamber is surrounded by unfamiliar lights and signs. The tapestry on an entire vast wall is covered with names, with red or green lights beside them. Large electronic scoreboards at each side of the chamber tick off fifteen minutes and indicate vote tallies, overall and by party. And up in the corners—can it really be?—television cameras. When it is all over, Rayburn is dumbstruck. What hath Congress wrought?

On a walk through the Capitol corridors and over to the Cannon Building, Rayburn is somewhat assuaged. Party offices—Speaker, majority leader, whip, and so forth—seem to be unchanged, and the names of the committees on the doors, from Appropriations to Veterans Affairs, are all familiar. But he keeps getting jostled by a series of mostly unfamiliar people (who seem to be members) running out of one subcommittee room and into another, or running to the floor when the bells ring, and they are ringing all the time. All this frenetic activity—and it is not even the end of a session. Not only that, but his newspaper tells him that today is *Friday*! Why, even the people from New York and Pennsylvania are here! He passes an open committee room door, stops, looks in, and sees a markup session in progress on an energy bill. "They must have forgotten to lock the door," he thinks, but then sees that the room is filled with staff, reporters, and spectators. "An open markup on a major bill. I can't believe it," he mutters to himself.

Rayburn walks into an office. Seeing three connecting rooms filled with desks, files, electronic equipment, and staff people, he assumes it must be the main quarters of the Appropriations Committee. He reels back in astonishment when a receptionist tells him that, no, this is the office of a freshman congressman from Texas.

On his way out, Rayburn counts fifteen staff people and notices a computer terminal and a television set playing the floor proceedings. Out in the hall, a set of blinding klieg lights ring several television cameras and reporters. "Oh," Rayburn thinks, "It must be the Speaker, or the Ways and Means chairman." The interviewee turns out to be a freshman Democrat, criticizing the windfall profits tax proposed by President Jimmy Carter and endorsed by O'Neill. Rayburn goes outside, sits on a park bench, slowly shakes his head, and drifts off into a troubled sleep.

He wakes up with a start. This was a comparative catnap; now it is April 1981. Rayburn is afraid to go into the House again. There may be even more frightening changes in store. So he strolls to the Senate side of the Capitol, picking up a newspaper on the way. He discovers that, while he slept, a Republican president has been elected—unfortunate, though nothing terribly unusual there—and along with him, a Republican Senate. Now that *is* unusual; Rayburn had seen only two others, for two years each, in his twenty-one years as House Democratic leader. To his relief, he reads that his beloved House of Representatives, at least, remains in the hands of the Democrats.

As Rayburn reaches the Senate side, he notices a door labeled "Budget Committee." "So they went back to the idea of separate budget panels," he muses. He walks inside to find Republicans voting in a solid bloc to support their president's budget package and thinks to himself that this new president is having an easier time with his own party in the Senate than Eisenhower did. When he discovers that the budget package calls for nearly $40 billion in budget cuts, he is doubly impressed. Why, these cuts total nearly half the entire budget when he left Congress! He notes that Democrats are deeply and bitterly divided on the budget question. "It's a good thing Lyndon isn't around to see this," he mutters.

Rayburn heads to the Foreign Relations Committee, where a confirmation hearing is going on. He is startled to see a Republican senator from North Carolina—politics have certainly changed in the South! But he is even more startled when the senator (Jesse Helms, a conservative like the president, he is told by a reporter) lambastes the nominee for assistant secretary of state for his leftist views and warns him—and the administration—that Senator Helms is not happy with the administration's nominees and will hold a large number of them in limbo indefinitely in protest. He thinks to himself that maybe this president is not in such great shape with his own Republicans, especially the conservatives.

A trip to the Senate floor presents a similar picture. A parade of self-identified conservative Republican senators criticize the president and his priorities, as well as their own Senate majority leader, arguing passionately that social issues cannot be delayed and that they will not sit idly by. "Ah," says Rayburn, "looks like we still have civil rights filibusters." No, he is told, the senators refer to such things as abortion, family planning, and prayer in the schools. But there is a marathon filibuster planned in the Senate over civil rights— conducted by liberals to prevent a rollback of major civil rights laws.

Continuing his stroll around the Senate, Rayburn is struck by the large number of people scurrying around the corridors of the numerous office buildings (including such converted landmarks as the Carroll Arms Hotel and the Senate Courts Apartment Building). These are not tourists, he realizes; they are staff. A tour of a typical senator's office shows five large rooms filled with staff, computer terminals, and equipment, along with three additional rooms in an annex. Rayburn is also struck by his realization that neither party nor ideology affect the sizes or apparent activities of the staffs— conservative Republican offices are as bureaucratic, overcrowded, and busy as those of liberal Democrats. Moreover, Southern senators do not seem to differ from Northerners in their use of staff. In a committee hearing, Rayburn sees senators constantly in whispered conferences with staff; staff feeding their bosses questions for witnesses; staff preparing speeches and amendments for their senators. "I saw *some* of this in the 1950s," he muses, "but not nearly so much, nor so universal!"

Rayburn walks outside again and finds another park bench. He prepares to drift off to sleep again, but this time he takes a sleeping pill first. After what he has seen, he does not want to wake up again for a very long time.

Our brief Rip van Rayburn fable, not the first spun by a scholar to highlight change in Congress, is designed to introduce a key question for this book—What has changed inside Congress that affects presidential leadership? We can first address this question by asking, Why was Rayburn so surprised, even stunned, by what he saw in 1980 and 1981? Obviously because much that characterized Congress in his heyday had changed. What changed—and what did not—can help us sort out the problems and potentialities that contemporary presidents face in dealing with Congress. Rayburn was a strong leader who worked closely with presidents from Franklin D. Roosevelt to John F. Kennedy. Our best place to start is with the core Rayburn era—the Congress of the 1950s.

Inside Congress in the 1950s

In the 1950s, as in the decade before and some years afterward, Congress was a closed system. Incentives, rewards, and sanctions all were internal to the congressional process. First, the absence of an outside focus of attention forced legislators to look inside their own system. Without an intense national media presence—especially a television presence—in Washington, relatively little public attention was paid to congressional proceedings or congressional members. A battle over policy between a committee baron and a maverick junior legislator, say, or a scandal involving one or more congressmen was paid little heed outside the confines of the Capitol. William Proxmire gained notoriety among political scientists as the quintessential "outsider" in the Senate after Ralph K. Huitt's seminal article in 1961,[1] but he was not a well-known figure outside Wisconsin or the political science fraternity.

As Michael Robinson has noted, a bribery scandal involving a prominent senator, Daniel Brewster of Maryland, was given virtually no coverage in the national media, even when Brewster was convicted and sent to prison (leaving Brewster both broken personally and obscure nationally).[2] Such goings-on—on the Hill, at least—were of only passing interest to a Washington press corps more involved with the behavior of the president and his coterie, and of even less interest to television networks centered in New York and attempting to establish a credible presence as sources of national nightly news.

This relative congressional obscurity was underscored in the social arena. Inside the Washington community at this time, social circles were more concentric than overlapping. While the style section of the *Washington Post* would report on fancy soirees attended by legislators, this was news of significance only to a handful of D.C. cognoscenti. The *Post* in the 1950s was not a national newspaper, with its stories syndicated nationally. Its focus on Washington social lions and lionesses would capture attention outside the capital only when the socializing involved the presidential circle (hence, Perle Mesta's notoriety). Only the handful of senators who sought presidential nominations were able to move into a more public spotlight—and even this was much less likely before 1960.

All of this meant that legislators could not easily find power, attention, publicity, or celebrity status away from the confines of the Capitol. To a member of Congress, virtually the only way to get ahead was to ride up the power structure inside the House or Senate. But the elevators were not self-run; rather, the operators were the senior party leaders and committee chairmen. These people pushed the internal button for numerous internal reasons. The formal rules of the House and Senate enhanced their power and influence in a variety of ways.

First, they protected committee chairmen from sanction or removal by their colleagues. Chairmen were basically selected at the beginning of each new Congress by a secret ballot vote in the majority party caucus, based on recommendations made to the caucus by a party committee. For House Democrats, in the majority for nearly the entire 1950s and 1960s, the group was called the Committee on Committees and consisted of the Democratic members of the Ways and Means Committee; the counterpart Senate group was the Democratic Steering Committee, chaired by the majority leader, who appointed the other members. In each chamber, the caucus was presented with a single slate of nominees for chairmanships, all routinely chosen on the seniority principle—that is, the Democrat with greatest continuous service on the committee—and arranged to provide for a single in toto vote. No procedure existed for a separate vote on any individual choice for a chairmanship. Though no rules mandated it, the party selection panels implicitly were governed by the seniority criterion. The same patterns prevailed for Republicans in the minority and on the rare occasions (1947–1948 and 1953–1954) when they were in the majority.

Second, formal rules gave the chairmen a near-monopoly over committee resources, especially committee staff. Chairmen could use the rules to control their committee agendas and to shape policy emphases and outcomes through their dominance over subcommittees (they could name the panels, choose the majority members, and select the chairmen) and through their ability to control when and if their committee would meet. Chairmen also controlled what other perquisites existed inside Congress for committee members: appointment to a conference committee, the ability to travel or "junket" on committee business at committee expense, and the giving of permission to hold a hearing in a member's home state or district.

Rules that kept most congressional negotiations closed to all except members and privileged staff multiplied the "inside" influence of chairmen. Chairmen were there overseeing their colleagues, making deals, and compromising or refusing to bend, while outside forces, such as the media and lobbying groups, were not present. True, lobbyists could still apply pressure and could always find out what went on in the closed rooms. But they could not supply their expertise or relevant data to members during the process of decision making, while chairmen had their expert staffs immediately at hand. Furthermore, with closed sessions, the members could put the best face on their actions or inactions when recounting them to groups or constituents.

Formal rules, especially in the House, also extended the control that chairmen had in their committees to actions on the floor. Chairmen controlled the time of debate for a bill, allocating the limited minutes to their designated spokesmen. Most important, House rules made amendments to bills difficult to attach and rarely subject to outside, or extra-congressional, influences. Chairmen, who tended to shape the bills in committee to their liking, did not want amendments added to their bills. The rules, which forced most amendments to be unrecorded, made it difficult for interest groups and the public to track the votes for or against their interests (while chairmen, who were there on the floor, could watch the voting more closely). The rules also placed a burden on anticommittee forces to get their allies to the floor to vote when amendments came up. Chairmen, however, merely had to convince potential opponents not to vote at all, an easy task since no records of attendance were kept.

Formal rules were supplemented by informal norms. Junior members were to be seen and not heard, to serve an apprenticeship until they were well steeped in the system. Violators of this norm received no great benefits in terms of public attention, but were quite likely to feel the sting of internal disapproval, with the amount of pain inflicted varying according to the gravity of the offense. The continuum of possible sanctions was large: no access to committee staff, no opportunity to ask questions of witnesses in a hearing, no room at the witness table for an important constituent who wanted to testify, no invitation to an interparliamentary exchange in Madrid, and no action on a coveted piece of legislation or amendment. With very limited resources available to the rank-and-file legislators, each of these perquisites was important. Sam Rayburn's most famous phrase was his admonition to junior colleagues: "to get along, go along." In this closed congressional system, few doubted the truth of his adage.

It is not surprising, then, that the House and Senate our fantasy Sam Rayburn saw in 1980 and 1981 came as a jolt. The latter-day Congress was oriented toward and dominated by junior members; open, to an incredible degree, to press, lobbies, and public; replete with overt challenges to the authority of party leaders, committees, chairmen, and the president; and filled with a seemingly endless army of staff and technical resources for everybody.

To a leader like Rayburn (or to a president for that matter), the most important contrast with the old was the fluidity of the new Congress. One key consequence of the old, closed system was that

Congress had been quite predictable, at least to the relative handful of close and seasoned observers (including the Speaker, the Senate majority leader, and usually the president's key staff aides). Bills from one set of committees were certain to pass easily and intact if they were reported out at all; bills from other committees were sure to elicit conflict, controversy, and amendment in committee and on the floor. How most members would vote or react was predictable long before the actual votes were cast. What amendments would be offered (and by whom) and which would be successful could usually be forecast. Of course, no one could determine the precise outcome of every piece of legislation or policy initiative. But one knew which votes would be close and which bills had no chance—and, on the close calls, which twenty or thirty members of the House or which five or six members of the Senate were the crucial swing votes.

The decisions governing these final outcomes were usually made at earlier stages of the process, shaped behind closed doors in committees, in conditions forged by committee chairmen, often negotiated with party leaders and presidential representatives. If and when agreements were worked out, the chairmen used their formidable resources within their committees, either to report a bill out with a united front or to quash a bill outright.

If the predictability of the system failed—if a bill that seemed certain to pass intact foundered on the floor—party leaders could swiftly withdraw the offending article from consideration and return to the proverbial drawing board, with few tremors that the embarrassment would make the front pages or the nightly television news. Indeed, it might not even make the wire services, given the small number of journalists closely following Congress and the general propensity of news editors to regard such stories as petty and boring internal congressional warfare.

This did not mean—as Rayburn himself would have readily admitted—that leaders like the Speaker ran Congress or that, as conventional wisdom would have it, the president could sit down with Sam Rayburn and Lyndon Johnson, work out an agreement, and that would be that. Rayburn's influence, and Johnson's, stemmed first from their relationship with committee chairmen and other senior powers—their ability to negotiate, to logroll, and to compromise with the oligarchs, to know when to back off and when to push.

Second, their influence was greater because they knew every member's political environment, strengths, weaknesses, and predilections. Thus they knew what could pass when. Lyndon Johnson was not powerful enough to push through the 1965 Voting Rights Act in 1957 or the 1957 Civil Rights Act in 1955. But he and Rayburn knew when *a* civil rights bill—any civil rights bill—could get through Congress, what it could contain, and what it would take to get the bill past a filibuster and the other major hurdles.

Third, the power of the leaders was enhanced by the closed nature of the congressional system. The Speaker and Senate leader could minimize overt defeats by their ability to control access of bills to the floor, and they could know with some reasonable certainty when they would win or lose. In the absence of substantial public or group attention to voting patterns, there was usually enough flexibility in the votes of their colleagues for the leaders to have a "reserve" in case things were going unexpectedly badly. The reserve of support included members who owed the leaders favors or who were afraid of sanctions or who were simply predisposed to help if needed. Moreover, the more often it appeared the leaders won and the less the attention paid when they lost, the more Rayburn and Johnson enhanced their reputations as powerful leaders. Thus they were all the more able to parlay those reputations into even more concrete successes, as rank-and-file legislators acted without prodding in anticipation of what the leader might want.

The formula for presidential success was not much different. The successful president, to begin, worked closely with congressional leaders, using their strength to expand his own. He accepted their judgments about what would pass and what to push, and he compromised with them, as they in turn compromised with committee barons. He provided his resources to them when necessary. As Senate Secretary Bobby Baker put it about the LBJ style of leadership:

> Much of the work of putting together a simple majority consisted of logistics. A senator who's for your cause down to his toenails is of no help if you can't produce him when the vote is taken. My first goal always was to produce one hundred percent of those senators who'd promised to help us; if I did that, no way in hell we'd lose—because LBJ was not one to call for a vote until he knew he had the horses. . . . When we had a Democratic president in the White House, I had Air Force One available to fetch them on short notice. Even when Republicans ruled the White House, we could command police cars and wailing sirens to round up the strays.[3]

Most important, the successful president emulated the successful congressional leader. He buried his failures in committee or in a conference in the Oval Office, before they escalated into embarrassing reversals in public forums. He only proposed initiatives he thought he could win (or, at least, he underscored and publicized only the likely successes). He built his reputation as a winner with Congress and used it to achieve more success, often with legislators acting on their own in anticipation of presidential action or approval.

Still the basic fact confronting presidents and congressional party leaders alike was that the constraints on them far outweighed their freedom to do what they wanted in the policy arena. When Rayburn and Johnson met with Eisenhower, it was most often to tell him what could *not* be accomplished—what was out of the question in Ways and Means; sure to be killed in Rules; absolutely unacceptable to Senator Richard Russell or Senator Robert Kerr. When Rayburn met with his own committee chairmen, it was not to tell them what the Speaker demanded or what the president insisted upon; it was to negotiate. Rayburn recognized full well the strong cards the chairmen held in their hands. Rarely would he take on a powerful chairman in a public setting. When he did, as with the challenge to Rules Chairman Howard "Judge" Smith in the attempt in 1961 to enlarge the Rules Committee, undertaken with the full backing of the popular new president, the outcome was very much in doubt until the actual vote (taken after a long postponement to enable Rayburn to scratch for more votes to provide a slender majority.)

Johnson and Rayburn knew their systems well and could operate as masters within them. But even before both left Congress—LBJ to move to the vice-presidency in 1961, Rayburn upon his death later that year—they saw the beginnings of change. Both saw it coming with the 1958 election, a "critical" election for Congress. While the 1958 elections ostensibly helped both party leaders, giving each of them many more members to fatten their majorities, they presaged greater problems for them and their successors. The Democrats gained forty-nine House seats and fifteen senators, most of the newcomers being liberals from the Northeast, the Midwest, and the West.

In the House, the freshman bloc, led by representatives like James G. O'Hara, helped form a new, structured liberal caucus, the Democratic Study Group (DSG). DSG became an ally of Rayburn's after liberal Democrat John F. Kennedy moved into the White House in 1961, but more important it became the moving force behind internal reforms implemented in the 1970s. These measures, which transformed the House, eliminated one by one the formal rules and informal norms that had created and nurtured the closed congressional system. In the Senate, the famous "class of '58" endured for nearly two decades, spurring the Senate toward the decentralized, democratized, junior-oriented institution that still prevails in 1982.[4]

Changes Inside Congress in the 1960s and 1970s

Changes in the internal rules, power, and customs of Congress began in the 1960s and culminated in the 1970s. The House of Representatives generally led the day in formal rules changes, the Senate lagging a bit behind.[5] The thrust of change, however, was the same in both houses.

First, power was decentralized. The insulation from removal of full committee chairmen provided by the rigid custom of seniority and by the omnibus-vote system of selection in the Democratic caucus was taken away by caucus reforms in 1971 and 1973. At the same time, the ability of chairmen to control their committees through subcommittees was hamstrung by reforms that took away the chairman's power to structure the subcommittees, to pick the subcommittee chairmen and members, and to control their jurisdictions and staffs. Subcommittees were given independent status and authority; their members were selected automatically according to set criteria; and their chairmen were elected individually by the committees' Democratic caucuses. Rules limiting legislators to one subcommittee chairmanship apiece gave an unprecedented number of gavels to rank-and-file members.

Second, resources available to subcommittees, to their chairmen and ranking members, and to all legislators were expanded. Chairmen in the past had been able basically to hire and fire all the committees' staffs—and the staffs had been small. In 1965, standing committees employed 571 people in the House and 509 in the Senate, an average per committee of 28 and 32, respectively. Reforms in the early 1970s allowed subcommittees and their leaders to hire their own personnel. Staffs then expanded rapidly; by 1979, the standing committees employed 1,959 in the House and 1,098 in the Senate, or an average per committee of 89 and 73, respectively.[6]

Personal staffs expanded rapidly as well. In the late 1960s, each House member could hire up to nine or ten employees, with a staff budget of about $150,000. By the end of the 1970s, House members were each entitled to hire eighteen employees, with a budget of nearly one-third of a million dollars. Adjunct research staffs—the Library of Congress's Congressional Research Service, the Office of Technology Assessment, the Congressional Budget Office—also mushroomed. So, too, did other resources available to members, such as computers, fancy telephone systems, data-processing equipment, and so forth. The net result was that each member of Congress, down to the lowliest minority freshman, became resource-rich, the possessor of enough staff and equipment to "stroke" all constituents, to monitor the legislative activities in all committees and other forums, to maintain a steady stream of press releases and media contacts, and to get involved, through speeches, bills, hearings, and amendments, in the full range of policy areas.

A third important change in the 1970s was that internal congressional deliberations were opened to public scrutiny. In both houses, reforms dramatically changed the nature of committee business. Before 1973, an open committee markup session, when a bill was actually put together, line by line, was as rare as a whooping crane. They were closed to all but committee members and a handful of staff (all beholden to the chairman). After 1973, nearly all the markups in the House and Senate were open to outside observers, whether press, lobbyists, or tourists wandering by.

This change further chipped away at the power of chairmen. They lost their near-monopoly of expertise; all the other committee members now had their own staff or even lobbyists whispering advice and amendments in their ears during the markups. Also, the chairmen's inside persuasion was less effective on members who faced conflicting outside pressures as well, because the members' actions were now directly viewed by the outsiders. Legislators could no longer put the best face on their votes or their rhetoric, as they had been able to do when the action took place behind closed doors.

It was not only meetings that were opened: in the House, votes, too, were opened. Before the 1970s, virtually all votes on amendments to bills were handled in a nonrecorded fashion, using a parliamentary procedure known as teller voting. To expedite business, members would walk down separate aisles, for ayes and nays, counted by colleagues as they passed. This took six minutes as opposed to the thirty or forty minutes for a roll call. Only the total number of votes was tallied, not who voted or how. With no records kept, attendance was low—less than half, on average, that for roll-call votes.

In the Legislative Reorganization Act of 1970, these votes were changed to recorded teller votes. Members signed cards—green for aye, red for nay—and dropped them in boxes, saving time while allowing votes and attendance to be published. This change doubled voting attendance at teller votes. More important, it reduced again the power of committees and their chairmen, this time to wheel and deal on the floor. A chairman in the past had been able generally to structure bills in his committee to his liking. Thus, amendments on the floor were discouraged, and nonrecorded votes helped in this regard. The burden was on the proponents of the amendment to get their supporters on the floor and voting. Chairmen could merely say to wavering members, "Don't cross me and don't violate your principles or constituents: don't vote at all. Without records, no one will know if you voted or how you voted—except me." With recorded, open votes, everybody knew who voted and how. Outside influences thus had more leverage, and many more amendments were offered and passed.

Fourth, in combination with these formal changes, informal norms and ways of behavior changed, too. The first to disappear was apprenticeship, the admonition long given to junior legislators to be seen and not heard. Tom Foley, initially elected to the House in 1964, described well his own experience at a time when apprenticeship was still strong:

> My first day on the Agriculture Committee . . . was spent listening to the strictures of the chairman, Harold Cooley of North Carolina. In the public arena of the committee room with the press present, he told us that he hated to hear new members interrupt senior members when they were asking questions. He went on to say that we would find, if we would only remain silent, that the senior members of the committee would ask all the important questions, discuss all the relevant issues, and decide them without our interference. He added that, unfortunately, for some it would take years; other, more clever individuals might learn in months, some of the basic information of the committee necessary for constructive participation. But, in the meantime, they could all help us—that is, the senior bench— by being quiet and attentive.[7]

In the years after Foley's initiation, committee chairmen lost their power to enforce such admonitions. Junior legislators expanded in number, and their resources expanded even faster. Party leaders became—out of both conviction and necessity—more indulgent in their attitudes toward the juniors. By the late 1960s, few sanctions existed to chastise the overzealous freshman. By the early 1970s, the norm of apprenticeship itself had disappeared: Junior members were encouraged to speak out and play an active role. Starting with 1974, freshman classes in the House organized, elected chairmen, took on staff, and aggressively acted to promote their interests, which included top committee assignments for class members and some substantive policy goals.

Through the 1970s and into the 1980s, freshmen offered amendments on the floor without ostracism and with legislative success. Some, like the Harkin Amendment specifying conditions for U.S. foreign aid, had important policy consequences. Likewise, freshmen

197

pushed their own bills and sometimes chaired their own panels. Nothing happened to reverse this pattern when the conservative Republicans captured the Senate in 1980.

As a norm of behavior, apprenticeship wholly disappeared. Other norms continued to exist as ideals, but faded in their expression and lost any power of sanction for violation. One such was reciprocity: the notion that a member should and would defer to the expertise and desires of committees and their leaders, and that the member in turn would be deferred to for his own committee recommendations.[8] Reciprocity had at times in the past been honored only in the breach, breaking down mainly for committees that were internally divided, like House Education and Labor. More often than not, it worked well, bolstering such panels as Ways and Means, Appropriations, Commerce, and Foreign Affairs on the floor. But by the late 1970s, the most prestigious panels, including Ways and Means and Appropriations, were suffering on the floor.

"Closed" rules, which bolstered the results of reciprocity by curtailing amendments to key bills, were virtually eliminated, and important committees were increasingly unable to keep their handiwork from being changed drastically on the floor by nonmembers of the committee, or rejected altogether. Ways and Means in the Carter years saw its proposal for a five-cents-a-gallon gasoline tax rudely rejected by the House; Foreign Affairs had its human-rights policy rewritten on the floor by nonmember Tom Harkin of Iowa; Commerce saw its version of the Clean Air Act redrawn on the House floor; Appropriations' proposals to cut back on impact aid for education were rebuffed by a broad bipartisan cross section of legislators. Some bills still emerged unscathed, of course, but the path of any given piece of legislation became more unpredictable, and the prospect diminished that a coalition built in a committee would hold together on the floor.

Reciprocity as an institutional norm had in the past gone hand in hand with specialization as an individual norm. Legislators were expected to dig into their committee work, learn it well, and devote their time and legislative activity to the relative handful of areas within their panel assignments. Dilettantes—those who were active in other areas and offered bills or, worse, floor amendments outside their specialties—were frowned upon, chastised, or ostracized. Their efforts were rarely successful.

Specialization, like reciprocity, worked in a system in which senior members (especially committee chairmen) dominated, in which staff resources were scarce and the substantive experts were monopolized by the committee seniors, and in which rules discouraged outsiders' efforts. Rank-and-file legislators would suffer if they challenged the committees; in any event, few had the time or staff to follow in sufficient detail the activities or issue areas of other panels, much less to draft the appropriate amendments or bills.

In the 1970s, of course, conditions changed. Senior authority waned, staff resources multiplied, rules opened things up. Every legislator had the opportunity and the ability to track every issue area and to introduce timely amendments to all bills as they hit the floor. Over time, the sanctions against such behavior declined. The norm remains in the legislature in the 1980s; specialization is still considered theoretically desirable and still has some meaning to many members. But its reach is far less than it was in the 1950s and 1960s, and, more important, it has little effect on actual congressional behavior.

One other norm that has recently been honored mainly in the breach is courtesy. Members of Congress used to go to very great lengths to praise their colleagues, even in disagreement. Former Speaker of the House John McCormack used to note proudly that he always referred to a fellow legislator as "the most distinguished member from . . ." or "the truly honorable gentleman." Once, in the heat of anger, he ignored his own advice and went so far as to disparage a colleague by saying, "I hold the gentleman in minimum high regard."

This restraint has changed. In the past decade, there have been many more incidents of personal animosity reflected in heated comments on the floor or in committee. Epithets like "liar" are used; personal motives or abilities are questioned. Shouting matches, if not commonplace, are no longer remarkable or notable. We have by no means returned to the physical violence of the nineteenth-century Congress, nor are such incidents of public acrimony applauded in the cloakrooms or accepted by members as necessary or inevitable. But clearly the norm of courtesy means less and is ignored more than it was in the 1950s. More open conflict means less ability for the legislature to compromise or even to act.

Along with changes in rules, resources, and norms, there have been significant changes in attitudes. The closed system of the 1950s had as an essential element a universally accepted sense of respect by rank-and-file members for their seniors. Party leaders and committee chairmen were revered, venerated, feared. So, too, were presidents and other such authority figures.

With the 1970s—and with Vietnam and Watergate—respect was replaced by distrust. Those with formal titles of authority or with age, status, or expertise were not to be given an additional measure of consideration by members of Congress, or the benefit of the doubt. To the contrary, they were to be discounted and downplayed. Party leaders, from the Speaker of the House on down, suffered from this change in attitude toward authority and leadership. So did the president and by extension the entire executive branch.

Outside Changes Affecting Congress in the 1960s and 1970s

Formal and informal changes inside Congress were accompanied by related and reinforcing changes beyond its confines. First, there were changes in the party system and thus the recruitment patterns for congressional candidates, resulting in different kinds of people getting nominated and elected. The political shakeups of the late 1960s (including disagreements over Vietnam and the riotous 1968 Democratic convention in Chicago) resulted in broad party reforms that diluted the role of public officials in the parties and strengthened the hand of grass-roots activists. Many of these same activists used their political organizing experiences, the assistance of their fellow activists, and their new clout to run in congressional primaries. Many won. By 1974, the mix of new members of Congress included a large number with no prior elective experience, little or no background in party affairs, and a deeper commitment to issue positions than to party or legislative organization. By the late 1970s, antiwar activists were drying up as a pool for new Democratic members—only to be replaced on the Republican side by anti–gun-control, anti-abortion, and pro-morality activists.

To many observers, the arrival of this new breed of legislator brought a decline in interest in compromise in Congress, a growing sense of personal acrimony, an enhanced distrust of leadership, and a growing pressure for more decentralization and democratization. Complained one veteran Democratic House member in 1975: "These new guys don't appreciate the value of compromise, don't believe there's a history of actions around here to learn from, don't trust anybody who's a chairman, and don't give a damn about the party." Virtually the identical words were uttered by a senior Republican congressman about his colleagues in 1980! The new legislators tended to be less predictable in their voting patterns, too—less likely, in other words, to be easily added to the columns of consistently liberal or conservative. This added to the unpredictability of action in the new Congress.

A second major outside change occurred in the mass media. Coverage of Congress, Washington, and government increased in importance and public visibility when the network news shows moved from fifteen minutes to a half-hour in 1963. But a more profound change occurred in the 1970s, as tension between citizens and government over the Vietnam War grew, tension between president and Congress mounted, and Watergate exploded. The press "discovered" Washington.

In 1957, there were 876 journalists accredited by the general Congressional Press Gallery, and 261 accredited by the Radio and TV Press Gallery, and 306 by the Periodical Press Gallery. By 1967, the comparable numbers were 986, 512, and 591. In 1981, they were 1,331, 1,028, and 1,004. The radio, television, and periodical press corps almost quadrupled in twenty-four years.[9]

Washington coverage was increasing rapidly before Watergate, but public interest in the nationally televised hearings by the Ervin Committee in the Senate and the Rodino Committee in the House, and in the investigative reporting of Bob Woodward and Carl Bernstein, added a new dimension to media attention. Coverage of Washington and of Congress moved beyond the front pages and the nightly news shows to the personality columns and prime time. The fact that Watergate was followed closely by congressional scandal—notably Wilbur Mills and the famed Tidal Basin incident, and Tongsun Park and "Koreagate"—accentuated and refocused the media coverage of Congress. A new generation of "Woodsteins"—investigative reporters inspired by the Watergate duo—began to zero in on scandal and sloth as well as policy on Capitol Hill.

This new media interest in Washington had several effects on Congress. Most important, it opened up Congress more than ever before to public attention and thereby created more opportunities than ever before for individual members to receive national publicity. In the 1970s, the high-circulation personality journal, *People* magazine, opened a Washington bureau and began to feature regular pictorials on congressmen in the news. The "Today" show, "Good Morning America," and "Nightline" expanded their coverage of Washington personalities. It became possible for any member of Congress to get national coverage and become a nationally recognized figure. Unshackled by norms or rules, aided by staff resources and new procedures, every member down to the most junior had the opportunity to seize attention.

Essentially, there were three ways to do this: become a victim of scandal, defy conventional wisdom and conduct, or publicize an issue. In the first category, we could put in recent years Wilbur Mills, Bob Bauman, Michael Myers, Charles Diggs, and many others. In the second category, there were members who denounced party leaders (Lowell Weicker and John LeBoutillier), denounced their institutions and colleagues (Bruce Caputo and Shirley Chisholm), denounced Washington (Ed Zorinsky and Paula Hawkins), defied presidents (Dennis DeConcini), used profanity (Bella Abzug), moved into their offices (Jim Jeffords), and tried singlehandedly to free U.S. hostages in Iran (George Hansen). The third group includes among others Jack Kemp (tax cuts), Les Aspin (Pentagon cost overruns), William Proxmire (government waste, a.k.a. the "fleece of the month"), Tom Harkin (human rights), Henry Hyde (abortion), and Jeremiah Denton (teenage sex).

Television and the mass media were not, of course, new phenomena on the Capitol scene. Such luminaries as Joe McCarthy, Estes Kefauver, and John McClellan had gained national attention through televised investigations in the 1950s. But the 1970s were different. As media coverage expanded, the number of members of Congress who were brought to public attention mushroomed, and more and more of the publicized members came from the rank and file. For Caputo, Hyde, Zorinsky, DeConcini, Denton, and LeBoutillier, fame of sorts came in their freshman terms. It came in every instance because of maverick behavior that in the old Congress would have resulted in ridicule and ostracism.

This trend toward personal publicity provided, in contrast to the Rayburn era, a range of tangible and possible outside incentives. No longer did a member have to play by inside rules to receive inside rewards or avoid inside setbacks. One could "go public" and be rewarded by national attention; national attention in turn could provide ego gratification, social success in Washington, the opportunity to run for higher political office, or, by highlighting an issue, policy success.

A third major change in the 1970s outside Congress was a striking expansion in the number, range, and activity of interest groups. The anti–Vietnam War movement fostered the growth in the 1970s of a number of groups claiming to represent the public interest in areas like consumer protection, environmental and defense policy, and general governmental reform.[10] The decentralization, democratization, and staff growth in Congress encouraged the creation and perpetuation of these and other groups, since more members of Congress, along with their staffs, could provide access and assistance to groups. As the access points expanded, the access process opened up, aided by recorded teller voting, open meetings, and open hearings.

It was not just (or mainly) public interest groups that grew in number and presence in and around Congress. Every type of group expanded. From 1970 to 1980, over 800 national trade associations moved to Washington, while the number of cities and towns directly represented tripled, to over 100. Another indication of the growth of groups during this period is the expansion of nongovernmental office space in Washington; this mushroomed from 39 million square feet in 1970 to 70 million square feet in 1980. The growth was not in commercial enterprises. By 1980, fully 40 percent of that office space was occupied by lawyers, accountants, and associations—compared with 19 percent in Chicago and 20 percent in Los Angeles.[11]

The growth in groups, combined with the "sunshine" reforms in Congress, contributed to the pressure for decentralization, strengthened the hand of junior members by giving them access to group information and resources, and added additional, outside pressures on members' voting decisions. Groups began to suggest or draft amendments to committee bills, to see that their friends introduced them, then to watch carefully when the votes—recorded votes—occurred in committee and on the floor. Groups began to pressure members of Congress on particular issues, using such weapons as targeted grass-roots support from constituents, issue-based "hit lists" of members on the wrong side, and contributions from political action committees (PACs) created after the passage of campaign finance reform laws.

In sum, as the result of a series of interrelated changes in internal operations and outside forces, Congress has become an *open system*. External incentives and rewards now compete with internal ones for members' time, attention, and behavior. The internal rewards, such as staff, trips, or chairmanships, have been democratized—they come automatically to legislators, without long waiting or testing. They cannot be withheld or removed for errant behavior. Moreover, what would have been defined as errant or maverick behavior in the past— challenging a committee's recommendations or expertise with amendments on the floor, criticizing the leadership or Congress itself, challenging the motives of other legislators—is no longer grounds for chastisement or even murmurs of disapproval. It may even bring two minutes of television exposure on the evening news, which would elicit widespread envy among colleagues.

In the open system, a high proportion of members (a majority of the Senate and 40 percent or so of the House) have chairmanships of one sort or another, usually with freedom to range widely in the scope of their hearings or investigations and with ample staff resources to assist. All 535 members have ample personal staff resources, which afford them the freedom to be active in all legislative issues and still attend to the more mundane constituency servicing. Inside committees, the open system spreads power and initiatives from the once-autocratic chairmen out to subcommittee leaders and rank-and-file members. Internal dissension in committees is not discouraged or quashed. Open meetings and hearings provide new opportunities for a variety of groups to observe members talk, deal, and vote and to influence members' actions as bills are marked up.

No longer internally cohesive or disciplined, committees are also unprotected on the floor. Major amendments to a bill might come from any direction, ranging from a dissident committee member challenging his own panel's product to an unknown freshman, whose foray into this policy area comes as a surprise to everyone. In an open system, unpredictability is the norm.

The Open System and the President

Rayburn, in our fable, was dazzled by these changes—accustomed, as he was, to operating within a closed system. But we can be confident that, in spite of his initial shock, he would quickly have adapted. Rayburn was a leader who worked in whatever system he was presented with, adapting himself and his resources to the available opportunities and constraints. And he would have realized that the open system of Congress, while unpredictable, erratic, diffused, and decentralized, also offered new openings for leadership and policy success that had been unavailable in the old era.

It is not much different for presidents. When Congress was characterized by a closed system, presidents had to work out deals and coalitions with the committee barons, or on occasion, find a broader group to persuade. The style that successful past presidents used was identical to that of the congressional leaders like Rayburn; indeed, the presidents would often rely on the leaders as brokers.

The challenge for a president in an open congressional system is, likewise, the same as the challenge to the contemporary party leaders. It requires a combination of new sensitivities and traditional skills. To prevail these days, a president first must accept a cardinal premise: he will be required to know and to deal regularly with a much wider array of players in the process, members *and* staff. Such dealings require a congressional liaison staff that works to know not just who the members are, but what they like and dislike, who needs to be sweet-talked and who can be bullied, who will be satisfied with a special White House tour for constituents or an invitation to a state dinner and who will insist on a substantive concession. Knowing the members also means maintaining an active, ongoing intelligence operation to achieve early warning of who might introduce a surprise amendment or oppose a presidential initiative or be vulnerable at a given future moment to a particular presidential plea.

Second, the open system requires much more frequent use of the most precious presidential resource—the president himself. Telephone calls to wavering members, meetings with important congressional groups, intimate give-and-take sessions with important legislators, and close working arrangements with congressional leaders are all necessary to maintain the broad net of relationships a president needs in Congress to get things done. A president who wishes to be successful with Congress will be willing to commit precious personal time to persuading members and will carry out the task of persuasion eagerly and cheerfully. While members of Congress have changed, and their institutions and incentives have changed, they are still human beings who respond to attention and favors, who understand political give and take, and who remain respectful and a bit awed by the presidency.

In knowing the members of Congress and in working closely with them, Jimmy Carter was deficient, while Ronald Reagan (at least at the beginning) was superb. Carter, as Eric Davis points out in chapter 3 of this volume, selected and retained a congressional liaison staff chief who was organizationally inept and ignorant of Congress. Frank Moore stories are legion—the unreturned phone calls, the gaffes—but the problem went far beyond Moore. One story epitomizes the Carter White House relationship with Congress: Congressman Norman Mineta, a Japanese-American Democrat from San Jose and a bright young Carter loyalist, was inadvertently and embarrassingly left off the guest list for the White House state dinner for the Japanese prime minister because the White House thought Mineta was Italian! And this from a White House that included a key congressional liaison staff member who had once been Mineta's administrative assistant.[12]

In spite of the presence of at least a few savvy lobbyists, the Carter liaison team had a difficult time assessing the members of Congress and keeping track of each one's needs and preferences. They were not helped by Carter's well-known distaste for personal politicking and friendly regular chats with legislators. They were hampered as well by Carter's lack of close friends on or from Capitol Hill.

Ronald Reagan, in part responding to the Carter experience, quickly established a strong and knowledgeable congressional liaison team, headed by Hill veteran Max Friedersdorf. Early in the administration, Friedersdorf and his colleagues made direct contact with all the members of Congress (sixteen months into the Carter term, one key Republican House member complained to me that he still had not been called by anyone from the Carter congressional liaison operation). The Friedersdorf team also began to size up the 535 members of Congress in the ways we have discussed above. They recognized early that long-term success is dependent on the accumulation of little things, such as returning phone calls and doing small favors for members.

They have been aided enormously by their president. Ronald Reagan likes to visit with congressmen and enjoys bargaining and bantering. He is charming and persuasive. Some of his best friends serve in Congress. He willingly devotes long hours to calling legislators and relying on personal persuasion. By all accounts, Reagan's personal efforts added at least a dozen Democrats to his side in the key vote on the budget reconciliation rule on June 25, 1981. As a *Congressional Quarterly* newsletter noted, "Reagan's prowess in the rule fight was undeniable. Vote counts by the GOP and Democrats the day before the House rules showdown . . . showed that the GOP had no more than 15 of 26 Democrats needed for their victory. That was before Reagan spent hours phoning undecided conservatives."[13] Similar comments were made after Reagan's stunning tax cut victory on July 29, 1981.[14]

Good political intelligence, political favors, and personal "stroking" of legislators are not always sufficient. There are too many members, too few inducements, and too many other persuasive elements out there. So a good president will also know to limit his priorities and to order them carefully. The new Congress is an anthill of activity, but that means much motion, and little movement. A president can use his resources, prestige, and power to focus congressional (and public) attention and to put a handful of his items at the top of the congressional agenda for action. Then, if he is lucky and skillful, he can use his abilities to succeed in these key areas. This has always been so, but Congress today is much more active and much less ordered—and everything is open and public. If a president asks for too many things and fails to put them in any strong order of preference, Congress will become overloaded, and much of his program will founder. Worse, it will look, under the glare of intense media coverage, as if the president said, "Do this," and Congress responded, "No." This is precisely what happened to Jimmy Carter, who early in his term proposed, among other things, a total overhaul of the tax system, a plan to contain health costs, a major change in the welfare system, a new trade bill, a gasoline tax, and a fifty-dollar tax rebate. All of these proposals—some vague pronouncements, others specific bills—were referred en masse to the House Ways and Means Committee. Most stayed there, the victims of committee gridlock. There were no specific instructions from the president on the order of consideration. Ironically, Carter's major early success—House passage of his comprehensive energy bill—was diluted because other, equal priorities of the president's simultaneously went nowhere. Carter looked like a weak leader as a result.

Reagan, on the other hand, started his presidency with one overriding issue to press: the economy. This focus translated into two initiatives, a budget proposal and a tax cut proposal. Reagan as president gave a nationally televised speech in February 1981, addressed Congress (also on television) in February, addressed Congress again (once more on prime-time television) in April, and spoke to the public via national television in late July—all on the subject of his economic recovery program and his two specific proposals. He set up timetables for action, devoted the full scope of his own and his administration's resources to get these two proposals ready for Congress and to persuade Congress to meet his deadlines and vote his way. The issues were magnified as a result of the Reagan emphasis, and his successes thus underscored and celebrated by press and public alike.

Just as important, the focus on the economic issue meant that simultaneous Reagan failures in other areas—the rejection of State Department nominee Ernest Lefever by the Senate Foreign Relations Committee; the postponement of advanced weapons sales to Saudi Arabia after overwhelming congressional protest; the passage of near-unanimous House and Senate resolutions condemning the administration's vote in an international organization on infant formula regulation; the rejection by House committees of administration proposals on surface mining, park land acquisition, and mineral leasing; the rebuff of the White House's proposals for funding cuts for public broadcasting; the rejection of the Reagan proposal to repeal the Clark Amendment banning American involvement in Angola—were downplayed in the press and ignored by the public, and thus had little negative effect on Reagan's overall image in Congress.

Reagan's early handling of the economic issue underscores another, traditional skill of presidential leadership, the ability to capitalize on political timing. A seasoned, savvy leader knows that momentum is a real force in politics and that reputation is more important than reality in the leadership game. It is as true today as it was in the 1950s that a president who can exaggerate his victories and minimize his losses is considered a leader, while a president who gets more blame and less credit than he deserves is dismissed as inept or is vilified.

Congressional cloakrooms still exist, and cloakroom banter about a president has a very real influence on how fearful legislators feel when they cast votes with or against the White House. The fear may be less than it was a few decades ago, given the reality that a president has fewer sanctions to apply to the recalcitrant. But it still exists.

Moreover, the president's reputation is not built entirely on the personal experiences of the legislators. Like the rest of us, they get most of their news and impressions of people and politics from the mass media: the *New York Times, Washington Post, Wall Street Journal,* and the networks. Thus, it is most important for a president to have a strong reputation with the media as a leader. It helps him not only with the public at large, but also with the Washington community. In the contemporary era, the access a president has to the enormous television audience multiplies the potential advantages he has in raising and fulfilling expectations, thus enhancing his reputation for further political leverage.

So, the sophisticated president knows how to maximize his public or political attention when success or drama are at hand. In Congress, Lyndon Johnson and Sam Rayburn were masters at delaying votes until just the right psychological and political moment. In the White House in 1964 and 1965, Johnson knew enough to take advantage of the momentum given him by the Kennedy assassination and his landslide election to steamroll legislation through and to look like a master doing it. Nixon timed his China trip and recognition announcement superbly, to disarm his foes and capture full world attention.

Jimmy Carter, in contrast, showed a consistent ability to deflate his opportunities—to bring public attention, interest, and expectation to a peak, only to follow with inaction. Energy policy is the best example. Michael J. Malbin elaborates on Carter's handling of energy policy elsewhere in this volume, but it is useful here to recount a little of one episode to show the importance of timing. After a few weeks of Senate and conference committee deadlock over his first comprehensive energy plan in 1977, Carter announced dramatically on national television on November 8 of that year that he was canceling his four-continent tour to stay in Washington to get the plan passed. At the time, the stalemate was with the Senate, where conferees were deadlocked 9–9 on natural gas pricing. They stayed that way for six and a half months, when the conferees finally voted 10–7 for a compromise. Much evidence suggests that during November 1977—incredibly—Carter did not apply face-to-face pressure to any of the nine opposing senators. Whether or not this is true, no savvy leader would dramatically cancel a trip, causing the public, Congress and press to take notice, before first arranging for a breakthrough to be imminent. Instead, as a result of Carter's inattention to political timing, he not only was unable to take credit for his plan and his persuasion, but his dramatic move served rather to highlight his ineptitude!

Note that we are not talking about charisma here. *Any* president has the ability to suddenly capture public and media attention, as Carter did. Note also that the energy plan ultimately passed; it does go down as a Carter accomplishment. But he received little or no credit for it, and his reputation in fact declined.

Carter repeated this pattern in July 1979, when he abruptly canceled a planned energy speech and retreated to Camp David, emerging days later to address the nation. The drama was palpable. Interest in this prime-time Sunday presidential address was as high as for any in recent times. The result was not wild enthusiasm, but still, mild approval. While well-delivered, the Carter speech gave few specifics and made no striking proposals or calls for sacrifice. But even worse, the president tripped over his own momentum a couple of days later by abruptly firing several members of his cabinet. The rather favorable response to his speech was forgotten, and once again the Carter reputation suffered.

In the "new" Congress, stage-managing is far more difficult than in the old, and far more risky. Reagan came within four votes of losing on his 1981 budget reconciliation vote; many things beyond his control could have occurred to turn a dramatic presidential victory into an equally important presidential defeat. The same is true of the vote in August 1982 on the Reagan tax increase bill. The point is, however, that a president must be sensitive to the importance of timing and must devote his resources to using it to his advantage. No matter how skillful a president is as a communicator, there are only a limited number of times that he can wholly capture public, press, and congressional attention, and heighten everybody's expectations. The successful president will hoard these opportunities judiciously, use them only when he can gain from them, and tie them directly to his expenditure of resources to persuade congressmen.

Finally, the savvy president will look at the new, open Congress and will devise ways of taking advantage of the permeability in the system. If Congress is more diffuse, no committee or "little group of willful men" can any longer bottle up completely and without recourse a pet presidential proposal, the way that chairmen like Wilbur Mills on Ways and Means, "Judge" Smith on Rules, and others did to pet initiatives of Truman, Eisenhower, Kennedy, and Johnson. In the old closed system, Jimmy Carter would never have gotten a vote in the House on his hospital cost containment plan; it would have died a definitive death in committee. In the new open system, he found ways to get the bill to the floor (even if he did end up losing on the vote there). Reagan's dramatic budget plan required bypassing many committees, overruling others, and turning the usual congressional decision-making process upside down. The new reformed budget process made his bold plan feasible technically; the fluid, unfocused atmosphere of the open congressional system allowed it to work politically.

The new Congress poses both new problems and new opportunities for a president. New sensitivities, creative leadership, and traditional political skills can overcome the problems and result in success. It will not be total success: no president in modern history has won all or even most of his legislative battles. But a skillful president today can do as well as his successful predecessors from the good old days. Even Sam Rayburn would acknowledge that.

Notes

1. Ralph K. Huitt, "The Outsider in the Senate: An Alternative Role," *American Political Science Review*, vol. 55 (September 1961), pp. 566-75.

2. Michael J. Robinson, "Three Faces of Congressional Media," in Thomas E. Mann and Norman J. Ornstein, eds., *The New Congress* (Washington, D.C.: American Enterprise Institute, 1981), pp. 55-98.

3. Robert G. Baker with Larry L. King, *Wheeling and Dealing* (New York: W.W. Norton & Co., 1978), p. 67.

4. On the impact of the class of '58 on the Senate of the 1960s and early 1970s, see Michael Foley, *The New Senate: Liberal Influence on A Conservative Institution, 1959-1972* (New Haven, Conn.: Yale University Press, 1980).

5. See, as examples, Norman J. Ornstein, ed., *Congress in Change: Evolution and Reform* (New York: Praeger, 1975); Roger H. Davidson and Walter J. Oleszek, *Congress Against Itself* (Bloomington: Indiana University Press, 1977); Lawrence Dodd and Bruce Oppenheimer, eds., *Congress Reconsidered*, 2d ed. (Washington, D.C.: Congressional Quarterly Press, 1981); and Mann and Ornstein, *New Congress.*

6. John F. Bibby, Thomas E. Mann, and Norman J. Ornstein, *Vital Statistics on Congress 1980* (Washington, D.C.: American Enterprise Institute, 1980), pp. 71-73.

7. Quoted in Norman J. Ornstein, ed., *The Role of the Legislature in Western Democracies* (Washington, D.C.: American Enterprise Institute, 1981), p. 163.

8. It should be noted that this definition of reciprocity is much broader than that used by Donald R. Matthews in *U.S. Senators and Their World* (New York: Vintage, 1960) in his discussion of folkways in Chapter 5.

9. Evidence gathered from appropriate *Congressional Directories.* See also Robinson, "Three Faces," p. 83.

10. On public interest groups, see Jeffrey Berry, *Lobbying for the People* (Princeton, N.J.: Princeton University Press, 1978) and Andrew MacFarland, *Public Interest Lobbies: Decision Making on Energy* (Washington, D.C.: American Enterprise Institute, 1976).

11. These figures come from Marc Kaufman, "Study Ties Growth to Lobbyists," *Washington Star*, October 6, 1980.

12. The incident was made even more embarrassing for the president when Mineta was asked by newsmen whether he was upset by the oversight. He responded that he was not unhappy at all: he thought that Prime Minister Ohira was the leader of Ireland!

13. *Congressional Insight*, vol. 5, no. 26 (June 26, 1981).

14. See Martin Schram, "Reagan the Tax Lobbyist: An Artist at Work," *Washington Post*, August 13, 1981, p. A3.

8

Rhetoric and Leadership: A Look Backward at the Carter National Energy Plan

MICHAEL J. MALBIN

Imagine it is May 7, 1981. Newspaper headlines are announcing President Ronald Reagan's first major budget victory in the House of Representatives. In a remarkable vote, 63 Democrats have joined with every one of the House's 190 Republicans to produce a 253 to 176 margin for the president. House Speaker Thomas P. (Tip) O'Neill, Jr., of Massachusetts says sadly that the vote marks "a fundamental change" of historic proportions. A *Washington Post* headline is "Shattered: Democratic Coalition Falls to Pieces."[1] News reports credit the victory, in part, to Reagan's masterly public speeches, particularly his triumphal April 28 televised address to a joint session of Congress—his first major public appearance after he was wounded on March 30 in an assassination attempt. They also point to his skill in establishing relations with Congress: he personally courted Capitol Hill in the month before Inaugural Day, selected an experienced team of White House lobbyists, used the Easter recess to send his surrogates into the districts of wavering Democratic members, and held private conversations with members of the House before the vote.

Some more cautious observers say they will reserve judgment for a while before they credit Reagan with a real victory. The budget resolution is only the first step in a months-long process, and the effect of the budget on the economy may take years to be known fully. But these voices are being drowned out. The day is the president's, and rightly so. Not since the administration of Lyndon Johnson has a president been so successful in the beginning of his term in pushing his program through Congress.

Now let the mind go back to another president with a different piece of top-priority domestic legislation. On April 20, 1977, the cardigan-clad Jimmy Carter gave the famous "fireside chat" in which he called the energy crisis "the moral equivalent of war." The president was slow in getting started: his energy bills were not even formally introduced until May 2, within a week of the date the House adopted Reagan's budget package four years later. Still, despite the slow beginning, Carter's speech was well accepted, his popularity was high, and his supporters were optimistic that most of the important elements of the National Energy Plan would become law.

For several months the optimism seemed justified. O'Neill, then new to the speakership, put his prestige on the line in support of his party's leader. On August 5, the House passed most of the National Energy Plan. That day, too, was the president's. But then the package began to unravel. In September, the Senate all but dismantled it. The House–Senate conference took weeks getting started, and almost a year to finish. On October 13, 1978—the last full day of the Ninety-fifth Congress—the ragged remains of the package were enacted with a margin of only one vote.

Thinking backwards, even only a few years, is enough to humble anyone who would predict the future. An administration's support in Congress can fall very far, very fast, at any time during the four-year presidential cycle. The importance of Reagan's initial victory, however, is that the reverse situation does not apply. Presidents, as Paul Light has said, may build up their political skills over time, but they cannot build up their power in the same way. An administration's power is at its peak at the beginning. Successes achieved during a four-year cycle are likely to be based on actions taken early in the first year.[2] As a result, mistakes made during the first year will color everything that follows.

For these reasons, the National Energy Plan—the highest domestic priority of President Carter's first year in office—is a good window through which to view the Carter administration's later problems. What happened to that package should also tell us something more general about the character of contemporary legislative–executive relations.

Any number of reasons were offered during the Carter administration for the energy package's legislative problems. Most seem partial at best, after Reagan's early successes. We were told at the time, for example, that the energy package failed because of the way it distributed costs and benefits. In pork-barrel bills, which are easy to pass, benefits take the form of discrete, visible projects while costs are small and largely invisible. The energy package had trouble, it was said, because it reversed this relationship, making discrete, organized groups of people bear clearly identifiable costs for a benefit that was diffuse, several years away, and speculative.[3] The explanation is correct, as far as it goes. Any bill that concentrates costs while diffusing benefits is bound to have a harder time than one that does the reverse. That explanation, however, does not begin to go far enough. President Reagan's budget package shared the same features: discrete beneficiaries were asked to accept budget cuts for the sake of speculative, long-term, diffuse benefits. Despite this, Congress adopted the first budget resolution. It follows that, although the relationship between costs and benefits may affect how difficult it is to pass a controversial bill, it cannot by itself tell us why Carter's proposals were decimated.

A second reason offered for congressional unwillingness to pass comprehensive energy legislation is related to Congress's internal decentralization after the reforms of the early 1970s.[4] Congress has always been structured to make it easier to kill or delay than to pass controversial legislation. The Constitution separates the House and the Senate, and gives the president veto power, precisely to slow down the process and force legislators to forge a broad consensus before acting. The number of congressional "veto points" increased over the years, as committees became more powerful and committee chairmen were given virtually automatic job protection through the seniority system. During the 1950s and 1960s, committee chairmen were clearly the most important people in Congress.

By the time President Carter was inaugurated, however, Congress had changed. Subcommittees were almost as important as full committees, and virtually every legislative committee in the House had a subcommittee dealing with energy policy. Party leaders had regained some control over scheduling pending bills, but both committee and party leaders found their positions open to amendment or defeat by unpredictable coalitions on the floor. To borrow the words of Roger Davidson: "Today's Congress is open, egalitarian, and fragmented. It lacks leadership or consensus, and its ideological or partisan commitments are uncertain. . . . The chief impression is buzzing confusion."[5]

There can be no question that the congressional fragmentation of the 1970s has made a president's work harder. Presidents can no longer be certain that anyone on Capitol Hill has the power to strike a bargain that will bind anyone else. During the spring of 1980, for example, Carter held a series of meetings with congressional leaders to put together an anti-inflation package. According to a press account of one such meeting:

> Part of the price of reaching a consensus [on inflation] with them [the congressional leaders] was that the President im-

pose an oil import fee and take the political heat for it. He kept the bargain. The Hill did not; the ink was still wet when Congress voted first to repeal the fee, then to override Carter's veto by a humiliating 335-to-34 vote in the House and 68-to-10 in the Senate.[6]

It would be hard to imagine something like this happening to President Eisenhower after he had struck a deal with Sam Rayburn and Lyndon Johnson.

Decentralization does make it more difficult to assemble coalitions, but it does not automatically make presidents less powerful. As Norman J. Ornstein argues elsewhere in this volume, politically sensitive presidents of past decades may not have suffered as many defeats in public, but defeated they often were. The openness of the 1970s makes it easier for presidents, as well as junior members, to get around chairmen when the need arises.[7]

In any case, whatever the fractionalizing effects of reform may have been, they did not prevent Congress from passing Reagan's first budget resolution in 1981. Of course, the budget may be a somewhat special case. The 1974 Budget Control and Impoundment Act works in exactly the opposite direction from most of the other recent changes in Congress, by providing mechanisms for central control where diffusion and fragmentation had previously been the rule. The budget resolution depended on a reconciliation process that would not have been possible without the budget reform act. Even so, Allen Schick has pointed out that reconciliation cannot work without the active cooperation of committee and subcommittee chairmen.[8] The rules may facilitate such cooperation, but it ultimately rests on something more pervasive in the political climate.

The Power to Persuade

Creating a favorable political climate is the most difficult task of contemporary presidential leadership. "Presidential power is the power to persuade," wrote Richard Neustadt in his classic study of the office.[9] But persuade whom? Of what? How? If a president were to limit his efforts to an attempt to persuade more than half of the Congress to accept his proposals on their merits, the job would be straightforward—and generally futile. Public issues involve more than two "sides." Sometimes there are as many sides, or opinions about the best possible public policy, as there are actors. So if the president hopes to persuade others to accept his proposals, he must work with committee and party leaders in Congress to structure a situation in which his proposals are accepted as the best of the alternatives that are practically available. Since structuring a vote means limiting the choices open to members, it presupposes maintaining good working relations with committee and party leaders, the people who hold the levers needed for structuring, and also with followers, whose choices will be limited.

Maintaining good relations leads to the most basic tool in Neustadt's account of presidential persuasion. "The power to persuade is the power to bargain," Neustadt wrote.[10] In his view, members of Congress and people serving in the administration help the president, and vice versa, because each expects to gain something from the transaction, either explicitly, in exchange for immediate support, or implicitly, by incurring an obligation. For the process to work well, there must be skilled bargainers on both sides of the relationship—people who are willing to engage in the process, who know what to offer to whom, and who have developed a reputation for constancy that will permit people to take risks, with the understanding that those risks incur mutual obligations. President Carter neither enjoyed this part of his job nor was very skilled at it. His reputation for inconsistency dogged him throughout the period Congress was considering the energy package, undermining the willingness of members to take risks on behalf of his program.

The close connection between persuasion and bargaining in Neustadt's account was based upon his understanding of what it is that the president has to persuade the members of Congress to believe:

> The essence of a president's persuasive task with Congressmen and everybody else, is to induce them to believe that what he wants of them is what their own appraisal of their own responsibilities require them to do in their interest, not his. Because men may differ in their views on public policy, because differences in outlook stem from differences in duty—duty to one's office, one's constituents, oneself—that task is bound to be more like collective bargaining than like a reasoned argument among philosopher kings. . . . This is the reason why: persuasion deals in the coin of self-interest with men who have some freedom to reject what they find counterfeit.[11]

The purpose of presidential persuasion, according to Neustadt, is to persuade people to adopt a president's ends out of their own self-interest. Thus, the typical act of presidential persuasion in Neustadt's portrayal involves logrolling more than deliberation—the latter is the coin of philosopher kings.

Neustadt's description of one form of persuasion seems accurate enough, but unduly restrictive and cynical. After all, the most convincing way to show a member that a proposal is in his interest is either to persuade him directly, using what used to be called deliberative rhetoric, showing that the proposal is consistent with his past beliefs and actions, or to "go over the member's head" with public rhetoric to persuade the member's constituents.[12] Neustadt had little to say about either direct (deliberative) or indirect (public) persuasion. The omission is serious.

It may well be futile, as we said earlier, for a president to rely solely on deliberative rhetoric; nevertheless, it does have an important role to play. As Neustadt suggests without elaborating, a member's perception of his interest partly involves his perception of his duty to his office. Few members are willing to stay long in office without feeling some genuine concern over policy. As Senator Thomas Eagleton told the *Wall Street Journal*'s Albert R. Hunt, "If on twenty major issues you steadfastly oppose the prevailing opinion of your constituents, you're probably in your last term." But, the Missouri Democrat went on, "you do pick some issues that you think are important and on these issues you owe your constitutents your judgment."[13] Presidents use deliberative rhetoric both to convince members of an issue's importance and to sway their judgments. A president who cannot persuade a fair number of members on this level makes the rest of his job just that much harder, if not impossible. There are not enough bargaining chips available to coalesce majorities around positions that do not have at least some clear intrinsic merit.

Indirect persuasion, or public rhetoric, is just as important to contemporary presidents as deliberative rhetoric.[14] As Senator Eagleton said, members cannot be expected to go against their constituents habitually. Presidents use public persuasion in two different ways. First, public rhetoric can be part of an effort to "go over the heads of Congress," which was President Carter's characterization of many of his own public speeches on legislation. In his view, the use of public rhetoric was designed to pressure members of Congress by showing them it would be costly to bow to the desires of special-interest groups. A less biased description of such rhetoric would see it as designed to persuade constituents to look at an issue from the president's perspective—that is, to narrow the gap between the perceived interests of the district and the nation. In either case, the first use of public rhetoric involves creating a political climate that all but compels members to go along with the president's program.

The second use of public rhetoric is more subtle. Presidents and members of Congress often will address the people to make them consider an issue that otherwise might escape their attention. The point of this is generally not to force members to bow to public pressure but to create counterpressures to the ones generated by the naturally attentive part of the public with a special stake in the outcome, the organized interests. If the strategy works, the pressures will cancel each other out, the member will be free to rely on his own judgment, and the president can turn to direct persuasion.

Neustadt's relative inattention to public rhetoric is probably justified for most issues. As he pointed out, people are "basically inattentive to what presidents and other political figures have to say."[15] If a president tries to appeal to the public too often, he is likely to induce boredom and confusion, not support. Presidents can take a few major issues to the public at a time, however. If these issues are presented persuasively, the public's attention can be galvanized long enough to achieve the desired result. Without public rhetoric, presidents are confined to bargaining within a framework dominated by habitually attentive interest groups. In general, this limits presidents to incremental actions that do not dramatically disturb the status quo. Presidents with only modest objectives may be satisfied with these limits, but a president who hopes to rearrange the status quo has to choose his issue carefully, put it at the top of his personal agenda, and rally public support behind the substance of his position. Effective rhetoric, matching deeds with words, can make an inattentive public attentive, changing every member's calculation of his political self-interest. It is the only choice open to a president who wants Congress and the attentive interest groups to accept major policy initiatives that go against the grain.

Carter's Rhetoric and the Energy Package

President Carter's legislative goals were certainly ambitious. When he came to office, for example, he wanted the House Ways and Means and Senate Finance committees to be prepared to rewrite the tax code, to reform the welfare system, to look at national health insurance, and to report new energy legislation. In each of these areas, and in others, Carter leaned in the direction of "comprehensive" bills. He explained the reason in a revealing interview published six months before he took office:

> Most of the controversial issues that are not routinely addressed can only respond to a comprehensive approach. Incremental efforts to make basic changes are often foredoomed to failure because the special interest groups can

benefit from the status quo, can focus their attention on the increments that most affect themselves, and the general public can't be made either interested or aware.[16]

Where Congress seemed reluctant to adopt his plans, Carter said he would not hesitate to criticize the legislative branch in public addresses, as he had done as governor of Georgia:

> I would use that influence of going directly to the people and identifying special interest groups that block good legislation. And I believe the President's voice would be much more authoritative and much more clear than any governor's voice could be, because of the close attention paid to the President's statements by the news media.[17]

These statements accurately forecast the way Carter used public rhetoric to promote his energy plan during his first year in office. He presented the details of his comprehensive plan once and then largely kept quiet about its merits, reserving his comments for occasions when he could attack "special interests."

It will be argued here that President Carter's almost entirely cynical view of the reasons people might have for opposing him hurt his efforts to persuade the Congress on all three of the levels just mentioned: bargaining, deliberative rhetoric, and public rhetoric. The conclusions will be based on a selective review of some of the events relating to the National Energy Plan. For a more complete history of what happened to the plan, readers are urged to look elsewhere.[18]

Jimmy Carter took office during a winter shortage of natural gas, which was causing factory slowdowns through much of the Northeast and Midwest. On the day after his inauguration, the new president announced he would submit emergency legislation and promised he would formulate a coherent energy policy "promptly."[19] Five days later, Carter submitted an emergency bill to Congress and told the press his chief White House energy adviser, James Schlesinger, would have comprehensive legislation ready "at an early date."[20] In another three days, on January 29, he told workers at a Westinghouse plant in Pittsburgh that a comprehensive package would be sent to Congress by April 20.[21]

Until Carter took office, there was no reason to believe that passing energy legislation would become as important for his administration as it did. Of course, Carter did speak about the subject during his campaign for office. From his formal announcement in December 1974[22] through the closing weeks of the 1976 campaign,[23] Carter spoke often about the need for a "planned," "rational," and "comprehensive" energy policy. Yet, during that long period, Carter never outlined in a public speech the basic principles that would guide the formulation of such a policy. Perhaps such principles could be gleaned from the relevant sections of the 1976 Democratic platform[24] or from campaign committee position papers,[25] but platforms and position papers are read only by specialized audiences and have little to do with building public support.[26] If anything, the campaign speeches suggest that building public support on the energy issue was not on the candidate's agenda. His acceptance speech to the Democratic national convention was silent on the subject. Its references to government reorganization, tax reform, welfare reform, and health insurance would lead one to expect these subjects to receive higher priority in a Carter administration than energy.[27] This impression was strengthened during the fall campaign, when the subject would get raised only in response to a specific question or as part of a discussion of such broader subjects as inflation.[28]

On the few occasions that Carter did try to develop a theme for his energy policies, the attempts were contradictory. Carter criticized the Ford administration on September 15, for example, for relying on a policy that would raise energy prices,[29] but wrote a publicly released letter to Oklahoma's Governor David Boren a month later in which he promised to deregulate the price of newly discovered natural gas.[30] (Both positions hurt Carter after he was in office: his 1977 National Energy Plan would have continued natural-gas price regulation and used taxes to raise the price of oil.) More often, however, Carter limited himself to safe statements tucked away in the middle of general speeches. As late as election eve, he portrayed his energy priorities and goals not as something he had already articulated but as something yet to be developed.[31]

There was nothing surprising about Carter's failure to take his energy program to the public during the campaign. The issues were complex, they divided the Democratic party, and the general public did not care much about them.[32] Under the circumstances, it would have been far more surprising had Carter chosen to stress the subject. The decision to downplay energy may have made sense in electoral terms, but it carried with it a governmental price. Although the public may be "habitually inattentive" to policy statements, as Neustadt has said, no time is better than a presidential campaign for gaining its attention. Presidents who want to make major policy changes that require public support will find it easier to win that support if the foundation has been laid during the campaign. If the issue has been developed sufficiently, the president even may be able to invoke his "mandate" to win over undecided members of Congress. In contrast, presidents who avoid policy statements to limit their campaign risks will find the task of governing just that much harder.

During the 1976 campaign, however, Carter may not have realized how important the energy program issue would become. The subject's absence from his inaugural address would seem to support that conclusion. Perhaps the natural-gas shortage in the winter of 1977 lead to a reordering, or even to the first crystallization, of his priorities. But, whether sudden or not, the decision to give top priority in early 1977 to a policy area that had not been a prominent campaign issue increased the already heavy odds that any president seeking major change must face. Sudden crises such as the winter gas shortage can be used to rivet public attention, but their transitory character makes it difficult to rely solely on them to sustain public attention over time, as a long-range program works its way through a slow-moving Congress.

Carter's difficulties were compounded by the way the energy package was put together. Two of President Carter's earliest decisions on energy were to name James R. Schlesinger head of a White House task force in charge of reviewing energy policy and then to give Schlesinger's group ninety days to propose a set of recommendations for congressional action. The ramifications of these two decisions were felt long afterward. Schlesinger, who had headed the Atomic Energy Commission, the Central Intelligence Agency, and the Department of Defense in the Nixon and Ford administrations, was an economist and policy analyst whose years at the Rand Corporation had honed his way of thinking about policy along lines that the new president and former engineer found compatible with his own. Carter wanted a comprehensive plan; Schlesinger could scarcely think of any other way to proceed.

Schlesinger circled his group's wagons for three months. Studies from outside consultants were commissioned and used, but Congress and the rest of the administration were kept almost entirely in the dark.[33] Whatever political judgments were brought to bear came from people on the White House staff who had worked on Capitol Hill and not from the members themselves.

The procedure had some advantages. Congress had been in stalemate over energy policy for three years.[34] A coalition of Republicans and Southern Democrats favoring oil and gas price deregulation controlled the Senate by a narrow majority. In the House, Northern Democrats favoring a continuation of the status quo held a narrow edge. In such circumstances, there may be something to be said for avoiding advance compromises in the administration's initial bill that would lock the administration into existing cleavages and patterns of thought.

But there also were costs. Unless the administration could devise a new way of defining and addressing the issue, it would have to face up at some time to the same facts and forces that produced the existing stalemate. The president learned this the hard way, as Congress repeatedly rejected those elements of his package, such as the gasoline tax, that were essentially identical to proposals Congress had rejected decisively in the past. By including the same proposals again, as part of his plan, Carter suffered needless defeats that politically damaged the prospects for success on other items whose fate might have been less predictable.

Instead of being a proposal that held out a new way of looking at this issue, the National Energy Plan was an amalgam of proposals, most of which had been offered in past Congresses.[35] What was new was that the proposals were joined together in a package that reflected a coherent, though controversial, set of underlying principles and assumptions.[36] These included three basic points: (1) domestic oil and gas production inevitably would decline sharply in the not-too-distant future, (2) conservation therefore represented the best short-term strategy for decreasing dependence on imports, and (3) conservation through governmental intervention was preferable to market-induced conservation through price. The last point was based on the administration's view of the government's ability to produce results more equitable than those of the market.[37] It was based, as David Davis has said, on "distinctly Democratic rather than Republican economics."[38]

Specifically, the energy package sought to achieve greater conservation by proposing, among other things:

- a series of conservation tax credits to homeowners and businesses
- a crude-oil equalization tax to raise the controlled price of domestically produced oil to world market levels
- a tax on gas-guzzling cars
- standby gasoline taxes of up to fifty cents per gallon
- mandatory utility-rate reforms
- mandatory industrial conversion to coal
- modest increases in the controlled price for newly discovered natural gas

The oil and gasoline taxes were coupled with rebates, the net effect of which was supposed to penalize wasters, benefit conservers, and leave the average person about even. The package contained little to stimulate domestic oil and gas production because its authors thought the supply picture was hopeless. Since in this view deregulation simply would have meant more money for producers rather than more supplies, the administration thought it more equitable to have the government raise the price with a tax instead. (For more on the package's details, including the fate of its elements in Congress, see table 8–1).

The administration's package was going to be a bitter pill to swallow. Interest groups immediately started lining up to challenge specific sections. The major labor and business organizations all opposed the gas-guzzler tax. Energy producers opposed continued price regulation and questioned the absence of production incentives. Consumer groups thought that regulated prices were being raised too high. Environmentalists questioned the emphasis on coal and nuclear development instead of mass transit and renewable energy sources. House Speaker O'Neill immediately sensed the danger: "The only way we can write a national bill is if they don't team up," he said. "If they logroll, you're in trouble."[30]

Against this array, the president had to persuade the general public to support a program whose only obvious immediate effects were to increase energy prices for the average consumer. To succeed, the president would have to convince people that cost increases were inevitable with or without an energy package and that the public would be better served if the revenues from price increases went to the government instead of to oil companies. To make its case, the administration had to show that the energy crisis was real, and that it was not, as many believed, a fantasy manufactured by the oil companies to increase their profit margins. The case was by no means an easy one to make, particularly since Carter took every opportunity to encourage the same public skepticism toward big oil that had led people to doubt the problem's existence in the first place.

Given the objective difficulties of his task, Carter's April 18 televised presentation of his program was effective. At Schlesinger's suggestion, Carter borrowed a phrase from William James, "the moral equivalent of war," to describe the seriousness of the situation. Using a theme that was to recur frequently in his speeches, Carter presented the issue as one that would test both the character of the American people and the ability of the president and Congress to govern the nation.[40] He repeatedly called upon people to distinguish their immediate from their long-term self-interest:

> Now we have a choice. But if we wait, we constantly live in fear of embargoes. . . . Inflation will soar; production will go

TABLE 8–1

NATIONAL ENERGY PLAN: PRESIDENT CARTER'S PROPOSALS AND THEIR OUTCOME, 1977–1978

President's Proposal	House Action	Senate Action	Conference	Final Act on
NATURAL GAS POLICY ACT				
Proposed April 20, 1977, to increase the controlled price of newly discovered natural gas from $1.45 to $1.75 per thousand cubic feet (mcf) in 1978, with further increases tied to the rate of inflation. Also extended controls to gas discovered and sold in the same state.	The House Commerce Subcommittee on Energy and Power voted 12–10 on June 9 to deregulate the price of newly discovered natural gas. The full Commerce Committee restored the president's proposal on June 24 by a 22–21 vote. After the Ad Hoc Energy Committee on July 21 expanded the definition of "new gas" to increase support for the measure, the House on August 3 defeated deregulation, 199–227.	The Senate Energy Subcommittee deadlocked 9–9 on deregulation, and reported the president's proposal without recommendation. The full Senate voted 50–46 on October 4 to: (1) Deregulate immediately all newly discovered gas onshore; (2) Lift the controlled price for offshore gas to $2.48 between 1978 and 1982, with deregulation in 1982.	After months of bargaining, conferees agreed in principle on May 24, 1978, to allow controlled prices to increase until 1985, after which the price of newly discovered gas would be deregulated. Final details were not worked out until August 18, when a conference report was filed.	Senate motion to recommit failed 39–59 on September 19, 1978. Conference report adopted 57–42 on September 27. House voted 207–206 on October 13 to adopt rule keeping all parts of energy in one package. Opponents of the compromise wanted a separate vote on natural gas. House adopted the combined energy package on October 15, 231–168.

ENERGY TAXES

Crude-oil equaliza-tion tax increased the controlled price of domestic oil through taxes that would be rebated to the public through income taxes. *Gas-guzzler tax* taxed new automobiles not meeting federal fuel efficiency standards. *Standby gasoline tax,* up to 50¢ per gallon, to be imposed in 5¢ increments if gas con-sumption one year exceeded previous year. *Tax credits*—for homeowner and busi-ness conservation, and for solar equipment.	Approved crude-oil equalization tax, gas-guzzler tax, solar and conservation tax credits. The Ways and Means Committee re-jected the standby gasoline tax on June 9, as did the full House on August 5. However, the Ad Hoc Energy Committee recom-mended, and the House approved, 4¢ per gallon gasoline tax (in addition to the existing 4¢ tax) with revenue to go into a mass transit and energy trust fund.	The Finance Committee rejected the crude-oil equalization, gasoline, and gas-guzzler taxes. Approved solar and conservation tax credits. Energy Com-mittee and full Senate approved ban on gas guzzlers instead of tax.	Approved only the solar and conservation tax credits and ban on gas guzzlers, October 12, 1978.	Senate and House passed conference re-port, October 15, 1978.

(Table continues)

President's Proposal	House Action	Senate Action	Conference	Final Action
UTILITY RATE REFORM				
Banned declining rate structures for large users; required utilities to offer different prices for peak and off-peak use to customers willing to pay for the needed meter.	Approved August 5, 1977.	Rejected by Finance Committee September 19, 1977.	Required states merely to consider the various rate reforms the administration would have required. Compromise reached December 6, 1977. Report filed October 6, 1978.	Senate passed October 9, 1978. House passed October 15, 1978.
COAL CONVERSION				
Proposed April 20, 1977, to prohibit new power plants and facilities from using oil	Approved with minor changes, August 5, 1977.	Following the president, the Senate Energy Committee required existing plant	Compromise reached on November 11, 1977. Report filed July 14, 1978.	Senate passed on July 18, 1978. House passed on October 15, 1978.

and natural gas as boiler fuels and to tax the industrial use of these resources by old plants at a rate high enough to encourage conversion to coal. The requirements for conversion under existing law would also have been simplified.

conversions by 1990 and prohibited new plants from burning oil and natural gas. The committee increased the list of exemptions, however, and added federal loans, loan guarantees, and grants. After adopting an amendment exempting all but the largest facilities, the Senate adopted the bill on September 8 by 74-8. The industrial-user tax was killed by the Finance Committee.

down; people will lose their jobs. . . . If we fail to act soon, we will face an economic, social and political crisis that will threaten our free institutions.[41]

To avoid such cataclysmic results, the president called upon people to sacrifice, as they would in a war, for benefits they themselves might never realize but which were necessary to preserve the nation's health for future generations:

> We've always wanted to give our children and our grand-children a world richer in possibilities than we have had ourselves. They are the ones that we must provide for now. They are the ones who will suffer most if we don't act.
>
> I've given you some of the principles of the plan. I'm sure that each of you will find something you don't like about the specifics of our proposal. It will demand that we make sacri-fices and changes in every life. To some degree, the sacrifices will be painful—but so is any meaningful sacrifice. It will lead to some higher costs and to some greater inconvenience for everyone. But the sacrifices can be gradual, realistic, and they are necessary. Above all, they will be fair.[42]

The battlefield rhetoric of this speech has been criticized unde-servedly. Given Carter's definition of the issue, the nature of his proposals, and his failure to prepare the public during the campaign, the tone was appropriate to the political urgency of the situation. If public opinion could not be galvanized quickly, the chance for favorable congressional action seemed remote. By likening the situa-tion to a war, Carter was able to acknowledge the program's obvious costs and to try to start turning them to his program's advantage. When the inevitable claims and counterclaims of energy experts began to be heard, Carter's position let him avoid making public responses to those claims in detail. People who questioned his con-clusions would publicly be treated as the moral equivalents of quislings —captives of "special-interest groups" who would rather surrender the nation than accept any sacrifice of their immediate private good.[43]

Early Reversals

Carter's April 18 address set a high standard. Unfortunately, the president did not seem to realize that, if public rhetoric was to succeed, his informal remarks and overt behavior would have to be consistent with what he wanted the public to believe. If rhetoric is to succeed, the public should never see the president treating it as "mere rhetoric"—hyperbole designed to embellish instead of state-ments rooted in principled conviction.

Carter stepped into this fatal error almost immediately. Almost as soon as the energy plan was unveiled, critics began lining up to suggest that it would involve more sacrifice and less benefit than the president claimed. House Minority Leader John Rhodes of Arizona reflected a general Republican consensus that the plan was a blueprint for a "no growth" economy.[44] Hobart Rowen, the *Washington Post's* influential economics reporter, seemed to support Rhodes's assertion in an April 21 article that said, "typically, private economists predicted that Carter's program would cause the economy to contract mildly, rather than expand" as the administration had predicted.[45] A *Washington Post* analysis published the same day concluded that "while President Carter's energy message is based on a 'worst case' diagnosis of America's energy future, his cures are fashioned on optimistic assumptions about coal production, cutting oil imports, and reducing the annual growth in energy demand."[46] In an editorial the next day, the same newspaper questioned the apparent gap between Carter's rhetoric and his program. "If the present national risk is as great as he described it on Monday, it requires a far more active response than he is now proposing."[47] Eventually, Congress's four support agencies—the Congressional Budget Office, the General Accounting Office, the Office of Technology Assessment, and the Congressional Research Service—independently weighed in with similar conclusions.[48]

Faced with criticisms such as these, Carter had three choices: to respond to their substance, to describe his program as a needed first step instead of as "comprehensive" and complete, or to moderate his rhetoric about the danger and the need for sacrifice. Astoundingly, given Carter's views on the importance of public persuasion, he decided on the last, thus reversing himself on the basic rhetorical underpinning of his position. This became apparent at a May 4 meeting with members of Congress. According to a press account of that meeting:

> President Carter, who two weeks ago told Congress his energy package is the "moral equivalent of war," is changing strategy and telling lawmakers it really isn't so tough politically. . . .
>
> "Until several weeks ago, I thought the sacrifice demanded of the average American family would be quite severe; I no longer believe that is true," one Congressman quoted the President as saying. . . .
>
> Some lawmakers at yesterday's meeting wondered about the President's changing strategy in selling his energy proposals. "It's difficult for me to understand how he ex-

pects Congress to respond when he starts off saying 'the sky is falling,' then goes to 'it isn't going to hurt much' and then to 'you'll like and make money off it'," said Rep. William R. Steiger (R.-Wis.), who was at the White House meeting.

Democrats weren't so willing to publicly question Mr. Carter's approach, but privately expressed similar doubts. "He may confuse people and in the process lose public support that's essential to pass any program," said one energy committee Democrat.[49]

Carter's widely reported rhetorical reversal undercut the well-orchestrated efforts of administration officials, who were busily promoting the program in hundreds of speaking engagements across the country.[50] The fact that the meeting was reported publicly is itself a symptom of an important institutional change. When Woodrow Wilson made different arguments for the Versailles Treaty in public speeches from those he made in meetings with senators,[51] he knew that he would not read about his private statements in the next day's newspapers. With the relationship between the press and Congress that exists today, it has become impossible to maintain so clear a distinction between public and deliberative rhetoric.

It would be wrong to put too much weight on any single incident. Carter's decision not to address energy issues prominently during the election campaign, his late start once in office, his continued public tongue lashings of the oil industry, and his inexplicable failure to follow up on the fireside address—all contributed to the problem. Whatever the cause, there can be no question about the result. President Carter's attempt to go over the heads of Congress was a complete failure. In a Gallup poll conducted April 1–4, two weeks before the president's fireside address, 41 percent of the people surveyed said they believed the energy situation was "very serious." The figure rose to 44 percent on April 29–May 2, and then dropped back to 40 percent on June 3–6, 38 percent on August 5–8, 40 percent on September 30–October 3, and 40 percent on November 18–21.[52] In fact, the figures remained remarkably constant into the summer of 1979, when they jumped to 47 percent after oil shortages resulting from the revolution in Iran produced a doubling of crude-oil prices and long lines for motorists at gasoline stations.[53] But in 1977 most people simply did not have any factual basis for being moved to the president's level of concern. On April 29–May 1, 1977, when half of the oil used in the United States came from abroad, only 52 percent of the people surveyed by Gallup knew the country had to import *any* oil to meet its energy needs.[54]

Of course, Carter's rhetoric was not completely without effect. The number of people who identified energy as the most serious problem facing the nation shot up from 1 percent to 15 percent between October 1976 and July 1977, according to Gallup, placing it third behind inflation (32 percent) and unemployment (17 percent). Given the other survey results, however, the increase did not amount to nearly enough for the president's purposes. (In January 1974, during the Arab oil embargo, the comparable figure had been 46 percent.)[55]

Missed Opportunities

Carter's failure to convince the public of the seriousness of the energy situation meant that he would have to work with Congress instead of against it. Yet his rhetorical reversals may have caused him even more trouble with this specialized audience than they did with the general public. The reactions of members attending the May 4 meeting with the president have been mentioned. The real problem, in members' minds, was that this was far from being an isolated incident. On April 14, four days before he was to explain his energy package to the public, Carter announced he was withdrawing the fifty-dollar individual tax rebate that was to have been the cornerstone of an economic stimulus plan he had announced in January. In a measured understatement, *Congressional Quarterly* described the decision as "a policy reversal that caught congressional leaders by surprise."[56] To many, the feelings went beyond surprise to betrayal. The rebate had survived a March 8 motion to recommit the bill in the House by a narrow 194–219 margin only because of support from Democrats who said they took a dim view of the rebate's potential effect, but felt they wanted to support the president.[57] By the time the plan was withdrawn, the administration had been working with similarly reluctant supporters in the Senate to get the bill out of the Finance Committee. Withdrawing the proposal pulled the rug out from under these people. Asked to comment on the effect this sudden shift had on the energy package, a White House lobbyist said the president "was hurt by the decision to change from the fifty-dollar rebate. I heard that example used every time—'well, are you going to stick with us on this one?'"[58]

Carter's statements on the energy package during 1977 did nothing to improve members' feelings about his steadfastness. The president made no public statements for more than a month after the May 4 meeting with members of Congress. He broke his silence the day after the House Ways and Means Committee rejected the standby tax on gasoline and the House Commerce Subcommittee on Energy and Power voted 12–10 to deregulate the price of new natural gas. On June 10, Press Secretary Jody Powell said the president saw the votes as "significant preliminary victories" by "the oil companies and the automobile companies and their lobbyists."[59] Carter repeated the charge himself the next day. In a question session with the Magazine Publishers Association, the president said the two votes resulted from "the extraordinary influence of the automobile companies and the oil companies in Washington."[60] The natural-gas vote was reversed later, but not the vote on the standby gasoline tax.

Through the rest of June and July, Carter said little to advance his case on the energy package. On a few occasions, he was able to bring the package into the daily news by attending events where the subject could be brought up. On other occasions, he responded to questions in interviews or larger question-and-answer sessions. None of these, however, gave the president a chance to educate the public further about his main concerns—as he might have done, for example, by announcing the government's monthly petroleum import figures himself instead of having them issued anonymously by the bureaucracy.

At no point was the sense of missed opportunities more evident than in early August. On August 1, the president issued a brief statement commending the House leadership for actions taken so far and stating his positions on the main amendments expected in the House floor debate scheduled for that week.[61] On August 5, the House adopted most of the president's energy package. Getting this far had required an extraordinary political effort in the months between April and August by everyone who had supported the president, particularly O'Neill. The Speaker used the powers recently granted him to create and stack an Ad Hoc Energy Committee that reviewed what the various legislative committees did to Carter's package. He also had the committees adhere to very tight schedules and worked with the Rules Committee to ensure that the package would be open to only a few amendments under tactically favorable conditions.[62] Yet Carter again failed to capitalize publicly on his victory to build momentum for Senate action. On August 5, the day the House completed work on the plan, Schlesinger was sworn in as secretary of the newly created Department of Energy. Carter allowed the event to slip by, making only a few innocuous remarks, instead of delaying the ceremony for a day to allow comments on the House's action.[63] The next day he all but invited the press to ignore the energy bill by calling a news conference to announce the details of his equally "comprehensive," equally complicated proposals to reform the welfare system. The only questions asked by reporters dealt with welfare and with the ongoing investigation of Office of Management and Budget Director Bert Lance.[64]

Congress then recessed for the rest of August. When it came back, the Senate began to dismantle the president's program. Any impartial observer surely could have told the president in advance that the Senate was going to be a less hospitable chamber for his package than the House. Unlike the House, the Senate had voted for natural-gas deregulation during President Ford's administration. The Senate's new majority leader, Robert C. Byrd of West Virginia, saw himself as a guardian of the Senate's prerogatives. As such, he was less inclined than the more partisan O'Neill to use his power to pass the president's bill. Had he been so inclined, he still would not have had O'Neill's authority to get committees to report bills in a way that would ensure floor votes on all of the plan's main items. Finally, the chairman of the Senate Finance Committee, Russell Long (Democrat, Louisiana), supported price deregulation and opposed increasing prices by means of taxes that would go to the Treasury. Since half of the plan's projected oil savings depended on taxes, Long's differences with House Ways and Means Chairman Al Ullman (Democrat, Oregon) were both crucial and predictable. Historically, Long voted with Southern Democrats and Republicans on the major divisive energy issues, while Ullman was on the other side. Each represented the position held by a majority of the members in his own chamber.

Despite the predictability of the House–Senate differences on energy, President Carter reacted to the Senate's actions as if taken by surprise (see table 8–1 for details). Indeed, he may have been surprised: by his own admission, he and his staff paid little attention to the energy package in the Senate until the bill passed the House.[65] The statements the president made while the Senate was considering natural-gas deregulation, coming after months of relative silence, seemed reminiscent of the tone he had adopted in June after he had suffered two defeats in House committee votes. On September 24, while campaigning for a Democratic gubernatorial candidate in Norfolk, Virginia, Carter threatened to veto any bill that immediately deregulated the price of natural gas.[66] Although none of the bills then pending would have done so, Carter ignored this. Instead, he focused on the administration's cost projections for a bill the gas industry would have preferred, but which contained none of the compromises that Senate deregulation supporters had put into their own bill. On September 26, the president went before the White House press corps with these irrelevant cost figures and said that, although "Congress has been lobbied continuously by the oil and gas industry to deregulate the price of new natural gas," he hoped the Senate would "act responsibly . . . to reject narrow, special interest attacks" on his plan.[67]

The statements came too late to make much of a difference, but the strongest opponents of deregulation naturally were heartened by the president's statement that he would be willing to veto a natural-gas deregulation bill. Led by first-term Democratic Senators James Abourezk of South Dakota and Howard Metzenbaum of Ohio, they decided to mount a filibuster, which they continued after cloture was invoked by demanding roll-call votes on hundreds of amendments. They were deeply shocked and embittered, therefore, when Vice President Walter F. Mondale, in his role as presiding officer of the Senate, joined with the majority leader just one week later, on October 3, to defeat them by ruling their amendments out of order. Perhaps the filibusterers had failed to notice that the bill Carter described in his veto threat was not precisely the one before the Senate. Or perhaps the administration decided, after it became clear that it was going to lose most of the plan's taxes, that it needed to move the natural-gas issue ahead to conference if it was going to have anything to show for its effort. Whatever the reason, the president's decisions to threaten veto after months of silence and then to have Mondale help break the filibuster led some of the administration's supporters to feel betrayed once again, as they had felt after the tax rebate was withdrawn.[68]

Immediately after the filibuster was broken, the president began, after long delay, to take his case again to the general public. On October 4, he issued a statement calling the Senate's bill "an injustice to the working people of this country" and vowed he would "not sign an unfair bill."[69] Then, in his opening statement to a news conference on October 13, the president repeated his April 18 statement that the energy crisis was "a moral equivalent of war" and warned:

> As is the case in time of war, there is potential war profiteering in the impending energy crisis. This could develop, with the passing months, as the biggest ripoff in history.[70]

Carter's stridently moralistic rhetoric backfired badly for three reasons. First, it insulted senators who opposed the president by suggesting that they must be beholden to special interests for adopting a position he had taken himself a year earlier. "It is patronizing when the president sets himself above us and suggests we are being manipulated by lobbyists," one Democratic supporter of the president's position was reported to have said.[71]

Second, the suggestion that senators were blindly following the oil companies was simply not borne out by the facts. Two studies of the votes on natural-gas deregulation concluded that people's votes were determined more by their ideologies than by lobbying or by the character of their districts.[72] Even though there may be some reason to question the sharpness of the separation between constituency and ideology in these studies,[73] there is enough evidence to dispel the myth that members were simply bending to pressure. Senators from the same state or members from neighboring congressional districts often ended up on different sides of the deregulation vote.[74] The vote showed, as we know from elsewhere, that senators and representatives often feel free to define their constituencies in ways that fit their broader political outlooks.[75]

Finally, Carter's attacks on big oil came at the same time that Schlesinger was reportedly trying to negotiate a compromise with the major oil companies.[76] But the tone of Carter's remarks made it difficult for senators to join in a compromise effort without fear of attack. Thus, just as Carter's remarks in his May 4 meeting with members of Congress had undercut his public rhetoric, so did his public rhetoric in October damage the administration's negotiations with Congress. The effects would be felt for months to come.

End Game

The time for quiet negotiation was now at hand. The Senate Finance Committee systematically gutted the plan's energy taxes in late September and early October, and Chairman Long made it clear that he had no intention of negotiating in conference until a gas-pricing compromise was achieved. The president's credibility was at stake; coming up empty-handed would have crippled his presidency. Everything hinged on reaching a compromise on an issue that had held the Congress in stalemate for years.

By the end of October, Carter began signaling that there was more to his position than his uncompromising rhetoric might suggest. At an October 22 panel meeting in Denver and in an October 28 press conference, the president renewed the claim, made originally in his April 18 fireside chat, that his plan was a first step toward deregulation.[77] The statements were completely disingenuous, of course. The National Energy Plan would have increased the price of gas sold in the interstate market, but it also would have regulated the intrastate market for the first time and would have continued regulation indefinitely, increasing the price only to keep pace with inflation and not to match the cost of alternative fuels. At the time, the remarks seemed baffling in the context of his previous strident attacks on deregulation; later they could be seen as a signal of the administration's new strategy for the House–Senate conference.

The administration went on to make several tactical errors early in the protracted conference negotiations. On November 8, three weeks after the conferees began meeting and four days after the first session of the Ninety-fifth Congress ended, Carter went on national television to give his first full-scale speech on energy since April. The speech was far less strident than earlier efforts and might have been effective had it been part of a careful strategy put into effect months earlier. Most of it was unexceptional,[78] but two points deserve notice. First, Carter described the three major purposes of the legislation as being to reduce consumption, to promote a shift from oil and gas to other sources of energy, and "to encourage production of energy" including "production of oil and gas here in our country."[79] That was the first time he mentioned production so prominently and confirmed the shift in signals of the previous two weeks. The second important point was Carter's announcement that he was postponing a major overseas trip until after Christmas "because of the paramount importance of developing an alternative energy plan this year."[80] As Norman J. Ornstein has argued, the postponement was a major tactical blunder. Carter had no reason to believe the conferees were anywhere near agreement. By delaying his trip, he merely increased the public's expectation that a bill would soon pass, and thus made himself look like a failure when agreement was not achieved on schedule.[81]

Not until May 24, 1978, did the conferees reach an agreement in principle on gas pricing. Another three months elapsed before details were settled and a majority of the conferees were willing to sign the conference report. Congressional mistrust of the administration was responsible for much of the delay.

The Energy Department's econometric models originally had predicted that the administration's position would mean more revenues for producers than the status quo, but significantly less than would accrue under deregulation. After the conference began, the administration decided to try to put together a centrist majority behind a phased-in deregulation proposal that pleased neither the most ardent foes nor the most ardent supporters of deregulation. In December, the Energy Department recalculated the cost of maintaining the status quo to support its new position. It now claimed that regulated prices under the old rules would shoot up faster than had been predicted and that phased-in deregulation therefore would cost consumers less, not more, than living under the existing law.

This convenient reversal simply confused the issue. The old set of predictions gave people opposed to deregulation a reason for not caring if the conference failed, while the new predictions had the same effect on lobbyists for the gas industry.[82] In truth, nobody seemed to believe either set of estimates. On December 5, an inter-agency Professional Audit Review Team issued a report that accused the administration of having changed its computer model earlier in the year to meet preconceived policy objectives.[83] The report simply confirmed what many members of Congress already suspected.

Despite these initial mistakes, the administration did finally show a degree of political skill and tenacity in bringing the lengthy conference to a successful conclusion. After rallying the public behind precedent-shattering policy changes had proved beyond its ability, the same administration that had so disdained and was so inept at incremental bargaining in its first year performed quite well at this lesser job in its second year. White House interventions prevented the conference from breaking down at several key points. The administration's lobbying of the business community, orchestrated by Robert Strauss and Anne Wexler, was crucial to the final victory. The president deserves credit for what happened in 1978, but that story has been told well elsewhere and needs no repeating here.[84] The real test was 1977—the year the administration tried to rally the public over the heads of Congress.

Conclusion

The administration claimed victory after the energy package was finally passed. By the time the president stood unsuccessfully for reelection, he was characterizing energy policy as one of his administration's most important achievements. The claims had some justification. After passing the remnants of the National Energy Plan at the end of Carter's first two years, Congress during the next two years set up a synthetic fuels program and coupled a windfall-profits tax with oil price deregulation. Also by the end of Carter's four years, domestic drilling for gas and oil was up while consumption and imports were down.[85] Still, the extent to which the administration can claim credit for all these accomplishments is limited. Consumption and imports were down because prices were up, more as a result of developments abroad than of events in the United States. In addition, the legislative victories of 1979–1980 turned out, even more than those of 1977–1978, to be incremental policy developments assisted but not led by the administration.[86]

So, if one looks at energy in incremental terms, the Carter administration can in some sense be called a success. Those were not the terms on which the administration asked to be judged, however. It came in asking for a comprehensive plan involving a radical shift in outlook. It went out not with a plan, but with a set of incremental changes that followed existing patterns of thought. There is nothing wrong with incremental policy change. The political structures of the United States were designed deliberately to prevent sharp, major policy shifts unless such shifts are supported by sustained majority opinion. What was wrong was not the way the system worked, but the way the president worked the system. Carter sought major changes, knowing full well that they could not be achieved without public support, but he failed to take the steps necessary to build the support he needed.

President Carter's failure thus was essentially a failure of public persuasion, or rhetoric. His efforts at persuasion were inadequate for reasons relating both to political-legislative strategy and to substance. Carter's strategic errors have been mentioned earlier: his slow start, missed opportunities, lack of priorities,[87] patronizing tone, and abrupt reversals. All of these contributed heavily to his problems with Congress. But one suspects those problems went beyond strategy to substance. His message simply seemed unequal to the job.

Carter's message essentially called upon people to accept sacrifices (taxes) now in order to avoid worse consequences later. His early speeches gave people little indication of what might be done affirmatively to avoid the stark choice between bad and worse. Contrast this with the messages conveyed by other presidents whose attempts to rally the people were more successful. Ronald Reagan says he wants to trim the role of government to unleash the genius of the American people. Franklin Roosevelt used speeches and government action to calm fears and reinvigorate nobler passions. John Kennedy's and Lyndon Johnson's speeches for civil rights urged white Americans to be true to their deeply held principles. In all cases, successful rhetoric joined an appeal to the people's character with a call for appropriate action. Moreover, the appeals to character were specific and positive. Moralistic sermons about malaise were the last things one would have expected from any of these leaders.

There are ways Carter might have redesigned his program to supply what was missing. Republicans, of course, would have called for deregulation, as Reagan does, to spur industriousness and creativity. Carter could not have been expected to follow a similar program, but he could have appealed to the nation's collective soul in much the same terms. He might have earmarked some of his proposed energy tax receipts for mass transit, synthetic fuels, and other advanced research and development projects. Many congressional Democrats had argued for such an approach before Carter took office; Carter eventually adopted it during the second half of his administration. Without getting into the merits of such a program here, there can be little question about its rhetorical advantages. Had Carter adopted such a program immediately, instead of two years later, he would not have been forced to offer the people a choice between suffering now and suffering later. Taxes could have been presented as an investment and not a bitter pill.

Americans are not a people who can easily be rallied under a banner of stoical suffering. They will accept sacrifice if it has a purpose. They like to be told what they can do, not what they cannot do. They believe in conquering nature, not in succumbing to it. In this, Americans remain a people of the Enlightenment who find it hard to accept the postmodern (or ancient) view of a world of limited possibilities. President Carter failed to persuade the American people because he did not connect his program to the passions and beliefs around which Americans can be rallied. His comprehensive program failed because it was not comprehensive enough.

Notes

1. David Broder, "Shattered: Democratic Coalition Falls to Pieces," *Washington Post,* May 8, 1981, p. A1.

2. See Paul Light, "The President's Agenda: Notes on the Timing of Domestic Choice," *Presidential Studies Quarterly,* vol. 2, no. 1 (Winter 1981), pp. 67-81.

3. See for example, Eric M. Uslaner, "The Congressional War on Energy: The Moral Equivalent of Leadership?" (Paper prepared for the Conference on Understanding Congressional Leadership sponsored by the Everett McKinley Dirksen Congressional Leadership Research Center and the Sam Rayburn Library, June 10-11, 1980); Eric M. Uslaner, "Shale Barrel Politics: Energy Policy and Institutional Decentralization in the Congress" (Unpublished paper, University of Maryland Department of Government).

4. See, for example, White House counsel Lloyd Cutler's "To Form A Government," *Foreign Affairs* (Fall 1980), pp. 126-43, esp. 135-36; Bruce I. Oppenheimer, "Policy Effects of U.S. House Reform: Decentralization and the Capacity to Resolve Energy Issues," *Legislative Studies Quarterly,* vol. 5, no. 1 (February 1980), pp. 5-30; Bruce I. Oppenheimer, "Congress and the New Obstructionism: Developing an Energy Program," in Lawrence C. Dodd and Bruce I. Oppenheimer, eds., *Congress Reconsidered,* 2d ed. (Washington, D.C.: Congressional Quarterly Press, 1981), pp. 275-95.

5. Roger H. Davidson, "Subcommittee Government: New Channels for

Policy Making," in Thomas E. Mann and Norman J. Ornstein, eds., *The New Congress* (Washington, D.C.: American Enterprise Institute, 1981), pp. 99-100 at p. 101.

6. "The Presidency: Can Anyone Do the Job?" *Newsweek*, January 26, 1981, pp. 35-42 at p. 41.

7. See chapter 7 of this volume.

8. See Allen Schick, *Reconciliation and the Congressional Budget Process* (Washington, D.C.: American Enterprise Institute, 1981).

9. Richard E. Neustadt, *Presidential Power* (New York: John Wiley & Sons, 1960), p. 10.

10. Ibid., p. 36.

11. Ibid., p. 46.

12. I am indebted to two papers by Jeffrey Tulis for opening my eyes to the utility of applying this ancient distinction to an analysis of the presidency. J. Tulis, "Thought, Speech and Deed: On Studying Presidential Rhetoric" (Paper prepared for the 1978 Annual Meeting of the American Political Science Association) and "The Decay of Presidential Rhetoric" (Paper prepared for the Conference on Rhetoric and American Statesmanship, University of Dallas, October 16-18, 1980). Also see James W. Caeser, Glen E. Thurow, Jeffrey Tulis, and Joseph M. Bessette, "The Rise of the Rhetorical Presidency," *Presidential Studies Quarterly*, vol. 11, no. 2 (Spring 1981), pp. 158-71 and Nicholas O. Berry, "The Foundation of Presidential Leadership: Teaching," *Presidential Studies Quarterly*, vol. 11, no. 1 (Winter 1981), pp. 99-105. For another critique of Neustadt along lines similar to mine, see Peter W. Sperlich, "Bargaining and Overload: An Essay on Presidential Power," in Aaron Wildavsky, ed., *Perspectives on the Presidency* (Boston: Little, Brown, 1975), pp. 406-30.

13. Albert R. Hunt, "Politicians Don't Play Politics All the Time," *Wall Street Journal*, May 14, 1981, p. 26.

14. I use the word "contemporary" advisedly. Tulis pointed out in his papers that before Woodrow Wilson, most presidential rhetoric on specific policies either was written or was spoken privately to members of Congress. Public rhetoric before Wilson, with few exceptions, was on broad themes and not on specific bills. Wilson set a new pattern by giving public speeches on behalf of the Versailles Treaty while it was before the Senate. Interestingly, Wilson's use of public rhetoric seems to have been connected to his low opinion of Congress and to his desire to reinvigorate the presidency. For an excellent discussion of this, see James W. Caeser, *Presidential Selection: Theory and Development* (Princeton, N.J.: Princeton University Press, 1979), chap. 4. Franklin D. Roosevelt, with his effective use of radio, married modern communications technology to a Wilsonian view of legislative–executive relations, transforming Wilson's experiment into an indispensable part of the office.

15. Neustadt, *Presidential Power*, p. 100.

16. Neal R. Peirce, "The Democratic Nominee—'If I Were President. . . .' ," *National Journal*, July 17, 1976, p. 999.

17. Ibid., pp. 998-99.

18. For example, see: Congressional Quarterly, *Energy Policy* (Washington, D.C.: Congressional Quarterly Press, 1978), pp. 1-44; David H. Davis, "Pluralism and Energy: Carter's National Energy Plan," in Robert Lawrence, ed., *New Dimensions to Energy Policy* (Lexington, Mass.: Lexington Books, D.C. Heath and Co., 1979), pp. 191-99; Charles O. Jones, "Congress and the Making of Energy Policy," ibid., pp. 161-78; James L. Cochrane, "Carter Energy Policy and the Ninety-Fifth Congress," in Craufurd D. Goodwin, ed., *Energy Policy in Perspective* (Washington, D.C.: Brookings Institution, 1981), pp. 547-600.

19. Jimmy Carter, *Public Papers of the Presidents of the United States, 1977* (Washington, D.C.: Office of the Federal Register, National Archives and Records Service, 1977), book 1, p. 7. "The Energy Shortage: Statement Announcing Initiatives to Deal with the Shortage," January 21, 1977.

20. Ibid., p. 21. "Natural Gas Legislation: Remarks at a News Briefing," January 26, 1977.

21. Ibid., p. 38, "The Energy Shortage: Remarks and Question-and-Answer Session at the Westinghouse Plant in Pittsburgh, Pennsylvania," January 30, 1977.

22. U.S. Congress, House of Representatives, Committee on House Administration, *The Presidential Campaign 1976*, vol. 1: Jimmy Carter (Washington, D.C.: 1978), pt. 1, p. 7.

23. Ibid., pt. 2, p. 1038.

24. "Democratic Platform: A Contract With the People," *Congressional Quarterly Weekly*, July 17, 1976, pp. 1922-23.

25. *Presidential Campaign 1976*, vol. 1, pt. 1, pp. 642-43 and 653-60.

26. For more on the connection between platforms and campaign speeches, and between platforms and government, see Michael J. Malbin, "The Conventions, Platforms and Issue Activists," in Austin Ranney, ed., *The American Elections of 1980* (Washington, D.C.: American Enterprise Institute, 1981), pp. 99-141.

27. *Presidential Campaign 1976*, vol. 1, pt. 1, pp. 347-52.

28. Ibid., pt. 2, pp. 748, 837, 1040.

29. Ibid., p. 748, September 15 address to the AFL-CIO.

30. Ibid., pp. 1060-61.

31. Ibid., p. 1116.

32. In October 1976, the Gallup poll reported that only 1 percent of a national survey identified energy as the major problem facing the country. In the same survey, 47 percent named inflation and 31 percent unemployment.

33. For a description of Schlesinger's team and of the ninety-day drafting process, see Cochrane, "Carter Energy Policy," pp. 551-56.

34. Richard Corrigan, "Waiting for the 95th," *National Journal*, September 25, 1976, p. 1359.

35. Elder Witt, "Carter's Proposals: A More Unified Framework, But

Many Familiar Elements from Earlier Debates," *Congressional Quarterly Weekly*, April 23, 1977, pp. 728-29.

36. For an analysis of the assumptions and econometric models that guided the administration, see Michael J. Malbin, *Unelected Representatives: Congressional Staff and the Future of Representative Government* (New York: Basic Books, 1980), chap. 9, esp. pp. 211-14 and 230-32. A shorter version of this chapter is available as "Congress, Policy Analysis, and Natural Gas Deregulation: A Parable about Fig Leaves," in Robert A. Goldwin, ed., *Bureaucrats, Policy Analysts, Statesmen: Who Leads?* (Washington, D.C.: American Enterprise Institute, 1980), pp. 62-87, esp. pp. 68-71 and 81-84.

37. Carter's basic approach paralleled that of the Energy Policy Project of the Ford Foundation in *A Time to Choose: America's Energy Future* (Cambridge, Mass.: Ballinger Publishing Co., 1974). S. David Freeman, director of the project, was a member of Schlesinger's White House energy staff. For a critique of the report see Morris A. Adelman et al., *No Time to Confuse* (San Francisco: Institute for Contemporary Studies, 1975).

38. Davis, "Carter's National Energy Plan," p. 195.

39. "The Energy War—Now It Is up to Congress," *Time*, May 2, 1977, p. 12.

40. "The Energy Problem," Address to the Nation, April 18, 1977, *Public Papers, 1977*, vol. 1, p. 656.

41. Ibid., pp. 658-59.

42. Ibid., p. 661.

43. Ibid.

44. John M. Goshko, "Carter Energy Program Draws Praise, Criticism," *Washington Post*, April 21, 1977, p. A18.

45. Hobart Rowen, "President Hopeful of Impact of Plan," *Washington Post*, April 21, 1977, p. A19.

46. J.P. Smith, "Carter's Energy Policy: A Melding of Pessimism, Optimism," *Washington Post*, April 21, 1977, p. A24.

47. "The Moral Equivalent of What?" *Washington Post*, April 22, 1977, p. A20.

48. Congressional Budget Office, *Natural Gas Pricing Proposals: A Comparative Analysis*, printed at the request of Senator Henry M. Jackson, Chairman, U.S. Senate Committee on Energy and Natural Resources, Publication 95-50 (Washington, D.C., September 1977); Comptroller General of the United States, *An Evaluation of the National Energy Plan*, Report to the Congress, EMD-77-48 (Washington, D.C.: General Accounting Office, July 25, 1977); Congressional Research Service, *Project Interdependence: U.S. and World Energy Outlook Through 1990*, printed for the use of the U.S. House Committee on Interstate and Foreign Commerce and U.S. Senate Committee on Energy and Natural Resources and U.S. Senate Committee on Commerce, Science and Transportation (Washington, D.C., November 1977); Office of Technology Assessment, *Analysis of the Proposed National Energy Plan* (Washington, D.C., August 1977).

49. Albert R. Hunt, "Carter Now Sees Energy Plan Causing Less Sacrifice, Little Political Fallout," *Wall Street Journal,* May 5, 1977, p. 18.

50. Mercer Cross, "Carter's Energy Program: The Sell Begins," *Congressional Quarterly Weekly,* May 7, 1977, pp. 839-41.

51. Tulis, "Thought, Speech and Deed," pp. 6-18.

52. George Gallup, "No Progress Being Made in Convincing Public of Energy Crisis," The Gallup Poll, press release, December 15, 1977.

53. George Gallup, "Public Changing Views on Seriousness of Energy Situation," The Gallup Poll, press release, September 2, 1979.

54. George Gallup, "Many Adults Would Flunk Test on U.S.-Energy Needs," The Gallup Poll, press release, June 2, 1977.

55. George Gallup, "Energy Crisis Seen As One of Top Three Problems Facing Nation," The Gallup Poll, press release, August 14, 1977.

56. Judy Gardner with Mercer Cross, "Rebates Dropped As Honeymoon Ends," *Congressional Quarterly Weekly,* April 16, 1977, p. 691.

57. Judy Gardner, "Carter Seeks Changes in House-Passed Tax Bill," *Congressional Quarterly Weekly,* March 12, 1977, p. 439.

58. Interview with the author.

59. "National Energy Plan, Statement by the White House Press Secretary," June 10, 1977, *Public Papers, 1977,* vol. 1, p. 1082.

60. "Interview with the Magazine Publishers Association," June 11, 1977, *Public Papers, 1977,* vol. 1, p 1092.

61. *Public Papers, 1977,* vol. 2, pp. 1396-97.

62. See Oppenheimer, "Policy Effects of U.S. House Reform," for more details.

63. *Public Papers, 1977,* vol. 2, pp. 1441-42.

64. Ibid., pp. 1443-58.

65. News conference, October 13, 1977, ibid., p 1986.

66. Ibid., p. 1658.

67. Ibid., pp. 1671-72.

68. *Congressional Quarterly* reported after the filibuster was broken that "longtime Capitol Hill observers described [it] as the most explosive confrontation in recent Senate history." Senator Gary Hart (Democrat, Colorado) was quoted as calling Byrd's rulings "outrageous." Energy Committee Chairman Henry M. Jackson (Democrat, Washington) said he had "never seen senators so raw-nerved as they were in the last two weeks." Alan Berlow, "Filibuster Fallout: Byrd's Role and Precedents," *Congressional Quarterly Weekly,* October 8, 1977, pp. 2127-28.

69. *Public Papers, 1977,* vol. 2, p. 1724.

70. Ibid., p. 1783.

71. Rowland Evans and Robert Novak, "Carter's Energy Package: A Problem with Tactics," *Washington Post,* September 30, 1977, p. A27.

72. Edward J. Mitchell, "The Basis of Congressional Energy Policy," *Texas Law Review,* vol. 57, no. 4 (March 1974), pp. 591-613; Pietro S. Nivola, "Energy Policy and the Congress: The Politics of the Natural Gas

Policy Act of 1978," *Public Policy*, vol. 28, no. 4 (Fall 1980), pp. 491-543, esp. 541-43.

73. Barbara Sinclair, "Coping with Uncertainty: Building Coalitions in the House and the Senate," In Mann and Ornstein, eds., *New Congress*, p. 218, fn. 25.

74. Malbin, *Unelected Representatives*, pp. 231, 234, and 271, fn. 45.

75. Raymond A. Bauer, Ithiel de Sola Pool, and Lewis Anthony Dexter, *American Business and Public Policy: The Politics of Foreign Trade*, 2d ed. (Chicago: Aldine, 1972), chap. 30.

76. Robert G. Kaiser and J.P. Smith, "Energy Bill Status Judged a Failure for Carter," *Washington Post*, December 14, 1977, pp. A1 and A4.

77. *Public Papers, 1977*, vol. 2, pp. 1880-81 and 1940.

78. Not everyone was this kind. Columnist Nicholas von Hoffman described the speech as "the most moving prose to come out of a first magistrate's mouth since Herbert Clark Hoover, who was also an engineer and wrote like one." "Carter's Energy Speech: A Fumbling Attempt to Rally The Nation," *Washington Post*, November 16, 1977, p. B13.

79. *Public Papers, 1977*, vol. 2, p. 1984.

80. Ibid., p. 1983.

81. See chapter 7 and Norman J. Ornstein, "Something Old, Something New: Lessons for a President About Congress in the Eighties" (revised draft prepared for the Conference on the Presidency and Congress, White Burkett Miller Center for Public Affairs, University of Virginia, January 24-25, 1980), p. 14.

82. Malbin, *Unelected Representatives*, pp. 213-14.

83. Ibid., pp. 269-70. For the report, see U.S. Professional Audit Review Team, *Report to the President and the Congress: Activities of the Office of Energy Information and Analysis* (Washington, D.C.: Federal Energy Administration, December 5, 1977), p. 29. The team was chaired by Richard W. Kelley of the General Accounting Office and contained staff level representatives from the Securities and Exchange Commission, Bureau of Labor Statistics, Federal Trade Commission, Bureau of the Census, and Council of Economic Advisers. The team and the Office of Energy Information and Analysis both were established by the Energy Conservation and Production Act dated August 14, 1976 (90 Stat. 1125). For another summary of the report, see Richard Corrigan, "Operation Manipulation," *National Journal*, December 17, 1977, p. 1967.

84. Nivola, "Energy Policy and the Congress," pp. 523-24; Congressional Quarterly, *Energy Policy*, pp. 5-28.

85. John Berry, "A Better Prepared U.S. Swallows Its Bitter Energy Pills," *Washington Post*, January 11, 1981, p. M1. According to Berry, 60,000 oil and gas wells were drilled in the United States in 1980, exceeding the 1956 record of 57,000. Imports in 1980 fell by 20 percent from 1979 to 6.2 million barrels per day, less than in any year since 1976 and only slightly above the level of 1973-1975. Gasoline consumption—277 million gallons or about 6.6 million barrels per day—was 11.1 percent below the

level of 1978. Gasoline cost an average of 65.2¢ per gallon in 1978 and $1.23 in 1980.

86. Oil price deregulation was mandated by the Energy Policy and Conservation Act of 1975. What Carter did in 1979 was sign an order phasing in the deregulation that would have come anyway and coupling it with a bill that recaptured some of the resulting profits for the Treasury. Whatever the arguments for or against the tax, it could scarcely be said to have had much to do with energy supplies or use. On synthetic fuels, Carter took the occasion of renewed gasoline lines to increase the dollar figures for a program that had already passed the House without his endorsement. By the time Congress finished with it, it looked very much like a proposal that had first been put forward by Vice President Nelson Rockefeller during the Ford administration.

87. While energy policy clearly was the most significant domestic policy initiative of the president's first year, he was not willing to treat it that way for months. From all appearances, the winter 1977 natural-gas shortage seems to have caused Carter almost to have stumbled into putting energy first. Earlier, we mentioned Carter's failure to give the issue prominence during the presidential campaign or in his inaugural address, as well as his long silences between public statements after the April 18 fireside chat. On June 22, Carter was asked at a question-and-answer session to name his top priorities. Instead of indicating priorities, he began rattling off a list of his major initiatives to date, concluding: "we've got about 60 or 70 other items on the domestic agenda that I'm going over with the Speaker and Majority Leader on. I won't list them all." (*Public Papers, 1977*, vol. 1, pp. 1146-47.) Carter's unwillingness to set clear priorities hurt all of his legislative efforts during his all important first year. That changed after a late 1977 review of White House lobbying efforts by Vice President Walter Mondale and an April 1978 conference at Camp David between Carter and his senior advisers. In mid-1978, the number of presidential priority bills was cut in half, top bills were given special "task-force treatment," and Carter's legislative performance began to improve. For the late-1977 to mid-1978 change, see Larry Light, "White House Lobby Gets Its Act Together," *Congressional Quarterly Weekly*, February 19, 1979, pp. 195-200.

9

A Mile and a Half
Is a Long Way

ANTHONY KING

The president and Congress. Both ends of Pennsylvania Avenue. It sounds so simple. But, as the chapters in this volume have made clear, it is not simple at all. Nearly two hundred years after the framing of the Constitution, politicians and political scientists still find it difficult to characterize the relationship between these two complex entities. In this final chapter, we look at the state of the presidential–congressional relationship today—and at one or two elements in the relationship that have tended to be overlooked.

Let us start by pretending that the relationship is in fact a good deal less complex than it actually is, by doing our best to strip it down to its essentials. To begin with, we shall be deliberately naive; out of naiveté is sometimes born wisdom. The analysis will become less simple-minded as we go along.

The Hypothesis of Randomness

Suppose that you are president of the United States. You sit in your office in the White House. You contemplate the problems of government. What is it that you want from Congress? More to the point, what is it that you *need* from Congress? If you are a president primarily concerned with foreign affairs, you will not need Congress as much as a president primarily concerned with domestic affairs. If you are a relatively unambitious president, you will not need Congress as much as a president who wants to pass a lot of laws in order to set the world to rights. But either way, you do need Congress —and you know it.

What do you need? You do not need the cheers of Congress when you deliver your State of the Union message (though these are nice to have). You do not need Congress's permission to marry a person not of the Protestant faith (unlike the British queen, who needs Parliament's). You do not need Congress's approval if you decide to give a state banquet for some visiting foreign dignitary (though at least some congressmen and senators will expect to be invited).

No, all you really need from Congress is votes, but you need those votes very badly. Moreover, under the American system, you need votes all the time and all kinds of votes: votes for and against bills, votes for and against amendments, votes to appropriate funds, votes not to appropriate funds, votes to increase the budget, votes to cut the budget, votes to enable you to reorganize the executive branch, votes to strengthen you (or not to weaken you) in your dealings with administrative agencies, votes to sustain your own vetoes, votes to override legislative vetoes, votes in the Senate to ratify the treaties you have negotiated and to confirm the nominations you have made, votes (every century or so) in opposition to efforts to impeach you. You need votes to enable you to build up a record, to win reelection, to win—who knows?—a place in history. Indeed, come to think of it, you need votes in Congress to enable the government to function at all. If appropriations are not forthcoming, or if a president for some reason vetoes those that are, the machinery of government simply grinds to a halt, as happened for a few truth-telling hours on November 23, 1981. The only kind of votes that you as president do not need, impeachment apart, are votes to sustain you in office. Unlike a prime minister in a parliamentary system, you at least have security of tenure until the next election.

In short, you are heavily dependent on Congress. You may think you are a splendid fellow to have been elected president, but you are really like Gulliver in Lilliput, a giant all right, but tied down. However devoted you are to almost any of your projects, great or small, if Congress opposes you, that is the end of the matter. The dome of the Capitol looks even larger at a distance than it does close up.

So much for the president. Now switch your perspective. Suppose you are a congressman or senator, sitting in your office at the other end of the avenue on Capitol Hill. If you are a Republican and the year is 1982, you probably have a signed photograph of President Reagan on your wall; if you are Democrat, the photo on your wall probably used to be one of Jimmy Carter (signed) but is now one of Franklin Roosevelt or John Kennedy (unsigned). As you sit there in your office reading your mail or talking to somebody on the telephone, what are your aims in life? Much, of course, depends on how old you are and whether you hope someday to run for a higher office (possibly the Senate if you are in the House, perhaps the

presidency itself). But in the normal course of events you probably
have three goals. The first is to be reelected later this year, or in two
or four years' time. The second is to be a big noise in the House or
the Senate, whichever you happen to be a member of—to wield power,
to be seen a lot on television, to be quoted a lot in the press, to win
for yourself a reputation as a skilled legislator, someone to be consulted, someone not to be crossed. The third is to play your part in
seeing to it that the United States of America is well governed,
according to your lights or maybe according to the lights of your
constituents.[1]

The people you need as a congressman or senator are the people
who will help you to secure these goals. In the case of your reelection,
it is all too obvious on whom you depend: the voters in your district
or state and, behind them, influential lobbying organizations, local
opinion leaders, the local media, the people who may or may not
contribute to your campaign. If you come from Iowa, the people who
matter to you are Iowans; if you come from Texas, the people who
matter to you are Texans.

Does the president matter to you? Can he help to secure your
reelection? How *might* he? In principle, there are two ways, by no
means incompatible, in which the president might help to get you
reelected. First, he might be a very successful, popular president.
If he were, and if he were of the same party as yourself, and if you
believed that people in large numbers at the next election would vote
the straight party ticket, so that if he did well, you would do well
too, then you would have a vested interest in helping the president
sustain his popularity, in helping him build up an impressive legislative record. In helping the president, you would be helping yourself
(call it "mutual self-help"). Second, the president, whether or not he
was successful and popular, might help you to get reelected if for any
reason he was moved to bestow favors on you, favors of direct benefit to your constituents or, alternatively, favors that made you appear
in the eyes of your constituents a very important person—a new
road, a new dam, a new post office, an invitation to the Rose Garden
for an important bill-signing ceremony, with plenty of photographers
on hand. One of the things likely to move a president to bestow such
favors, highly valuable to yourself, might be your support for him
in key votes on Capitol Hill. In this case, in helping the president you
would not be helping yourself directly; rather you would be hoping
to receive help from him (call it "exchange of favors").

Two or three generations ago, many members of Congress undoubtedly made both of these kinds of calculations, but it is very
doubtful that many make them today—at least often enough to alter

significantly the pattern of voting in either house. The first calculation, mutual self-help, has been undermined, as Austin Ranney points out in chapter 5, by the increase in the number of safe congressional seats, especially in the House, by the fact that primary elections, in which it is harder for the president to intervene, have become more important to the electoral fortunes of members, and above all by the decline of straight-ticket voting—and party voting generally—since the early 1960s. The electoral relationship between presidents and congressmen has been uncoupled. Members no longer believe that their electoral fortunes are closely bound up with the president's or even with their party's; whether they achieve reelection will depend largely on their own success in providing what Morris P. Fiorina calls "nonpartisan, nonprogrammatic constituency service," on the few public stands they take that directly affect their constituents and are visible to them, and on national political trends that may overwhelm them irrespective of anything they themselves do.[2] If presidents no longer have coattails, there is no point in congressmen's clinging to them. On the contrary, it will sometimes be to their advantage to distance themselves from the president, as Republicans distanced themselves from Richard Nixon and many Democrats distanced themselves from Jimmy Carter.

The second calculation, exchange of favors, is probably still of some importance, even in the 1980s. Incumbent members of Congress in swing districts and states need all the help they can get from whatever source. A favorably disposed president can assist from time to time by influencing the location of a veterans hospital, by preventing the closure of a defense installation, by steering an important government contract in their direction. Most of the time, though, this kind of activity is but the small change of electoral politics. Presidents do not have all that many favors at their disposal, and anyway, the favor disposed on one member is liable to be a favor denied to another. Moreover, of the universe of selective benefits that the executive branch as a whole has to offer, the greater part, in practice, is in the hands not of the president but of other government agencies, which may use them as much to further their own ends as to further the president's.[3]

In any case, the electorally oriented member of Congress, as he sets about the business of "advertising, credit claiming, and position taking," has no choice but to rely largely on his own efforts, not on those of the executive branch.[4] What matters to him are his constituency newsletters, his personal contacts with newspapers and television stations, the quality of the services he provides to individual constituents and local interest groups, his relations with district and state opinion leaders, and not least the stands he takes on major issues—and the ways these stands are perceived and evaluated by voters. From the perspective of such a congressman, the president of the United States most of the time is merely "noises off."

It is striking that scholarly writings focusing on presidential–congressional relations attach some importance, though usually not much, to the favors that a president can confer on congressmen, while writings focusing on the congressman's own political world scarcely mention the president at all. David Mayhew and Morris Fiorina both depict members of Congress as inveterate vote-maximizers; they do not, however, portray the president as being at all important to this activity.[5] Likewise, in Richard Fenno's brilliant study of members of the House in their home districts, presidents make only occasional walk-on appearances.[6]

If the president of the United States cannot help you much in your reelection campaign, can he be of assistance to you in your efforts to build a reputation as a man of power and influence on Capitol Hill? The short answer is: a little perhaps, but not much, and only occasionally. The reputations of men on the Hill are over-whelmingly made by their peers on the Hill—in the course of committee hearings, marking up bills, negotiating face to face, determining committee assignments, and making speeches on the floor. The president has little to do with any of this. To be sure, a party leader or committee chairman may occasionally believe that his prestige in Congress will be enhanced if he is identified as the major backer of the president's program, and a hitherto unsuccessful legislator may seek responsibility for some part of a president's program in hopes of making a record for himself. Thus, in 1977 House Speaker Tip O'Neill is said to have taken up President Carter's energy program partly because he "recognized that if he could demonstrate his ability to lead the House on this one issue by securing the passage of the President's proposal, his reputation for power on Capitol Hill would be secure."[7] In the same year, Rep. Jack Brooks, chairman of the House Government Operations Committee, dropped his opposition to Carter's proposals for reorganizing the executive branch, partly because he sensed that a majority of his own committee was against him, but partly also because he had already succeeded in wresting maximum advantage from his committee chairmanship: "The President had invited him to Georgia to discuss the reorganization bill in the first place and had sought out his support."[8] But in general, power and prestige in the House and Senate are determined within the House and Senate. O'Neill calculated that it would be to his advantage to espouse Carter's energy program; Robert Byrd, the Senate majority leader, simultaneously calculated that it would be to his advantage to do the opposite. The president figured to some extent in both men's calculations, but their fellow members of Congress figured far more.

The president thus cannot greatly help you to secure reelection, and it is most unlikely that he will be able, to any significant degree, to raise or lower your standing on Capitol Hill. He lives in his political house at one end of Pennsylvania Avenue; you live in your political house at the other end. He needs you, but on the face of it you have no great need of him.

At this point, it is worth pausing to take stock. Suppose that this were all we knew about the American political system: The president is elected for four years by one electorate; congressmen and senators are elected for two or six years by another; the political futures of members depend very little on the man in the White House. If this were all we knew, what would we conclude about the chances that, on any given matter of public policy, the president and Congress would produce the same policy? We would probably conclude that the chances were no greater than random: fifty-fifty if only two policy options were available, one in six if three were available, one in twenty-four if four were available, and so on. Differences between the president and Congress would be the rule rather than the exception. To use Nelson Polsby's metaphor, quoted by Charles O. Jones in chapter 4, the presidency and Congress would be like "two gears, each whirling at its own rate of speed"—and, on coming together, they would clash more often than not.[9]

This "hypothesis of randomness," of president and Congress living in two wholly separate political worlds and coming together only by accident or in response to some factor external to both of them, is of course not wholly realistic. Nonetheless, it is a useful reminder of the very large number of occasions on which the president and Congress do in fact pull in different directions, and it also encourages us to seek some positive explanation when the policies of president and Congress do coincide, when the two branches of government actually do appear to be working together. If noncoincidence is taken to be the norm, and if instead we observe instances of coincidence considerably more often than would be expected by chance, then there is clearly a mystery to be solved.

Power, Personality, Opinion, Climate

One part of the explanation lies in the shared powers of the president and Congress as specified in the Constitution and the laws. The United States cannot have two public policies, one congressional, one presidential; it has to have one—one budget, one tax code, one strategic arms limitation treaty (or none, as the case may be). And the Constitution and the statute book provide numerous mechanisms —the presidential veto, legislative vetoes, senatorial confirmation of appointments, senatorial ratification of treaties, and so on—for determining what that one policy shall be. These mechanisms are also a factor in determining, in each case, where the balance of power between president and Congress will lie. This balance is, of course, of prime importance, but there is no need to explore it in detail here since its main features (for example, the president's veto power) are well known and since many good studies of the subject exist.[10] As Allen Schick points out in chapter 7, changes in the law and even in the Constitution subtly alter the balance of power between president and Congress from one generation to the next.

Given any current state of the Constitution and the law, how important a part does the president himself play—his personality, his political skills, his standing with the American public—in ensuring that his wishes and the wishes of Congress coincide more often than would be expected by chance? (We focus on the president's active role, though of course a supine president could bring about presidential–congressional coincidence of view simply by agreeing to everything that Congress required of him. That often happened in the last century. Since FDR, however, presidents have been made of sterner stuff.)

In the matter of presidents' personalities and legislative skills, there is a marvelous discontinuity between American folklore and the findings of a good deal of recent political science. There is easy agreement about wherein the relevant elements of a president's personality and political skills lie: warmth, accessibility, an intimate knowledge of the workings of Congress, sensitivity to congressmen's power stakes as well as his own, a willingness to work with congressional leaders, a willingness to talk with members with a view to finding out what is on their minds as well as telling them what is on his own, a shrewd instinct for timing, knowledge of whom to bully and whom not to bully, a capacity for remembering who might like to use the White House tennis court—and so on into the middle distance. But there agreement ends. The folklore, remembering Lyndon Johnson and fed on press photos of the president, feet on desk, talking on the transcontinental telephone to some wavering senator or other, imputes enormous importance to the personality of the president. A warm, strong president with skills (like Kennedy or Johnson) gets his way; a cold, weak president, unsure of himself, without skills (like Carter) fails to get his. More precisely, and to be fair to the folklore, the claim is that, in any given political situation and with any given balance of political forces, a president with skills is more likely to get his way than a president without them. It is a matter of probabilities.

Some political scientists, however, dispute this general line of argument. They maintain that a close examination of the record shows that presidential skills are of only minor importance. Other factors—public opinion, the balance of opinion in Congress, the partisan balance in Congress—matter far more. George C. Edwards, for example, examined *Congressional Quarterly* presidential-support scores between 1953 and 1978 in a search for evidence that presidents widely adjudged to possess first-class legislative skills got their way with Congress substantially more often than similarly placed presidents who did not possess them. Edwards could find no such evidence. Presidential legislative skills, he concluded, "do not seem to affect support for presidential policies, despite what the conventional wisdom leads us to expect."[11]

Edwards's evidence cannot be gainsaid; it should remind us that, other things being equal, "the president," in Edwards's words, "is in a weak position with regard to Congress. His burdens are great and his assets are few."[12] But analyses of this kind typically overlook the importance (even though they may recognize the existence) of two points. The first is simply that some congressional outcomes matter far more to presidents than others. In 1919, Woodrow Wilson would probably have been content with a *Congressional Quarterly* support score of near zero if he could have got the Senate to ratify the Treaty of Versailles—and it was his lack of legislative skills that undoubtedly led to his defeat. Likewise in 1974, Nixon would happily have jettisoned the whole of his legislative program to escape those few but lethal votes on the articles of impeachment. The second point, following from the first, is that in this context overall scores, so useful in other contexts, can be hopelessly misleading. The slightest upward shift in the score may conceal some overwhelming legislative triumph; an ever-so-slight downward shift may conceal disaster. In assessing the legislative skills of presidents, the analyst in fact has no alternative but to conduct a series of "thought experiments": What would have been the outcome of a given legislative struggle if President B instead of President A had been in the White House? Any reader who conducts such experiments (for example, Johnson instead of Carter on energy policy) is bound to conclude that the exercise of presidential legislative skills may on occasion be crucial. One such occasion will be discussed later in this chapter.[13]

There is, then, something to be said for the folklore—a conclusion also implied by Jones's analysis of a variety of presidential styles in chapter 4 of the present volume. That said, however, it would be quite wrong to conclude that a president's warmth, charm, and knowledge of congressmen's susceptibilities can ever be crucial except at the margin (however important that margin may be to any particular president). Harry Truman could not have got national health insurance through the Eightieth Congress had he been Lyndon Johnson, John Kennedy, Franklin Roosevelt, Machiavelli, and Odysseus all rolled into one; it is very doubtful that Jimmy Carter ought to be blamed for failing to get the strategic arms limitation treaty (SALT II) through the Senate in 1979–1980 (though he may be blamed for having negotiated it in the first place). The important point is that, in the pursuit of their third goal, the good government of the United States, what matters to members of Congress is not primarily the president's views, interesting though these may be, but their own views and their perceptions of their constituents' views. Every study ever undertaken of voting in the House and the Senate points hard in this direction. Forced to choose between his own views and his constituents', a congressman will usually choose his constituents' (if he knows what they are and believes they could seriously affect his chances of reelection). Forced to choose between his own views and the president's, a congressman will almost always choose his own— unless he is given some powerful incentive not to (which presidents, for the reasons already given, are not usually in a position to provide), or unless, as can happen, the president manages to persuade him to change his mind.[14] In presidential–congressional relations, the political opinions of the two parties to the relationship, if not quite all that matters, are nevertheless nearly all.

This simple statement suggests a large part of the solution to our original mystery: why two such politically disparate bodies as the president and Congress from time to time—indeed quite frequently—produce public policies satisfactory to both. If they do so, it is because they agree with each other or are responding similarly to political pressures, often emanating from public opinion, bearing down on them both. Contrariwise, if they clash, it is because they disagree. It is (almost) as simple as that. One corollary is that hard evidence and rational arguments play a larger part in presidential– congressional conversation than the outsider, obsessed with talk of "power" and "deals," often realizes. As Ralph K. Huitt, political scientist turned executive branch lobbyist, once put it, "The most effective tool is so simple it sounds naive, and so it is hard to credit. It is knowledge, expertise, and a command of the business at hand."[15]

Studies of President Carter's dealings with Congress similarly testify to the damage done to the president by his and his aides' inadequate knowledge of the facts and by their proneness to cut intellectual corners.[16]

What role does party play in affecting the balance of opinion within the two houses of Congress and therefore the probability that Congress as a whole and the president will agree? This is not an easy question to answer, for reasons suggested by the very different legislative experience of the British House of Commons. In the House of Commons, most votes are "whipped." That is, every member of Parliament (MP) is under considerable pressure to vote with the other members of his party, whatever his own private views. On whipped votes, almost all members of one party vote one way, almost all members of the other party the other. But a few votes in the House of Commons are "free," with MPs permitted to vote as they want, entirely free of government and party pressure. It might be thought that the differences in the behavior of MPs between these two types of votes would provide a reasonable indicator of the strength of party in the British parliamentary context, and up to a point it does. The only trouble is that, even on free votes, MPs divide to a very considerable extent along party lines, their partisan affiliation remaining the best single predictor of their votes.[17] In other words, party-as-organization (present in the whipped votes) has to be distinguished from party-as-body-of-sentiment (present in the free votes)—and this distinction is by no means easy to make in practice, since we cannot be sure how the MPs would have voted on the whipped votes had they been free. Members of each party might have been almost as united unwhipped as they were whipped.

Much the same problem arises in analyzing voting in the United States Congress. To be sure, all votes in Congress are, in the British sense, free votes; but one would still like to be able to distinguish between how congressmen would behave if left entirely to their own devices (in which case any partisan effect that emerged would be a pure party-as-body-of-sentiment effect) and how they would behave if subjected to some sort of party pressure—or, more modestly, received unambiguous party signals. As Ranney shows in chapter 5, some efforts have been made to detect a party-as-organization effect in Congress by, for example, comparing how far congressmen change their pattern of voting on specific issues when the president's party changes; and the evidence does indicate a modest amount of vote switching of this kind.[18] But the amount is modest; and the best first approximation to the truth is still to say that voting in Congress is overwhelmingly a function of members' political opinions—and their perceptions of how best to get reelected. Party voting, in short, is mainly opinion voting in another guise.

This stripped-down approach to the explanation of presidential–congressional convergences leaves a good deal out of account, of course. There is authority inherent in the presidential office; the president of the United States is both prime minister and monarch, and, other things being equal (which they occasionally are), if the president wants something, then that in itself is reason enough to give it to him. The president is well provided with information and expert advice. He is better able than anyone else in the country to command media and public attention. Partly for all these reasons, he is well placed to take legislative and other policy initiatives, to determine the agenda of America's politics. Members of Congress may decide in the end to reject presidential proposals; they usually find it hard to ignore them. In addition, there is some evidence that a popular president is assisted by the mere fact of his popularity. The influence of a president's public prestige, it would appear, is greatest on members of his own party, and is also boosted if at the previous election the president has run ahead of members in their own congressional districts.[19]

The factors affecting the presidential–congressional relationship mentioned so far are all familiar. They are mentioned in all the books on the subject. But there may be present on occasions another factor, which political scientists seldom mention except in passing (perhaps because, analytically, it is so hard to handle). That factor is "mood," or "atmosphere," or "climate." The precise term is not important, but the idea behind it is.

Presidents live in a world of uncertainty; so, much of the time, do members of Congress. A congressman's own views are important to him, as we have seen—but on a given issue he may not have fixed views. His constituents' views are also important to him—but on a given issue his constituents may not in fact have views; or he may not know what they are; or he may not know how stable or strongly felt they are; or he may find that they are divided in such a way as to leave him uncertain as to how he should vote. Members of Congress, like everyone else, may know in general where their interests lie; but they may not know in practice how their interests should be pursued. The business of politics, after all, is in large part the business of exercising judgment, of taking risks, of following hunches, of making educated guesses.

Under these circumstances, mood or climate may be of considerable importance. A political mood is hard to define and seemingly impossible to measure. Nonetheless, everyone can feel a mood when he or she is in the presence of one. Moods condition thoughts and feelings; they facilitate some courses of action and inhibit others. They occasionally determine outcomes.

This is not the place to undertake an essay on the phenomenology, genesis, and dynamics—to use Fred I. Greenstein's terms—of political moods, atmospheres, and climates. But two thoughts are relevant to the relations between presidents and members of Congress.[20] The first is that the presence of a political climate is likely to have as one of its component parts the widespread belief that some political force is all but irresistible—or, alternatively, that a political force once thought to be irresistible is no longer so. Civil rights in the 1960s, for example, became "an idea whose time has come." In the early 1980s, the pro-Israeli atmosphere that had enveloped American politics since 1948 began to dissipate, at first gradually, then more rapidly. It was hard to say precisely why, but the change was evident. Under these circumstances, supporters of fading ideas suddenly become defensive; proponents of new (or old, formerly unpopular) ideas suddenly realize it is safe to go on the attack. Congressmen, in deciding how to cast a crucial vote, do not mind being on the losing side; sheer numbers are not at issue. What they do mind is being on the wrong side; and high levels of political uncertainty may make members more prone than usual to seek the safety of numbers. "I will set this foot of mine," said Casca cautiously, "as far as who goes farthest." Political climates influence judgments about how many people are likely to be prepared to go how far. Climates can create tip-over effects, with once-solid majorities becoming ineffectual minorities astonishingly rapidly.

If the first element in a political climate consists of judgments about the balance of political forces, a second element has to do with ideas. There are intellectual atmospheres as well as political atmospheres, and there is always a chance that the former will become the latter. A cause may become hard to defend not merely because a majority is known to be opposed to it, but because people have, for whatever reason, become unreceptive to the theories and values underlying it. The reverse can also happen, with the hitherto unthinkable suddenly widely thought. In this context, lip service becomes an oddly important kind of service—because it is a useful indicator of which ideas are and are not generally acceptable, and also because it is a mode of expression that in practice often commits the person who pays lip service to more than mere rhetoric. It is hard, for example, for a politician to pay lip service to "waste in government" without finding that he cannot in practice vote against presidential attempts to eliminate such waste. Politico-intellectual moods of this kind may be sweeping in their effects when, as in the early 1980s, democratic electorates are unpredictable and when there is no prevailing, generally accepted public philosophy.[21] Seeking to explain why previously inconceivable innovations happen, Lewis Anthony Dexter referred a generation ago to "the simple fact that people who are important and influential either (a) change their perspectives or (b) lose their self-confidence."[22] It might be hypothesized that President Reagan's victories in Congress in 1981 owed a good deal to atmospheric changes of precisely this kind.

In the light of that possibility, it is worth looking in some detail at the events of Reagan's first year, especially at his stunning—and to a considerable extent unexpected—victories on his proposed budget and tax cuts and on the sale of AWACS (Airborne Warning and Control System) aircraft to Saudi Arabia. There is no reason to believe that, with regard to presidential–congressional relations, 1981 will prove typical of the Reagan presidency. On the contrary, many in his administration were very soon looking back on his achievements in 1981 with something approaching nostalgia. Historians will nevertheless be fascinated by Reagan's first year, just as they are by Roosevelt's hundred days. More to the point, the year serves to illustrate a number of the general points already made in this chapter.

Reagan, the 1981 Budget, and AWACS

The story of the 1981 budget and tax cuts is quickly told. President Reagan took office on January 20 pledged to getting the American government off the backs of the American people (the implication: budget cuts) and to releasing for the first time in generations the full productive energies of American individuals and businesses (the implication: tax cuts). A month later, he proposed to Congress eighty-three major cuts in domestic programs, a drastic reduction in the spending levels envisaged in the Carter budget, drastic cuts in the levels of taxation, especially of income tax, and at the same time considerable increases in defense spending. During the next few weeks, he ordered further budget cuts as federal spending appeared to be soaring even higher than had been anticipated. The Democratic leadership in the House meanwhile worked on the details of an alternative package, which would save many of the Great Society programs being threatened by Reagan.

In late March, shortly before the attempt on Reagan's life, the Senate Budget Committee heralded a long series of presidential victories by adopting unanimously a package of spending cuts even greater than the one the president had recommended. The full Senate confirmed the committee's recommendations in early April by 88 votes to 10. The president's real problem, however, lay in the House, where, despite the 1980 election, the Democrats still had a majority. Fortunately for him, some sixty Democrats, mainly from the South, the "Boll Weevils," were making it clear that they preferred the president's proposals to those of their own leadership and were looking for a compromise. In the event, the president adopted as his own a compromise worked out in the House, "the Gramm-Latta substitute," and in early May a coalition of Republicans and conservative Democrats rejected the liberal Democratic proposals by 253 votes to 176. The House then adopted an only slightly modified version of the Reagan package by 270 to 154. Sixty-three Democrats deserted their party on the first, crucial vote. In late June, twenty-nine Democrats voted with the Republicans when the House confirmed the detailed budget cuts that had been worked out in committee. Finally, in July, after an emotional television appeal by the president for "the first real tax cut for twenty years," the Senate adopted his plan for cutting income tax by 25 percent over three years by 89 votes to 11. The House adopted it by 323 votes to 107. Again, Democratic desertions were on a large scale. The president signed his package of budget and tax reductions into law on August 13. Few had expected him to go so far so fast.

What had happened? Two plausible answers can be dismissed straightaway. The first is that Reagan won because he was enormously popular with the American people, that members of Congress were swept along on an immense wave of pro-Reagan popular emotion, a wave given added impetus by the March assassination attempt. The only trouble with this theory is that Reagan was not in fact especially popular. Not only had he won the 1980 election with only 50.8 percent of the vote (27.4 percent of the electorate), but his standing in the polls, never buoyant, tended to sag as time went on. Six months into his presidency, Reagan's Gallup poll rating was somewhat lower than Nixon's and Carter's at the same stage in their careers and considerably lower than Kennedy's and Johnson's.[23] People liked Reagan, but there is no evidence that they thought he was doing an especially good job.

The other theory that can be dismissed out of hand is the idea that the president got his way so easily because there was an overwhelming consensus among congressmen, senators, academic economists, businessmen, and the media that he had stumbled upon a sure-fire cure for the country's economic ills. On the contrary, one of the oddest things about Reagan's 1981 triumphs in the field of economic policy is that almost no one believed that they stood much of a chance of achieving the desired results. The consensus of informed opinion, indeed, seemed to be that their most probable effect would be the damaging one of fueling inflation. Representative Buddy Roemer (Democrat, Louisiana), who voted for the president's budget, captured the overall mood nicely: "Nobody knows for sure what's in it. It was purely a take-it-on-faith matter. And I think that few members can forecast how it will affect the economy or the country."[24]

If congressmen voted for the budget even though they did not think Reagan was enormously popular, and if many of them voted for it even though they had no confidence it would work, why did they vote for it? To be sure, they were responding to the positive policy initiatives of a newly elected president, but many presidents before Reagan had launched similar initiatives without achieving anything like the same success. During the passage of the Reagan package, few explicit theories were advanced to explain what was happening, but one or the other of two implicit theories was contained in almost every speech and newspaper article.

One was the Reagan-as-Superman theory. According to this version of events, Reagan won his famous victories chiefly because of qualities inherent in himself: his personality, his persuasiveness, the warmth he generated, his mastery of legislative skills. This is the theory embedded in press commentary and headlines like the following:

> [Following Reagan's recovery from the assassination attempt] he returned to the wars riding an extraordinary surge of personal sentiment and irresistible political force.
>
> . . . a measure of the real triumph of Reagan's hundred days: his success at clothing his presidency—and smothering his opposition—in a blanket of personal goodwill unmatched since Dwight Eisenhower.
>
> The Reagan Steamroller
>
> Even the solidly Democratic House of Representatives fell to an irresistible force named Ronald Reagan.
>
> . . . the most powerful political force in America.
>
> Reagan Shows Skills as Master of Politics[25]

The clear implication is that Reagan, the man and the president, was crucial to the achievement of his legislative successes and that some other president, even though elected on the same platform, would not have done so well.

The alternative theory, seldom stated explicitly but clearly present in many people's minds, might be dubbed the Reagan-as-surfboarder theory. This version of events does not deny that President Reagan is a likable fellow, adept at talking wavering members of Congress around to his point of view. The theory stresses, however, the extent to which both congressmen and the president were borne along, like surfboarders on a tidal wave of political sentiment. There was something in the atmosphere:

> "Let 'em read the election returns," said O'Neill of his critics.

> Sen. Byrd [the Senate minority leader] waived any pretense of party discipline, saying before the debate began that despite his doubts about the "tenuous assumptions" underlying Mr. Reagan's budget, he would vote for it because "the people want to give him a chance."

> "They say they're voting for it," said Rep. Toby Moffett, a Connecticut liberal, "because they're afraid."

> The evidence of the polls [on the budget cuts], and of the Speaker's own tip sheets on last week's voting in the House, suggested what was for him an unhappy ending: that Reagan and his antifederal revolution are ideas whose time has come—and settled in to stay.[26]

But the most eloquent expositor of the surfboarder theory was Meg Greenfield, in her column in *Newsweek*:

> The basic all-important fact about the Reagan budget-cutting triumph . . . is that there was no opposition to it. Yes, there was resistance, some of it very sensible and impassioned. But when Reagan pushed what was supposed to be the opposition, it collapsed. It simply isn't *there*. It has been retired or enfeebled or frightened by what it perceives to be the prevailing political opinion in the country.[27]

The Superman and surfboarder theories are not incompatible; Superman would probably have made an expert surfboarder. But their emphases are quite different, one on the man, one on the *Zeitgeist*. No one can ever know which is more nearly correct, because Reagan and not someone else won for the Republicans in 1980. The analytic problem is complicated by the fact that Reagan the candidate, as distinct from Reagan the president, had himself done so much to create the *Zeitgeist*. The man and his times were of a piece.

Even so, it is hard to escape the conclusion that Reagan won because of a certain mood, a certain climate, rather than because of his own personality or any special legislative skills that he possessed. In the first place, most of those who supported him in both the Senate and the House were Republicans; and the great majority of Republicans shared (and share) his economic philosophy. In the second place, those Democrats who supported him, chiefly the Boll Weevils, did so not because they had been snowballed or charmed or threatened by the president but because their own disposition was to agree with him in any case; as Representative Charles W. Stenholm of Texas said of the tax-cut proposals, "This particular issue is about 80 to 85 percent of the platform I campaigned on."[28] Finally, the Reagan-as-Superman theory is hard to reconcile with the sheer scale of the president's numerous victories. Given congressmen's goals and the great weight of political pressures bearing down on them, it is seldom possible for any president, however skillful or charming, to shift more than a handful of votes. Yet Reagan consistently won by wide margins. On only one vote, that in the House on June 26, when an attempt by the Democrats to force a series of separate roll calls on different proposed spending cuts was defeated by 217 votes to 210, was the result anywhere near close. Some force greater than the president was clearly at work.

That force, which created an entirely new climate in both houses of Congress, was a compound of many elements. First was the results of the 1980 elections, which increased the number of economic conservatives in both houses. Second was the way in which the 1980 election results were interpreted ("Nothing is more important in Capitol Hill politics than the shared conviction that election returns have proved a point").[29] Third was the widespread belief, based on phone calls, opinion polls, and congressmen's mailbags, that Reaganite economics was what the voters wanted ("because they're afraid"). Fourth was the equally widespread belief that the budget and tax cuts were all but unstoppable ("I've been a politician long enough to know when to fight and when not to").[30] Fifth, and not least, was the weary sense among many Democrats that they had no economic doctrines with which to oppose those of Ronald Reagan, however implausible the latter might seem. Intellectually as well as politically —and sometimes politically because intellectually—you can't beat something with nothing. In the 1981 debates in Congress on budget and tax cuts, Reaganism rather than Reagan was the true victor.

The AWACS story was altogether different. The issues it raised were ones of high politics, not ones that directly affected the great majority of Americans or caught their attention. The only groups intensely concerned were Jewish-American lobbying organizations like the American Israel Public Affairs Committee. AWACS also differed from the budget and tax-cut issues in raising questions not just of policy substance but of the president's right to make policy in a particular field. On the economy, no one denied that Congress had just as much right as the president—perhaps more—to determine tax rates and spending levels. On AWACS, by contrast, the view was advanced that, whatever the legal position, if Congress vetoed the deal with Saudi Arabia, it would be undercutting the president's capacity to determine the general course of American foreign policy. In the end, AWACS differed from the economic issues, too, in that the outcome turned on the votes of only a handful of individuals. Face-to-face persuasion in this case became crucial.

Negotiations for the sale of the aircraft and other advanced military equipment to Saudi Arabia began under the Carter administration. The Reagan administration carried on the negotiations and on August 25, 1981, formally notified Congress that a contract had been signed. The contract would go through unless vetoed by both houses of Congress; one was not enough. From the beginning, it was clear that the administration's prospects were far from good. Members of Congress objected to the deal on the grounds that the possession of such sophisticated military equipment by Saudi Arabia would threaten Israel's security and also because of the danger that, if there were a leftist coup in Saudi Arabia, the AWACS planes might fall into enemy hands. The House Foreign Affairs Committee voted by 28 to 8 to oppose the deal on October 7, and the full House followed suit by 301 votes to 111 a week later. Everything now depended on the Senate. Senators were warned that, if they insisted on vetoing the sale, peace and American security in the Middle East would both be threatened, American oil supplies would be endangered, and anyway the Saudis could buy similar aircraft from the British. Later, when those arguments had apparently not carried sufficient conviction, the president and his advisers raised the ante, claiming that what was at stake was the president's ability to make foreign policy, to negotiate with other nations in America's name. The whole debate was turned into a vote of confidence in both the man Ronald Reagan and the presidency as an institution.

Still, the omens were not good. Just over half the members of the Senate, 51, signed a motion opposing the deal, and on October 15, by a majority of 9 to 8, the Senate Foreign Relations Committee pronounced against it. Concern in the White House, by all accounts, turned into desperation, as administration officials realized that defeat of the deal would not only undermine the president's authority in foreign policy but would also alienate, possibly permanently, the Saudi Arabian leadership. Wavering senators were shown through an AWACS airplane conveniently parked at nearby Andrews Air Force Base and were assured that, although the planes would be Saudi-owned, U.S. personnel would be involved in flying and maintaining them until into the 1990s. President Reagan meanwhile threw himself and his prestige into the battle. Between mid-September and late October, according to the press reports, Reagan saw 75 of the 100 senators, talking alone to 44 of them, 17 of them between Monday morning, October 26, and two o'clock on the afternoon of October 28, when the vote in the Senate was finally taken.[31] His efforts paid off. A considerable number of senators committed to voting against the deal—Robert Jepsen (Republican, Iowa), Charles Grassley (Republican, Iowa), Edward Zorinsky (Democrat, Nebraska), William Cohen (Republican, Maine), Orrin Hatch (Republican, Utah), John Melcher (Democrat, Montana), Slade Gorton (Republican, Washington)—changed their minds after talking with the president, and a substantial number of waverers also came down on his side. The vote not to block the AWACS deal was won by 52 votes to 48. Afterwards, everyone who had met the president was emphatic that he had not used strong-arm tactics or even tried to make deals. He had stuck to the issues. He had appealed to them straightforwardly to support him as president.[32]

Consider this episode in the light of our earlier discussion. The president's activities had little effect on the power balance in the Senate (though the majority leader, Howard Baker, came out of the fight with his reputation as a persuasive head-counter enhanced). They had no effect on senators' chances of reelection (and to some extent may actually have reduced those chances, since senators who voted for the deal were likely to come under pressure from the Jewish lobby). All that the president had to offer the waverers was his conception of good public policy and his conception of the proper role of the president in the making of U.S. foreign policy, both buttressed by the authority inherent in the presidential office, of which Reagan made subtle and imaginative use. Power matters in politics—but, where power stakes are neither paramount nor clearly defined, good arguments effectively deployed can matter too.

A week after the confirmation of the AWACS deal, the cover of *Time* magazine referred back to the budget and tax cuts, depicting a smiling Reagan under the headline, "AWACS: He Does It Again!" The implicit idea, that AWACS was in effect simply a repeat performance of the budget, was understandable, but wrong. Reagan had not done "it" again; he had done something different. In the case of the budget and tax cuts earlier in the year, the paramount factor had been, not the man in the White House, but the politico-economic mood of Congress and the country. In the case of AWACS, by contrast, the president's own personality and skills had genuinely come into their own. If Reagan was to be faulted, it was not for his conduct once the crucial vote in the Senate was imminent, but for having, in earlier weeks, permitted his administration to drift so close to the brink of a potentially damaging congressional defeat.

Metaphors and Prospects

In the AWACS case, as we have seen, President Reagan and many members of the Senate were in direct personal communication. In the economic-policy case, Reagan likewise lobbied members of both houses extensively, and in addition was a larger-than-life presence addressing joint sittings of Congress and the whole nation on tele-vision. But if this chapter and this book have a theme, it is that these occasions of prolonged, intimate presidential–congressional conversation should not be regarded as typical. The presidency and Congress are indeed separate institutions, politically as well as physi-cally. Members of Congress have their own political needs and priorities, which the president, whoever he is, is mostly powerless to affect. Members of Congress spend their days conferring with staff, attending hearings, making speeches, marking up bills, and attending to the needs of constituents; they do not normally spend their days attending to the needs of presidents. Weeks, even months, may go by without the average member of Congress so much as catching a glimpse of the president; some congressmen leave Wash-ington after long careers without ever engaging a president in private conversation. Members of Congress learn about presidential goals and capacities from fellow members of the Washington community and emissaries from the executive branch—and also, like everybody else, from reading newspapers and watching television. In practice, the relations between the president and most congressmen and sena-tors are no more intimate than those between a typical college presi-dent and his college's students and faculty.

The truth of this observation emerges most clearly when the focus of attention is not the presidential–congressional relationship as such but the inner workings of Congress. In 1959, for example, the Brookings Institution in Washington organized a series of round-table conferences at which House members were invited to talk can-didly in an open-ended way about the House of Representatives and their working life within it.[33] Anyone reading the report of the proceedings will be struck by how seldom the president and the executive branch are mentioned. Committee chairman? Fellow members of one's party or state delegation? These are people who have to be taken into account in all of one's calculations. But the president? He is mainly heard, to use a phrase we used before, as "noises off." The author of the report remarks at one point: "None of the Republicans attending the Brookings sessions had ever received a personal phone call from the president requesting their support for or against a measure, and the majority stated that no direct pressure had ever been applied to them."[34] The Eisenhower era was not the Reagan era. Even so, a presidential phone call, or even a call from someone close to the president, is still a relatively rare event—something to tell the family about over dinner.

The relationship between the American president and Congress is altogether an unusual relationship, one foreign to the experience of most people who study it, as well as to the experience of most other democratic countries. Not surprisingly, the analyst looks for metaphors, for suitable language in which to describe this strange institutional interface.

There is a language, commonly used, that probably ought not to be. It has the wrong resonances. This is the language of "conflict" and "cooperation." To be sure, there occurs from time to time straightforward conflict between Congress and the president, as when the president vetoes a major bill or, as during the later Nixon years, when many in Congress come to perceive the presidency as an alien and hostile institution. To be sure, too, it is not hard to find instances of active cooperation, as in the late 1940s, when Truman worked closely with senior members of Congress to develop the Marshall Plan. But, as a way of thinking about the presidency and Congress, the language of conflict and cooperation has two specific disadvantages. One is that it strongly implies that the president and Congress ought to work together, that cooperation ought to be the norm, that conflict is to be deplored, whereas, as Ranney points out at the beginning of chapter 5, the Founding Fathers were determined that the two bodies should act as checks on each other. Secondly, and more seriously, terms like conflict and cooperation subtly overstate the degree to which the presidency and Congress are involved with one another. Presidents may have Congress always on their minds, but members of Congress by no means always have the president on theirs. Most of the time they are neither conflicting nor cooperating; they are just going their own ways. If a simple metaphor is needed, Polsby's "two gears, each whirling at its own rate of speed" is nearer the mark.

Anyone on the lookout for analogies between American presidential–congressional relations and similar relationships elsewhere in the universe could do worse than consider the relations between two sovereign states that are members of the same diplomatic and military alliance. Each depends on the other, but neither can control the other—and each is always in some danger of misunderstanding the other. Neustadt's classic study of the relations between the United States and Britain in the 1950s and 1960s, *Alliance Politics,* is full of remarks suggesting that the relationship between the president and Congress is but one element in a larger set of inter-institutional relationships. The following references are specifically to Anglo-American intergovernmental relations, but the more general implications are evident:

> What went wrong in those instances [Suez and Skybolt] . . . was their external impact, *not* their internal logic. The makers of these choices did not err in their own terms. Rather, their choices ran afoul of someone else's terms. . . .
>
> In every instance, players on the one side failed to understand the stakes of players on the other. They failed to do so because they misread the interests which the other men pursued. They misread interests because they misunderstood, to some degree, the precise nature of the game in which the others were engaged: its positions, or its channels, or its history. . . .
>
> However much they mingle with each other, every player carries in his head the rules of his own game. On those his head depends.[35]

Neustadt refers to the distinct possibility, under these circumstances, of "muddled perceptions, stifled communications, disappointed expectations, paranoid reactions."[36] Incoming presidents are advised to read Neustadt's *Presidential Power;* Jimmy Carter probably ought to have read *Alliance Politics* in addition—or instead.

The international-relations metaphor suggests yet another note of caution that should be sounded in the ear of anyone contemplating the subject of this book. Politicians and political scientists frequently write about the president and Congress as though both were single political actors, as in such sentences and phrases as:

> Congress insists on being treated as a partner. . . .

> But Congress will accept strong presidential leadership . . .

> Congress often rewrites and revises the statutory bases of agencies . . .

> . . . as Congress itself interprets them.[37]

The use of shorthand phrases like these is natural and much of the time does no harm. It can lead the unwary, however, into imagining that Congress, like the president, can be construed as some kind of rational, purposeful, decision-making individual. In fact, of course, for the great majority of purposes there is no such thing as "Congress"; there are merely 535 members of the House of Representatives and the Senate—individuals, committees, subcommittees, parties, caucuses, state delegations, study groups, and prayer groups. In the twentieth century, even "the president," flesh-and-blood individual, is often very different from "the president," the higgledy-piggledy collection of people who work in the White House and speak through the real president and in his name. For analytic purposes, these corporate abstractions need to be decomposed into their constituent parts. Graham T. Allison's Model I—the notion that the behavior of collective entities can be interpreted as though it were the behavior of single, rational individuals—is usually misleading when applied to foreign governments. It is equally misleading when applied to Congress.[38]

What of the future of the presidential–congressional relationship? In 1982, the age of suspicion has passed. The president of the United States is a man emollient, anxious to please, transparently honest. Indeed the reader of Charles O. Jones's passages on Lyndon Johnson in chapter 4 will have been struck by the uncanny resemblance between Johnson's and Reagan's legislative styles, despite the two men's different personalities:[39]

Know what is going on. Reagan, unlike Johnson, never served in Congress, but he behaves as though it were his natural metier. His relationship with his first head of congressional liaison, Max Friedersdorf, was close; Friedersdorf's relations with friendly and potentially friendly congressmen were equally close. An aide said of Reagan in his first few weeks: "We had to keep him off the Hill when he first arrived or he'd have been there every day."[40]

Know thyself. Like Johnson, Reagan has naturally adopted "a congressional perspective." It is doubtful whether he or his aides spend as much time as Johnson did on the details of how federal programs are being administered in states and districts, but Reagan is every bit as anxious as Johnson was to involve members of Congress in the making of administration policy. On the budget in 1981, he adopted Gramm-Latta as his own. On AWACS, he made effective use of a letter to senators in which he assured them that the deal would not proceed unless the Saudis supported the Middle East peace process. The letter was signed by the president, but it originated at a meeting between senators and top White House aides and by the time it was published it had been amended by several of the Senate waverers. "The object is to let a lot of Senators get their fingerprints on it."[41]—a Reagan official, Johnsonian language.

Act fast. It would be hard to imagine a president moving faster than did Reagan at the beginning of his term of office to have his plans and priorities accepted as the nation's. Reagan knew the climate was favorable. He was determined to act before it changed.

Be persistent. Set priorities. Be accessible. Implicate the members. On the budget, if not on AWACS to begin with, Reagan again behaved as though he were a true disciple of Johnson. Every political commentator in the first nine months of 1981 remarked on how Reagan's almost exclusive concentration on the economy enabled him both to set his own priorities and to address himself to the priorities and concerns of congressmen in a way that Carter never had.

Make party leaders look good. Reagan's position in 1981 differed from Johnson's in that, whereas majorities in both houses of Congress were of the president's party under Johnson, Reagan's party had a majority only in the Senate. But Reagan's concern to make Howard Baker, the Republican leader in the Senate, look good was evident even before Inauguration Day. The president first refused to countenance any move to unseat Baker as majority leader, even though Baker had fought him for the Republican nomination. He then, during both the budget and AWACS debates, went out of his way to share with Baker the credit for his successes. The relationship began to resemble that between Eisenhower and an earlier Senate majority leader, Lyndon Johnson.[42]

Go to the public last. At this point, the Johnson and the Reagan paths appear on the face of it to diverge. Johnson was notoriously reluctant to appeal to the people over the heads of members of Congress. As Jones points out, he did not want to pick fights with Congress, and he knew that congressmen believed that they were just as entitled as the president to represent the people. Reagan, by contrast, appealed to the people repeatedly during the legislative debates on his budget and tax cuts. His television appearances became part of what amounted to an elaborate three-way conference call, taking in the president, the congressmen, and the American people.

The two men's strategies were not, however, as divergent as they seemed, because their political situations were different. Reagan was not appealing to the people *against* Congress. Rather, he was trying to keep in existence that mood, that atmosphere, that climate of opinion, which had won him the election and which he believed was essential if enough Democrats in the House were to be induced to desert their party's leadership. Politically, Reagan's television ad dresses were the equivalent of Johnson's efforts at the very beginning of his administration to keep alive the spirit of John Kennedy. On the one occasion in 1981 when Reagan might have appealed to the people against Congress, over AWACS, he notably failed to do so. His instincts, like Johnson's, told him that private persuasion was much more likely to be effective than public declamation.

As we have seen, Reagan began well. But it would be a rash person who would draw any general inferences, even about the later phases of the Reagan administration, from the experience of this one president in his first year. Not only is it the case, as every chapter of this volume has made clear, that presidential–congressional relations are as variable as the personnel and the issues of American politics, but there is reason to think that American politics itself during the 1960s and 1970s entered a new, more febrile era, an era in which elected politicians are on their own, in an increasingly hostile world, without the benefit of any generally accepted structure of political and economic ideas.

Two claims have been made about the first phase of the Reagan administration. One is that the alliance in early 1981 between the Republicans in the House of Representatives and the Democratic Boll Weevils represented a revival of the old pre-1970s conservative coalition in Congress. The other, alluded to earlier, is that Reaganism is an idea whose time has come—and settled in to stay. No one can be certain, but it seems doubtful whether either of these claims is valid. Both the coalition and the philosophy appear to the outside observer to say less about fundamental changes in American politics than about the mood of the American people—and even more, of American politicians—in response to adverse economic circumstances and the failure of the philosophy of the New Deal and the Great Society to contend with these circumstances. If Reaganism as an economic policy fails to work, the pressures on the incipient new-style conservative coalition will be intense; it will probably disintegrate as the congressmen who make it up seek their own dependent ways to electoral salvation. Even if Reaganism does work and a new public philosophy for the 1980s does begin to emerge, the centrifugal forces in American politics—the growth of primaries, the decline of party voting, the new methods of campaign finance—seem much too powerful to permit the creation of substantial political blocs that will endure for any considerable length of time. American politics in the 1980s seems more likely to be characterized by the making of largely independent political judgments by very large numbers of people—in other words, by continued political atomization.

If this is so, presidents and members of Congress may sometimes respond in unison to what they perceive to be prevailing national moods. Indeed presidents and presidential candidates are likely to try to create such moods. But for the most part the presidency and Congress will continue to dwell apart in their separate political households. The hypothesis of randomness will still be a useful hypothesis. It is only a mile and a half between the White House and Capitol Hill, but politically it is, and will remain, a very long way to travel.

Notes

1. On congressmen's three goals, see Richard F. Fenno, Jr., *Congressmen in Committees* (Boston: Little, Brown, 1973), chap. 1.

2. The quotation is from Morris P. Fiorina, *Congress: Keystone of the Washington Establishment* (New Haven, Conn.: Yale University Press, 1977), p. 37. With regard to national trends, Mayhew writes: "All in all the rational way for marginal congressmen to deal with national trends is to ignore them, to treat them as acts of God over which they can exercise no control. It makes much more sense to devote resources to things over which they think they can have some control." See David R. Mayhew, *Congress: The Electoral Connection* (New Haven, Conn.: Yale University Press, 1974), p. 32.

3. See Fiorina, *Congress*, pp. 67-70, and R. Douglas Arnold, *Congress and the Bureaucracy: A Theory of Influence* (New Haven, Conn.: Yale University Press, 1979).

4. The quotation is from Mayhew, *Congress*, p. 73.

5. For example, none of the references to Lyndon Johnson in Mayhew's *Congress* (pp. 31, 107, 127, 138, and 170-71) is concerned with Johnson as someone who could help congressmen get reelected. On the contrary, as Mayhew points out, "The election cycle adds its own kind of perversity; the vigorous enactment of President Johnson's Great Society legislation (by all the survey evidence popular) was followed in 1966 by the largest Republican gain in House popular vote percentage of the last quarter century" (p. 31). The Fiorina volume referred to in footnote 2 likewise contains only about a dozen references to post-1961 presidents.

6. Richard F. Fenno, Jr., *Home Style: House Members in their Districts* (Boston: Little, Brown, 1978).

7. Rochelle Jones and Peter Woll, *The Private World of Congress* (New York: Free Press, 1979), p. 39.

8. Ibid., p. 124.

9. Nelson W. Polsby, *Congress and the Presidency*, 2d ed. (Englewood Cliffs, N.J.: Prentice-Hall, 1971), p. 147.

10. Notably Louis Fisher, *President and Congress: Power and Policy* (New York: Free Press, 1972) and the same author's *The Constitution Between Friends: Congress, the President, and the Law* (New York: St. Martin's Press, 1978).

11. George C. Edwards III, *Presidential Influence in Congress* (San Francisco: W.H. Freeman, 1980), p. 202. Presidential-support scores indicate the extent to which the various members of Congress supported the president on those roll-call votes in which he indicated a clear preference for a particular vote.

12. Ibid., p. 205.

13. See pp. 262-65.

14. The number of studies bearing on these points is large. See, in particular, the classic article by Warren E. Miller and Donald E. Stokes, "Constituency Influence in Congress," *American Political Science Review,* vol. 57 (March 1963), pp. 45-56, and Aage R. Clausen, *How Congressmen Decide: A Policy Focus* (New York: St. Martin's Press, 1973).

15. Ralph K. Huitt, "White House Channels to the Hill" in Harvey C. Mansfield, Sr., ed., *Congress Against the President,* Proceedings, vol. 32 (New York: Academy of Political Science, 1975), p. 83.

16. The case of natural-gas deregulation is a good one. See Michael J. Malbin, *Unelected Representatives: Congressional Staff and the Future of Representative Government* (New York: Basic Books, 1980), chap. 9.

17. See Peter G. Richards, *Parliament and Conscience* (London: George Allen and Unwin, 1970), chap. 9.

18. See pp. 144-45.

19. Kathryn Newcomer Harmon and Marsha L. Brauen, "Joint Electoral Outcomes as Cues for Congressional Support of U.S. Presidents," *Legislative Studies Quarterly,* vol. 4 (May 1979), pp. 281-99; and Jon R. Bond and Richard Fleisher, "The Limits of Presidential Popularity as a Source of Influence in the U.S. House," *Legislative Studies Quarterly,* vol. 5 (February 1980), pp. 69-78.

20. Fred I. Greenstein, *Personality and Politics: Problems of Evidence, Inference, and Conceptualization* (Chicago: Markham, 1969).

21. On the absence of a public philosophy in post-LBJ America, see Samuel H. Beer, "In Search of a New Public Philosophy" in Anthony King, ed., *The New American Political System* (Washington, D.C.: American Enterprise Institute, 1978), pp. 5-44.

22. *The Sociology and Politics of Congress* (Chicago: Rand McNally, 1969), p. 206.

23. "How Reagan Compares in the Polls," *U.S. News & World Report,* July 20, 1981, p. 16. The percentages of the American people approving of the way the last six American presidents were handling their job at midsummer of their first year in office were: Kennedy, 74; Johnson, 74; Nixon, 65; Ford, 39; Carter, 63; Reagan, 59.

24. Quoted in *Time,* July 6, 1981, p. 17.

25. *Newsweek,* May 11, 1981, p. 24; ibid.; *Newsweek,* May 18, 1981,

p. 28; ibid., p. 29; *Newsweek,* July 6, 1981, p. 20; *Washington Post,* August 2, 1981, p. A8.

26. *Newsweek,* May 11, 1981, p. 26; *International Herald Tribune,* May 18, 1981, p. 4; *Newsweek,* May 18, 1981, p. 29; ibid., p. 30.

27. "The Democrats' Vanishing Act," *Newsweek,* July 13, 1981, p. 88.

28. Quoted in *Newsweek,* May 11, 1981, p. 26.

29. Mayhew, *Congress,* p. 71.

30. Tip O'Neill at a press conference shortly after the Democratic leadership in the House had lost its first important vote. Quoted in *Newsweek,* May 11, 1981, p. 25.

31. *Time,* November 9, 1981, pp. 12-13.

32. See "The Man with the Golden Arm," *Time,* November 9, 1981, pp. 25-31.

33. Charles L. Clapp, *The Congressman: His Work as He Sees It* (Washington, D.C.: Brookings Institution, 1963).

34. Ibid., p. 155.

35. Richard E. Neustadt, *Alliance Politics* (New York: Columbia University Press, 1970), pp. 61, 115, and 117.

36. Ibid., p. 56.

37. Richard M. Pious, *The American Presidency* (New York: Basic Books, 1979), pp. 177-78.

38. Graham T. Allison, *Essence of Decision: Explaining the Cuban Missile Crisis* (Boston: Little, Brown, 1971). For an attempt to decompose the legislatures of three European countries, see Anthony King, "Modes of Executive-Legislative Relations: Great Britain, France, and West Germany," *Legislative Studies Quarterly,* vol. 1 (February 1976), pp. 11-36.

39. See pp. 108-111.

40. *Newsweek,* May 18, 1981, p. 30.

41. *Time,* November 9, 1981, p. 26.

42. Both Eisenhower and Johnson construed "Make party leaders look good" to mean "Make the leaders of *both* parties look good." Reagan, by contrast, was concerned in 1981 only with making the Republican leaders look good. He appeared to take pleasure in humiliating the leaders of the Democratic majority in the House, almost certainly to the detriment of his relations with Congress in the long term.

A NOTE ON THE BOOK

This book was edited by Carol Rosen
and by Elizabeth Ashooh of the
Publications Staff of the American Enterprise Institute.
The staff also designed the cover and format, with Pat Taylor.
The text was set in Palatino, a typeface designed by Hermann Zapf.
Hendricks-Miller Typographic Company, of Washington, D.C.,
set the type, and R. R. Donnelley & Sons Company,
of Harrisonburg, Virginia, printed and bound the book,
using paper made by the S. D. Warren Company.

SELECTED AEI PUBLICATIONS

Public Opinion, published bimonthly (one year, $26; two years, $48; single copy, $5.00)

War Powers and the Constitution. John Charles Daly, mod. (1984, 29 pp., $3.75)

Humanism and Capitalism: A Survey of Thought on Morality and the Economic Order, Bernard Murchland (1984, 62 pp., $3.95)

A Muslim's Reflections on Democratic Capitalism, Muhammad Abdul-Rauf (1984, 74 pp., $4.95)

Aliteracy: People Who Can Read But Won't, Nick Thimmesch, ed. (1984, 59 pp., $3.95)

Making Economic Policy in Congress, Allen Schick (1983, 282 pp., cloth $19.95, paper $10.95)

The American Elections of 1982, Thomas E. Mann and Norman J. Ornstein, eds. (1983, 203 pp., cloth $16.95, paper $8.95)

After the People Vote: Steps in Choosing the President, Walter Berns, ed. (1983, 39 pp., $3.95)

Prices subject to change without notice.

• *Mail orders for publications to:* AMERICAN ENTERPRISE INSTITUTE, 1150 Seventeenth Street, N.W., Washington, D.C. 20036 • *For postage and handling, add 10 percent of total; minimum charge $2, maximum $10* • *For information on orders, or to expedite service, call toll free* 800-424-2873 • *When ordering by International Standard Book Number, please use the AEI prefix—0-8447* • *Prices subject to change without notice* • *Payable in U.S. currency only*

AEI ASSOCIATES PROGRAM

The American Enterprise Institute invites your participation in the competition of ideas through its AEI Associates Program. This program has two objectives: (1) to extend public familiarity with contemporary issues; and (2) to increase research on these issues and disseminate the results to policy makers, the academic community, journalists, and others who help shape public attitudes. The areas studied by AEI include Economic Policy, Education Policy, Energy Policy, Fiscal Policy, Government Regulation, Health Policy, International Programs, Legal Policy, National Defense Studies, Political and Social Processes, and Religion, Philosophy, and Public Policy. For the $49 annual fee, Associates receive
  • a subscription to *Memorandum*, the newsletter on all AEI activities
  • the AEI publications catalog and all supplements
  • a 30 percent discount on all AEI books
  • a 40 percent discount for certain seminars on key issues
  • subscriptions to two of the following publications: *Public Opinion*, a bimonthly magazine exploring trends and implications of public opinion on social and public policy questions; *Regulation*, a bimonthly journal examining all aspects of government regulation of society; and *AEI Economist*, a monthly newsletter analyzing current economic issues and evaluating future trends (or for all three publications, send an additional $12).

Call 202/862-6446 or write: AMERICAN ENTERPRISE INSTITUTE
1150 Seventeenth Street, N.W., Suite 301, Washington, D.C. 20036